# Praise for *The Plot to Destroy Trump*

"The DEEP STATE conspired to take down TRUMP. This book fills in all the details, and names names. All patriots need to read it."

—Alex Jones, founder, *Infowars*

"This Dan Brown-style page turner is based on fact, not fiction, and it is a great read."

—Harold Fickett, CEO and publisher of *SCENES*

"The attempt to destabilize and destroy President Trump is one of the most disgraceful episodes in modern political history. This is an important book that will help to dispel the myths."

—Nigel Farage, *LBC Radio* and *Fox News* contributor

"The Red November conspiracy details how an unelected deep state sought to depose an elected president. As a political scandal, it doesn't get bigger than that."

—Francis Buckley, *New York Post*

"This book is simply unputdownable!"

—Freddy Gray, *The Spectator*

"Providing a fact-based counter-narrative to that of the establishment media, Dr. Malloch represents what should be the real American interest in the 2016 election and beyond—that Russia and other nations have an inherent interest in weakening the legitimacy of the President of the United States. The media—alongside Democrats and even former British spies—are actually assisting Kremlin interests."

—Raheem Kassam, editor, *Breitbart*

"With his characteristic no-nonsense approach, Ted Malloch certainly makes you wonder why government investigators spent so much time and taxpayers' money on giving such credence to a clearly politically slanted document. With so much of the deep state against him, it's a miracle President Trump—the people's choice—is still in the White House! This book reveals what Trump is up against."

—Tim Newark, author of *Protest Vote* and political commentator for the *Daily Express*, among others

"Courageous! That's Ted Malloch, who sacrificed elite-style comfort and prestige to be a freedom fighter."

—Joseph Farah, founder and CEO, *WND*

"This book connects all the dots in the plot to destroy Trump. It is the most politically explosive book of the year."

—Caroline Wheeler, *Sunday London Times*

"To the list of worldly ills—the unethical knaves in big business and the fools in big government—author Theodore Roosevelt Malloch has now added the cowards in "big conspiracy," who secretly traffic in worldly falsehoods so as to reap the whirlwind of political strife. Why do they do it? Because their thirst for power knows no bottom, and because they hope to gain the political upper hand in the ensuing confusion. No one loses more in the exchange than the ordinary citizen, who knows his world is at least partly run by these manipulative liars, but who cannot quite bring himself to reject the beautiful lies being spun. *The Plot to Destroy Trump* pulls open the veil behind which these manipulators operate. It is a view of jaded and world-weary malevolence, leavened with the essence of pure self-interest. In so many ways, the liars have the upper hand because they are selling "wishes come true," and because the truth itself can be hard to hear—e.g., work hard, compete, don't accept handouts—but the ordinary citizen knows something is deeply crooked about this world. It is a crookedness for which the only remedy is Truth. "Let there be Truth," says author Malloch—a declaration that every citizen who wishes to live in reality can embrace as their own."

—K .W. Bickford, *Times-Picayune*

"In stunning detail, *The Plot to Destroy Trump: The Deep State Conspiracy to Overthrow the President* exposes the biggest political scandal of our lifetime. A must-read!"

—Jim Hoft, *Gateway Pundit*

"This thriller reads like a Tom Clancy novel. It unpacks a conspiracy theory on Red November."

—*Daily Caller*

"To patriots, national election results matter. Following Trump's stunning upset victory in 2016, globalists and deep state allies went into overdrive. Each day, more evidence emerges demonstrating just how many Americans conspired to defy the expressed will of the electorate. *The Plot to Destroy Trump* is historical fact, yet it reads like a thriller. Ted Malloch brings us a cautionary tale that must be remembered each time we vote, in all free nations, under rule of law."

—Charles Ortel, *Charles on Sunday*

# THE PLOT TO DESTROY TRUMP

## The Deep State Conspiracy to Overthrow the President

# THEODORE ROOSEVELT MALLOCH

### Foreword by Roger Stone

### with a New Afterword by the Author

Skyhorse Publishing

Skyhorse Publishing books may be purchased in bulk at special discounts
for sales promotion, corporate gifts, fund-raising, or educational purposes.
Special editions can also be created to specifications. For details, contact
the Special Sales Department, Skyhorse Publishing, 307 West 36th Street,
11th Floor, New York, NY 10018 or info@skyhorsepublishing.com.

Skyhorse® and Skyhorse Publishing® are registered trademarks of Skyhorse
Publishing, Inc.®, a Delaware corporation.

Visit our website at www.skyhorsepublishing.com.

10 9 8 7 6 5 4 3 2 1

Library of Congress Cataloging-in-Publication Data is available on file.

Cover design by Brian Peterson
Cover photo: AP images

ISBN: 978-1-5107-5273-3
Ebook ISBN: 978-1-5107-5274-0

Printed in the United States of America

*Vox Populi, Vox Dei*

# CONTENTS

*Christopher Steele is the head of Orbis Business Intelligence, Ltd., in London, England. He pulls a dossier out of his office vault. Composed of disinformation to compromise presidential candidate Donald J. Trump, it triggers investigations, court warrants, and endless "fake news" stories. Steele himself has to go into protective hiding when the dossier he prepared goes viral and the Russian intelligence service puts him in their sights. The dossier is shared with both British and American Intelligence Services and becomes the basis for wiretaps, surveillance, unmaskings, and indictments. After Special Investigative Counsel Robert Mueller interrogates Steele, his inventions become the trigger in a witch hunt to bring down the US president. Is it a modern Watergate, a devilish trick, or a plot to destroy the president? Follow the path and connect the dots in this Red November conspiracy.*

# FOREWORD

## By Roger Stone

IT HAS BEEN MY PLEASURE TO work for four American presidents and to be involved in ten presidential campaigns. One was a libertarian candidate, Gary Johnson; the others were Presidents Richard Nixon, Ronald Reagan, my great friend and a great patriot, Senator Bob Dole, George Herbert Walker Bush, of which I have some regret, and of course now Donald J. Trump.

I would say that the 2016 election was an election in which all of those things that I thought were absolutely necessary and true about American politics, about micro politics in the age of mass communications, all proved *not* to be true or at least to be suspended for the time of this most recent election.

Donald Trump was successful and elected president without benefit of sophisticated professional polling, focus groups, message testing, hundreds of millions of dollars, or paid broadcast advertising.

He was the candidate who operated solely and completely on the basis of his instincts, on the basis of his gut.

Trump had no speechwriters. He had no press secretary. He had no prepared talking points for him to read from. He was very much his own man. There was no Karl Rove in front of him and there never has been. I suspect there never will be, certainly not Roger Stone, and most definitely not Steve Bannon.

The fact is that he was massively outspent, while it's very hard to get precise numbers on the intersection of hard and soft money. A reasonable estimate would be that the forces supporting his opponent, Hillary Clinton, raised on the order of $2 billion dollars, perhaps a bit more. Those supporting Donald Trump, although not Trump himself, spent about $237 million dollars.

Additionally, I would make a case that the traditional old media and the new media were *both* actively working against his election.

The old media I define as the three US-based television networks, and I label with them the cable networks.

While they certainly gave Trump a disproportionate amount of coverage during the primaries, they did that not to boost Donald Trump. They did it because somebody this freewheeling, somebody this unscripted is "interesting"—and being interesting is the most important thing in politics.

The *only* thing worse in politics than being wrong is being boring. Donald Trump as a candidate was never boring. And that drove ratings and ratings drove their ability to charge more for their virtual advertising.

I would also argue that in the general election phase of the campaign that coverage turned largely negative, very nasty, indeed.

I would also make a case to you that the new media was rigged against Trump. We see that for example at Google, when the Trump campaign put out a press release it was marked as "Promotion." When the Hillary Clinton campaign put out a press release it was marked as "Update."

That is the difference between literally tens of millions of people reading it and others not following it at all. That's just one example of the bias.

I think it would be a mistake to view the Trump election solely as the rise of an interesting and flamboyant populist candidate.

He was far more than that. He was the total rejection of a two-party duopoly. Although they endeavor to sound different at election time, they are really bringing the country one set of identical policies.

The Republicans and Democrats, the elites of both parties, were working together, the Bushes and the Clintons, whose policies and truths were largely indistinguishable. They brought us endless wars, where our inherent national interests were never clear.

The erosion of our civil liberties, the reading of our emails, the reading of our text messages, the wiring of our phone calls, the collection of metadata on Americans, is in violation of the Fourth Amendment of the US Constitution, borrowing and spending of debt that my grandson's children will end up paying for, immigration policies that are unfair, that do not reward those who wait their turn and go through the process, that have rendered some of our neighborhoods and streets unsafe.

Our international trade policies where we were promised by both the Bushes and the Clintons were not an economic panacea but instead sucked the jobs out of America as one populist candidate, Ross Perot, once said. Economic policies that brought devastation to the central part of our country, the rust belt, left in desperation. These were the policies of the Republican and Democrats working together.

These are the policies of the political elites; these are the policies of the Bushes and Clintons alike, when they find their way to the White House.

How, for example, could Barack Obama promise us that Guantanamo would be closed, and instead it is still open?

Why could they promise us that the war in Afghanistan would be ended and it is still going on? Why would we march off to war in Iraq where our inherent national interest was never clear? Why do the wars have the combined partisan support of the elites and no one else?

I believe that Donald Trump's election was a rejection of all of that.

I also, having worked for a number of presidents and spent some time in Washington, realize that when the establishment cannot defeat you, they first try to discredit you. When they cannot do that they try to co-opt you. After that they try to delegitimize you. And failing that they try and depose you.

Yes, I am disappointed that we are still in Afghanistan. Yes, I think sending more troops has been a mistake. Our largest troop deployment to date has been unable to win that war.

Yes, I do not think that Donald Trump can accomplish everything in only one year.

But it is interesting to me that we were told that if he were elected our stock market would collapse and our economy would go into deep recession. Under this president we have now created almost two million new jobs.

The stock market has roared to unprecedented levels. Unemployment has hit longtime lows. African American unemployment, one of the most intractable problems in the country, is at the lowest number, ever.

Yes, I want to see Trump's plan to rebuild our urban centers realized. He promised us this during the campaign.

He has only been president for one short year. We have multinational corporations who have left, repatriating money back to the United States, coming back to the United States. Companies like Apple, hardly Trump supporters, announcing that they're repatriating $250 million dollars and they are going to spend another $350 billion dollars in a US-based expansion.

By any stretch of the imagination the president has had a *very* successful first year.

The reaction to his election is something that is worth looking at closely.

First, there was the argument that the Electoral College should overturn his election. Mr. Podesta, the manager of Hillary Clinton's losing campaign, a man who spent $2 billion to get his brains beat in, suggested that the Electoral College should be briefed on the Russian collusion.

It would have been a very short briefing.

This is because, so far, the claim of Russian collusion has proved to be a complete delusion.

Yet despite the fact that we have had multi-million dollar tax-payer financed investigations by the House and the Senate, we do not have any evidence of any effective action, of anybody in the Trump campaign or the Trump family or by Trump associates, who successfully coordinated or colluded or conspired with the Russian State. None.

We do know that the handful of aides around Bill Clinton, and the Clintons, made millions of dollars from the oligarchs around Vladimir Putin.

There's the gas deal, the uranium deal, which you may have heard of, and there is the banking deal to boot.

You see, the president has the intractable opposition of what we call the "Deep State."

Some people say, Stone, you are a conspiracy theorist. For example you said that maybe Lee Harvey Oswald didn't kill Kennedy or didn't act alone. Well, perhaps we learned in the documents just released that the government has lied from the beginning about their knowledge of Oswald, where he came from, and his various movements.

I wrote a book about that which is a *New York Times* bestseller. No, I am not a conspiracy theorist. I am a conspiracy realist. I simply go where the facts take us.

There is no shortage of data to show the second phase of the opposition to Trump. Since the Russian collusion delusion has centrally collapsed, we have seen some of the seeds of this emerge. I suspect you will hear more of it: the president is "crazy." He is out of his mind and he is not competent.

He needs to be removed.

He is not able to discharge his duties. Well, I have known him almost forty years and he is the same person he has ever been.

Is he eccentric? Most definitely, he is. So was Franklin Roosevelt. So was Theodore Roosevelt. Go back and read what they said about Teddy, an egomaniac, a lightweight, a braggart, one of our greatest presidents. Lincoln was considered to be eccentric too. He slept in bed with a man.

All of our greatest presidents have changed the presidency in their own image.

Trump has a unique style. He is not a cookie-cutter, blown-dry, polling-fueled career politician. He is a force of nature and he is an actual phenomenon. He has his own unique leadership style.

If that style gets you two thousand points in the stock market and two million new jobs, I like it. Most people do.

The seeds of this entire narrative that the president is mentally unbalanced—which I believe to be manifestly untrue based on all the evidence, both anecdotal and personal and now medical—are based on a 25th Amendment strategy being propagated by some leftists that he may need to be removed from elected office.

This too is based on the intractable opposition of the same Deep State. Dwight Eisenhower called them the "Military Industrial Complex." How can it be that Robert Gates would be a cabinet member and Secretary of Defense for both George W. Bush and Barack Obama, if their policies were so different?

As I said earlier, why is Guantanamo still open? Why do we have the same people in the second and third levels of the intelligence agencies serving the last two or three previous presidents?

It is very simple and I can explain it to you. Hillary Clinton promised these folks an expansion of a proxy war in Syria. I see no winners in Syria, with Assad propping up Hezbollah and Hamas and himself being propped up by the Russians, is certainly no friend of ours or of human rights.

ISIS on the other side is propped up by the Saudis, whose involvement in 9/11 is the subject of legislation on which they do not want to be sued. You have one hundred or more small subsets of terrorist fanatics funded by the Saudis.

I am sorry, this is not worth one drop of American blood or one borrowed American dollar.

We have seen graphically in Libya what happens when you topple a regime with American bomber planes without thinking through the implications.

You can look at the videos of the slave markets in which black Africans are being sold as slaves in Tripoli. They are chilling to say the least.

So the intractable opposition to Trump is based in many cases on his unwillingness to expand the war or make new ones, while cutting bureaucracy and defunding excesses.

Trump was not only the law and order candidate from a rhetorical perspective, he was the only "peace" candidate. Does he have any delusions about the evil of the Russian system?

Does he think Vladimir Putin is a good guy?

Absolutely not. But when the other folks in the world, such as the Russians, have thermonuclear weapons, a guy who wants to work with them is probably a pretty good idea.

The war over Syria is much closer geographically than it would look on a map. It is not a sound idea because our national interests there are not at all clear.

We are witnessing the beginning of the collapse of an illegitimate effort to reverse what the Deep State could not do in the 2016 election.

We now know almost certainly and most certainly we will get more information shortly, as in this book, that the entire claim of Russian collusion and the unconstitutional and illegal surveillance of the Republican candidate for president and his top associates, including yours truly, is based on—a lie.

It is based on a fabrication, a dossier that is not based in truth.

Donald Trump did not meet with prostitutes and did not urinate on a bed in Moscow.

It just didn't happen.

The documents (you have to give those guys from Fusion GPS credit) sold the same information three times to three different buyers.

First, it was sold to the Republicans funded by hedge fund manager Paul Singer and Marco Rubio, who was running for president

Then he sold it to Hillary Clinton and the Democratic National Committee.

And then, finally, sadly, and most incredibly, he sold it to the FBI.

It is due to this dubious document that this administration has been questioned; it is the same document which the Obama administration took to the FISA court and asked permission to surveil Trump and his associates. In July of last year they were stunned when initially their first request was flatly rejected.

It is important to understand that under the FISA court rules there need be no probable cause for action. The government doesn't say we want to spy on someone because we have evidence that he is involved in treason or we believe he is involved with Russia. They could spy on you simply because they want to. In fact, 99 percent of the government requests that go to the FISA court are rubber-stamped and the surveillance is undertaken.

We now know that the highest level officials in the Obama administration went back to the FISA court, to a different judge, never acknowledging to the second judge that the previous judge had turned down their request, because these proceedings are all *secret*.

They got illegitimate permission to conduct surveillance on the basis of the fake evidence.

What you had was collusion by the highest levels of the Intelligence Community in the United States. They were interested in the expansion of the war in Syria, convinced had they had a choice between Hillary Clinton and, say, Jeb Bush and that that expanded proxy war would have been in the bag.

Desperate to dislodge this president, who they were shocked was elected with to begin with, this is a nothing short of a *coup d'état*.

The idea, having failed with their Russian argument, then turned to the 25th Amendment.

How does the 25th Amendment work?

You would need a majority of the president's cabinet and the vice president to agree that the president is no longer mentally capable of discharging his or her duties. Then the president would have the constitutional right to take that to either the highest legal office or to appeal it. That appeal would go to the House of Representatives under control of Speaker Paul Ryan.

Such a strategy may sound far-fetched but it cannot work without the hysteria built up by the folks at, oh I don't know, how about CNN, that the president is mentally unbalanced.

It is already the next phase of the effort to dislodge this president who threatens their business as usual and the Deep State.

More chilling is an effort to put the toothpaste back the tube.

As I said back in 2016, it was the year in which the mainstream media lost their monopoly stranglehold on political dissemination of political information. The invention of the internet changes things.

It opened the door to the broader alternative media—left, right, and center.

What we now see is an effort to censor those on the internet by Google, Facebook, Twitter, and Amazon. This flies exactly in the face of American tradition.

If you are going to leave the caps square then everyone has to have access to the town square. We should be opposed to any censorship of any voice, right or left. It doesn't matter if you are the wackiest far-out leftist or whether you are a right-wing nut, you should have a chance to speak and to be heard.

I am one who has been banned for life from Twitter. Is it coincidental then that they shut off the president's Twitter feed for eleven minutes? Was it coincidental that Julian Assange's Twitter feed went down? Or that it popped back up?

Was it an accident that somebody spilled Coke on the keyboard and that's what made Sean Hannity's Twitter feed disappear?

Are they playing games with us?

These companies have First Amendment responsibilities. They have what many would consider to be antitrust responsibilities.

They also have the other problem, which is that people who want to have a robust dialogue can pick up and go elsewhere. They'll go to other internet alternatives where you can have a dialogue.

One of the most interesting things that we just went through is the disintermediation of the media.

Almost everything that we have been told about this is wrong. Yes, we had under Barack Obama a near state takeover of government by the Deep State and an attempt to overthrow President Trump before, during, and after he was elected.

Comcast, AT&T, Verizon, they all had to give equal access to everybody. Not the content providers. They can defame you, they can block you, they can ignore you, they can censor you, they can literally erase you from history, and they were unfettered.

True networks require that everyone have an equal voice and the new rules will lend themselves to that. Now we have Mr. Pompeo, the former CIA Director and now presumptive Secretary of State, saying that the Russians are going to interfere with the 2018 elections.

Has anyone been able to produce any evidence whatsoever that they interfered in any meaningful way in the 2016 elections?

I wonder what the basis of this information is?

Some of you may not know that a group is suing me in the District of Columbia courts by the name of Protect Democracy, which is a front group for Barack Obama.

Their allegation against me is that I worked with the Russians to hack the Democratic National Committee's email and gave the information to WikiLeaks.

Not only is there no evidence of that, none of it is true, they will be hard-pressed to prove it in court if we get that far.

What interests me most is that the president's lawyers filed a motion in court in essence saying that given *The New York Times v. the United States* case, the famous Pentagon Papers case, the publication of classified information by a journalist is not a crime.

That's what journalists do. If you are going to bust Julian Assange, then you have to bust the *New York Times,* the *Washington Post,* the *Wall*

*Street Journal,* and many others who have had enormous scoops by tainting from sources.

It is the role of a free press to share information. It may be inconvenient and it may be embarrassing to the government but it is most definably not illegal.

How can it be that campaigns were being sued? In a courtroom Trump's lawyers asserted that there is no violation of law, therefore there can be no conspiracy, as you can't conspire to commit a crime at the same time.

Pompeo and Sessions, the Attorney General, are arguing that Julian Assange be extradited to the United States for a crime of publishing classified information. Now you cannot have it both ways. Assertions that I knew in advance that Julian Assange would publish Hillary Clinton's emails are false, other than to say that I can read what he said in a dozen interviews. I did re-tweet what he said.

The idea that I interfered in John Podesta's email is also patently false. I never said that but I did read the Panama Papers.

In January 2016 they outlined his shady business dealings in Eastern Europe, including Russia.

So there is no evidence whatsoever. On the other hand, this lawsuit is a great fundraising device for these folks.

It will lead exactly nowhere. The point to bring it all back to my central point is that censorship is the last step in this effort to discredit and destabilize this president.

I don't think the 25th Amendment narrative will work. I think in the end censorship will not work because in the end free speech will win out. I don't think the toothpaste can be put back into the tube. We like our Twitter feeds and our Facebook posts and any other number of up-and-coming social media outlets.

Gone are the days when the three major networks said something that didn't happen or just did not cover it, as if it just didn't happen. It is like the proverbial tree falling in the forest. No, I think if we are going to have a robust debate we should be ready and happy to have it

Make no mistake: there was a clear attempt, call it a plot, to take down the duly elected president of the United States. His name is Donald Trump.

Now what are we going to do about it?

# INTRODUCTION

THE STORY WE HAVE HERE IS truly stranger than fiction. You can't make this stuff up; I couldn't if I tried. What is presented in this book is the truth as I see it, after carefully analyzing countless texts, articles, documents, interviews, and speeches.

This combing through documents to verify their authenticity is a process that today, it seems, has fallen by the wayside. A process that has shifted from the ones who should be doing it, the news media, to the ones who shouldn't have to, the general public. To be sure, this cultural shift has an unintended consequence: a transfer in autonomy. No longer are the ones supplying the information responsible for fact-checking their sources before releasing them for public consumption. Instead, the responsibility now lies in the hands of the public.

Like most historical trends, this didn't happen overnight. It was a slow and gradual shift that occurred in tandem with the rise of the internet and other social media platforms that allow news to travel twice around the world before anyone thinks to question its veracity. Yet there is a silver lining to this shift: a newly forged path has been carved out, creating platforms for independent voices to reach a wider, more discerning audience without the constraints of traditional media broadcast.

There's a quotation often attributed to Mark Twain: "A lie can travel halfway around the world while the truth is putting its shoes on." Twain's sentiment continues to ring true today—perhaps even more so now than when it was first written well over a hundred years ago. With countless media outlets, a decline in journalism, and general disregard for the truth—where the measure of success is through ratings and likes and clicks, not accuracy—it's no wonder that a document like the Trump-Russia dossier, which is undoubtedly fabricated, has cemented its place as a political fork in the road, blurring the once-drawn line in the sand between fact and fiction.

And yet it's not just the media that bends the truth. These news outlets are often just the last line of defense, a buffer of sorts, between the truth and the public. Sometimes they're reporting what they were told. To find the truth, we have to go back further and deeper. Like a game of telephone, the farther we go back, the more the message and story is distorted. And yet, if we step away from it all as we try to connect the dots from a distance, we see it's part of a bigger picture—something more than just media, which is a mere cog in this great machine. This machine, as we've come to know it, is what we call the Deep State: a collective group of government agencies and select individuals who hold great power to manipulate, distort, and downright falsify the information that will be released to the media and then to the public, ultimately changing the course of world history.

This Deep State is at the heart of our hunt for Red November: a conspiracy orchestrated by anti-Trump forces that begins with memos written by former MI6 agent Christopher Steele for Fusion GPS, an intelligence firm. From here, the trail opens up, spreading its reach throughout Washington—including the FBI, the DOJ, and the CIA—as these forces work together to fabricate a narrative to delegitimize, subvert, and ultimately depose President Trump. This is Red November.

And yet as this story of Donald Trump's alleged nefarious connection to Russia continues to unfold—a complicated, tangled web of people and places and meetings and questionable timetables and events—we're missing one piece to this puzzle: tangible proof of any wrongdoing or collusion between Trump and his Russian adversaries. Despite this, the mainstream media continues to run this story that makes you dizzy just trying wrap your head around it. It's far too complicated. And it only gets complicated if you're lying. It's not complicated if you're telling the truth.

As so it has become in our world today, the information out there from the left media is both disparate and confusing, each outlet and talking head offering cloudy versions of the story that only further overwhelm consumers. These news outlets force readers and viewers to sift through the information and disseminate what is truth and what is not.

The purpose of this book is to cut through the clutter and to provide you with an alternative to the mainstream media's foregone conclusion that relies solely on salacious, unverified gossip that will produce higher ratings that translate into high ad revenue. And more, they know that this is what their audience wants to read. They know that their consumers will sop up this gossip and come back for seconds because it fits in nicely with their narrative—reaffirming their political beliefs, not challenging them—further deepening their echo chambers. This is dangerous: it's an attack on true discourse and open dialogue. If we can't tolerate alternative opinions that question our own beliefs and ideological stances, then the result is paralysis: the slow and inevitable death of a nation.

This book serves as a challenge to mainstream media and thinking and to the widespread notion that there is some sort of nefarious collusion between President Trump and Russia. My aim is to lay the facts out as clearly as possible for you, the reader, to see the difference between fact and pure fiction.

The story I present to you on the pages that follow is an attempt to peel back the layers, tracing that telephone line back to the source and revealing the real story: a story that was still putting its shoes on while a great big lie was traveling halfway around the world. This story, as Winston Churchill once put it, is a riddle, wrapped up in a mystery, inside an enigma . . . but perhaps there is a key.

—Theodore Roosevelt Malloch
March 2018

# PART I

# ORIGIN STORIES: THE MAKING OF RED NOVEMBER
## JUNE 2016—NOVEMBER 8, 2016

# 1

# STRANGER THAN FICTION

CROSSING VAUXHALL BRIDGE IN LONDON, ON the south bank of the River Thames, stands a modern, monolithic fortified structure: the headquarters of the Secret Intelligence Service of the United Kingdom. Londoners know it as MI6—short for Ministry of Intelligence, Section 6—where agents work on external and foreign affairs. Surely, any passerby on a Sunday stroll down the river would view MI6—a rather imposing building—as a place where serious business takes place. The agents inside, however, have grown quite fond of the nickname given to their section: "The Circus."

MI6 gained international fame through novelist Ian Fleming's James Bond, a fictional character who works as a "Double-O" agent within these very walls—which Fleming simply refers to as "Six." In Hollywood's cinematic interpretations of Fleming's novels like *Golden Eye* and *The World Is Not Enough*, MI6 is shown front and center. Again it appears in *Skyfall,* this time under explosive attack. In *Spectre*, Bond's nemesis traps him inside the soon-to-explode building. But in true Fleming fashion, Bond escapes near-certain death with a beautiful girl clutching his arm just moments before the inevitable explosion, leaving his adversary to suffer a painful death inside a crumbling MI6.

And yet, without a sworn enemy, what would Bond be? With every new chapter in the series, Bond is pitted against a new, more sinister evil. And more often than not, that enemy is Russian. Ever since the death of Dr. No, the evil forces behind SPECTRE have been busy exacting revenge on MI6. In *From Russia With Love*, Sean Connery's character is face-to-face with none other than Donald "Red" Grant, an aptly named adversary. This archetypal rivalry with Russia is so ingrained in American and British culture—in a real, political sense and on the silver screen—that one questions whether it is art imitating life or the other way around. The very notion of Russia as an enemy is so deeply embedded into the so-called water supply that we view any political interaction with Russian officials as suspect. Is there any truth behind this rivalry with Russia, or is it a false narrative concocted by government officials in attempt to create a bogeyman, so to say—an evil force that opposes everything we stand for?

Though fictional, James Bond has become a permanent fixture in global pop culture, transcending generations while maintaining cultural relevance and adoration in the eyes of men and women alike. His fictional status as the ultimate spy has yet to be matched . . . that is, until we meet Steele.

# 2

# STEELE, CHRISTOPHER STEELE.

AT THE HEART OF OUR TWISTED labyrinth of a story, we have one man with one mission. His name? Christopher Steele. His mission? Dig up dirt on the Republican candidates for president of the approaching 2016 US presidential election. His mission begins in June of 2016.

Steele and our fictional hero do share a common background: Like Bond, Steele was a former MI6 agent himself, snagging the coveted position right after graduating from elite Cambridge University in 1986, where he was a member of the Fabian Society, a socialist organization that seeks the "betterment of society" by democratic socialist principles. The logo of the group was a tortoise for its predilection of gradual transition to socialism—as opposed to revolution. The globalist society has as its coat of arms a wolf in sheep's clothing. Even to this day, Steele still considers himself a socialist.

Could our British spy have something against his capitalist American adversaries?

After Cambridge, he began at the Foreign and Commonwealth Office (FCO) for two years. Then, after in-depth training, Steele underwent diplomatic cover as an agent in Moscow during the closing years of the Cold War. Serving at the UK mission in the Soviet Union with a pseudonym, he was a deep agent whose identity was suppressed. He ran a ring of informants and collected highly confidential and secret information using established but clandestine collection techniques and methods.

Steele's expertise on Russia remained valued, and he was selected as case officer for that unlucky FSB defector Alexander Litvinenko, whose state-sponsored assassination in 2006 affected him deeply. Steele had many associations down the years with Russia and Soviet defectors and continued with a string of informants in Moscow and the former USSR well past his retirement from active service in MI6.

Over time he mastered the Russian language and culture and became very knowledgeable about how things work—or more accurately, how they don't—in Moscow. In short, he mastered his craft. As a spy, he was adept at collecting raw information, stringing together disparate sources, and bending people and facts to fit his mission and subject matter—a skill that would be *very* useful in 2016.

In 1993, he returned to London after the collapse of the Berlin Wall and once the Soviet Union had imploded. Steele then moved to Paris, where he continued his Russian espionage and spy game until 2000, when he was outted. After Paris, he found himself in war-torn Afghanistan working with Special Forces on "kill or capture" missions aimed at Taliban targets. Steele recruited other agents and specialized in training them. From 2004 to 2009 he headed the all-important Russia Desk at the very pinnacle of MI6. In March 2009, Steele, now retired from MI6, founded a private intelligence agency, known as Orbis Business Intelligence, with a fellow MI6 retiree.

So, how then does a retired MI6 British agent find himself on one final assignment to meddle with the outcome of the US election? Who is funding the mission—and for how much? Do they want more than just "dirt," or is there a grander scheme at play? Could there be something more than just money in it for Steele—a man who pledges his loyalty to socialism? Does he have it out for Donald J. Trump—a living, breathing emblem for everything that represents American capitalism?

With the 2016 US election just months away, Steele begins on his mission—one that will culminate in the release of a thirty-five-page dossier of seventeen memos written from June to December 2016 that will rock the political establishment. Though he's on a solo mission, surely there are more hands at play here in this orchestrated plot to subvert Trump . . .

# 3

# THE WATERS RUN DEEP

SOMETIMES ART TRULY DOES IMITATE LIFE. "Deep State" is a fictional television miniseries about a retired MI6 agent called back to do just *one* more job.

Sound familiar?

In the real world, the Deep State is synonymous with a shadow government—a permanent yet formless administrative state that exists in contrast to the tangible public structures we've all come to know.

This Deep State is secretive. It entails a fluid network that includes intelligence agencies like the NSA, FBI, CIA, and Defense Department—agencies that run on secret surveillance, in-the-know intel, and cryptic communication. Agencies that play for high stakes, willing to do anything to make sure they don't lose it all. This Deep State isn't your local town council or the Department of Agriculture. In other words, it ain't your grandpa's government.

The term has been thrown around in political circles for years, but it quickly reentered our national discourse in early 2016 when Trump talked about a cabal—a secret political faction—that operated in Washington DC of unelected officials—that "swamp" that had to be drained, as he so demanded.

Back in 2014 Eric Snowden, the NSA whistleblower, exposed the reach of government surveillance, saying: "There's definitely a deep state. Trust me, I've been there."[1]

---

1 Garvin, Glenn. "Is the Deep State Real—and is it at war with Donald Trump?" *Miami Herald*. Feb 2 2018. http://www.miamiherald.com/news/politics-government/article 198038824.html.

Internet activist and founder of WikiLeaks, Julian Assange—who has gained international recognition as an advocate for truth—publicly released a trove of classified CIA documents that have been dubbed the "Deep State Files." Following an arrest in 2010, Assange has lived under political asylum granted by Ecuador since 2012, where, to this day, he currently lives at their embassy in London. Assange, who can't leave his confined space, rarely speaks to outsiders and has almost no human interaction. Clearly, the stakes for going against this Deep State are high.

Perhaps it is Mike Lofgren, a former congressional aide, who accurately captures the essence of the Deep State, calling it "a hybrid association of elements of government and parts of top-level finance and industry that is effectively able to govern the United States without reference to the consent of the governed as expressed through the formal political process."[2]

Its origins echo the long-standing politico term "military-industrial complex," first referenced by President Dwight D. Eisenhower in his 1961 farewell address when he discussed its potential risks: "In the councils of government, we must guard against the acquisition of unwarranted influence, whether sought or unsought, by the military-industrial complex. The potential for the disastrous rise of misplaced power exists and will persist."

Some believe the military-industrial complex makes up only the private part of the Deep State. However, it also involves leaders in finance and technology who, too, are tied to the Intelligence Community and defense establishment.

In his book *The New Freedom*, published in 1913, Woodrow Wilson, US president during the First World War, had this to say, "Since I entered politics, I have chiefly had men's views confided to me privately. Some of the biggest men in the United States, in the field of commerce and manufacture, are afraid of somebody, are afraid of

---

2  Longley, Robert. "The 'Deep State' Theory explained." Thoughtco. Jan 31 2018. https://www.thoughtco.com/deep-state-definition-4142030.

something. They know that there is a power somewhere so organized, so subtle, so watchful, so interlocked, so complete, so pervasive, that they had better not speak above their breath when they speak in condemnation of it."

Make no mistake: the Deep State is the central actor in the Red November plot to destroy the president.

Without it, the whole thing would not exist.

This Deep State works together to help fulfill their collective yet sometime conflicting political agendas in hopes of extending its ever-growing reach. To do so, they orchestrate either for or against a political candidate come November.

# 4

# OLD DIRTY TRICKS

EVERY FOUR YEARS AMERICA PUTS ON a show that is too big to miss. The world watches with bated breath for the outcome. The stakes are as high as the cost to run, clocking in to the tune of around two billion dollars. All parties involved will do anything to win. For political contestants, the means most definitely justify the end. But in order to win, someone has to lose.

After eight years of Democrat, left-leaning Barack Obama, the country faced a monumental decision in 2016: Should they continue in the same direction with a so-called "third term"—electing the establishment and politically connected Hillary Rodham Clinton—or turn 180 degrees and run in an opposite direction?

Clinton's hands were notoriously dirty and she had been known to rig a situation to her own advantage, not to mention collect cash for the family foundation.

Nothing is "fair" when it comes to the Clintons.

Politics is a blood sport for them. Disappointed about her 2008 loss to the immature and less-than-experienced young community organizer, then-Senator Obama, Clinton was not going to lose this time around.

The Republican primary, on the other hand, was wide open since there was no incumbent. All kinds of candidates thought they were right for the times: senators, governors, pastors, congressmen, a former CEO—you name it. Seventeen candidates competed in all.

And one candidate was even more outrageous: a heavyweight, foul-mouthed, brash New York blue-collar billionaire who wanted to turn the entire system upside down. He was running against bad trade deals, lax immigration, high taxes, and the decline of America, which he saw as "crippled." His slogan? "Make America Great Again!"

Against this backdrop both sides and certain American foreign friends and adversaries saw an opportunity to influence, perhaps steal, or at least try and win the election.

And like a game of chess, sometimes the best defense is going on the offensive—searching for insurance, so to say, to make sure your opponent loses. We've come to know this strategy as opposition research—the political pros simply call it "oppo." And all candidates partake.

To be sure, this tactic is by no means new. Politicians have built their livelihoods on this type of research in hopes of maintaining secure footing in an ever-shifting political realm. Sun Tzu, the great fifth-century Chinese general, wrote about this in his classic work *The Art of War*, prescribing his followers to focus their aim on their opponents' moments of weakness. The English Whigs, echoing Sun Tzu, further perfected the technique, which they called "scandalmongering." Thomas Paine, the English-born American activist, brought this very idea across the Atlantic to bolster himself and his patron Benjamin Franklin when they published their pro-independence tracts during the American Revolution.

Nearly two hundred years later, in Richard Nixon's White House, the president systemized the notion and kept files on just about everyone he came across and even had an "enemies list." Nixon was helped by Roger Stone, then a young operative, who would go on to perfect this bag of so-called "dirty tricks." Stone used such tricks to bring down then-New York Governor Eliot Spitzer about his perpetual affinity for prostitutes, particularly "Client 9." Politicians who rely on opposition research use trackers to follow a target. This kind of research utilizes databases of public and private records and speeches that stretch back decades, and of course human intel. But such information doesn't come cheap.

In fact, an entire industry—replete with data shops, gumshoes, listening devices, and K Street consultancy firms—has sprung up to cash in on this ripe business opportunity. One business in particular, Fusion GPS, has risen to the top and become the go-to for all of Washington's dirty tricks needs. The company has become the epicenter of this sordid game and the heart of this Red November tale.

# 5

# THE DOSSIER:
# A FAILSAFE INSURANCE POLICY

THE OPENING LINE OF STEELE'S NOW infamous dossier begins with an explosive claim: the "Russian regime has been cultivating, supporting, and assisting Trump for at least five years. The aim, endorsed by Putin, has been to encourage splits and divisions in the western alliance."

Make no mistake about it: Russia has a clear strategy. After its devastating loss in the Cold War, under Vladimir Putin, Russia has two agendas. The first is to be respected as a proud nation in the eyes of the world and seen as an important European power and as an equivalent superpower. The second item on their agenda is simply the demise of the West.

Moscow wants a complete reversal of the historical undoing that began in 1989 when Eastern and Central Europe peacefully reclaimed freedom and eventually brought down the Soviet empire. As James Kirchick at *Politico* put it, "Shorn of Marxism-Leninism, the Kremlin today is driven by an ideologically versatile illiberalism willing to work with any political faction amenable to its revisionist aims."[3]

Russia wants to reset the Trans-Atlantic Alliance using destabilizing efforts. Like a studied disciple of Sun Tzu's *Art of War*, Russia exploits its opponent's weakness and moments of crisis in a calculated attempt to exacerbate the situation by its malign intentions.

---

3    Kirchick, James. "The Road to a Free Europe Goes Through Moscow." *Politico*. March 17 2017. https://www.politico.com/magazine/story/2017/03/russias-plot-against-the-west-214925

Fomenting disintegration, its motives revolve around predatory strategies to divide and conquer its enemies—namely the West, or more accurately: America.

Using aggression and subversion, Russia no longer has to depend on the deployment of the Red Army on its western flank. With the Communist ideology long since out of fashion, Russia continues to meddle with its capitalist enemies by inciting confusion and chaos by any means necessary to achieve this demise of Western governments and societies and to restore their own footing as a political power player.

Russia had perfected the technique called *kompromat,* whereby you entrap a target and blackmail them using sex, money, or ambition. Ideology was not so important any longer. This was only about raw political power and national interests.

Russia had a reputation for meddling in other countries' elections going back decades. In Western Europe and elsewhere, they played dirty and did as much as possible to influence regimes and select and depose leaders.

Well, for that matter, so had the US, toppling numerous regimes, bribing officials, and putting up CIA fronts. In the Ukraine alone, the US spent over a billion dollars to get rid of the elected regime of Viktor Yanukovich, a crooked Putin ally.

The question in a new era of social media and cybersecurity was what *could* and what *would* Russia do to influence an American electoral decision?

Would Hillary Clinton exploit this long-established rocky relationship between the US and Russia to her advantage? Would she use Steele's dossier as a failsafe "insurance policy" should she lose the election?

When in doubt, blame Russia. After all, they have a history of meddling in elections.

Russia has, as Winston Churchill described it, long been "a riddle, wrapped in a mystery, inside an enigma." But as he astutely warned, the key is Russian national interest.

Carrying a dark past and something of a chip on its shoulder, Russia in recent decades was a shadow of its former Soviet self.

Shedding an empire and many of its republics, Russia, while resource-rich, had become an inferior place and hardly a first world economy. Sure, it still had a decrepit nuclear arsenal, and its secret police were to be feared, but not as much as in the Stalinist past or even the Kremlin of Mr. Gorbachev.

Russia was now a materialistic autocratic kleptocracy with ambitions to restore its own greatness, but it lacked the means to do so.

The intent was there but it seemed inept, clumsy, less than efficient and often bumbling, even if it was at times proud, xenophobic, and ardently nationalistic.

The Russians were always good at thumping their own chests.

The Soviet peace dividend never really materialized on either side. Russia opened to crass materialism and allowed an oligopolistic regime of friends to get rich quick and cash in, but it didn't hold much international clout or sway the way it used to in the "good old Communist days."

At the UN it had a veto power but little muscle. It had no Warsaw Pact and faced enemies on its every border. It felt surrounded—caged in.

The one thing the Russians continued to do well, besides drinking too much vodka, was espionage . . .

# 6

# FUSION GPS: PROPAGATING PROPAGANDA

In October 2015, with the 2016 election just over a year away, the *Washington Free Beacon*, a conservative website, hires the American research firm Fusion GPS to conduct opposition research on Donald J. Trump and other Republican presidential candidates.

Why would a Republican-funded website be looking for dirt on their own nominees?

Well, Trump, as we've come to know, is no ordinary politician: He's unpredictable, volatile, and shoots from the hip. Unlike every other politician, he's anything but boring—he's a showman. And when a man like Trump throws his red hat into the ring of the biggest show on Earth, he is bound to be the star of the show. And the star of the show is always subject to the most attack. Even his Republican counterparts want dirt on him.

The world of conservative journalism exploded during the Obama years. They attacked everything he did—from his birth certificate, to his health care plan, to his socialist outlook, to his anti-Israel Muslim-favoring foreign policy.

The *Washington Free Beacon* was launched into this competitive and vituperative political environment in the spring of 2012.

The new rag was dedicated to uncovering the stories that "the powers that be hope will never see the light of day" and producing "in-depth investigative reporting on a wide range of issues, including public policy, government affairs, international security, and media."[4]

There was nothing they wouldn't touch—so long as it fit their neocon agenda and attacked Obama. The *Free Beacon* wanted "No Bama."

This blatantly neoconservative publication regarded its role as a mobilizer for citizens by publicizing stories that would influence coverage in mainstream media.

They wanted to get attention and didn't care how they did it.

One thing is certain: the *Free Beacon* is at the core of the hunt for Red November. Leading up to November, they'll instigate and thrive on anti-Trump venom, broadcasting their views widely in an attempt to take him down.

One man in particular is the financial backing behind this diatribe: Paul Singer, a huge hedge fund magnate who has also been an activist investor.

Singer is also founder of NML Corporation, a Cayman Islands offshore unit that is tied to his hedge fund. It is based offshore for a reason.

*Forbes* put Singer's total wealth at just shy of three billion dollars.

As a very big donor to various Republican candidates, his real philanthropic cause has been LGBTQ rights.

Both Singer and his allies in his firm have for years been the top source of contributions to the National Republican Senatorial Committee. He counts among his close friends Jeb Bush, the former governor of Florida, and the junior Florida senator, Marco Rubio.

Both were also candidates in the 2016 Republican presidential primary.

Singer has been described as one of the "smartest and toughest" money managers in hedge world. He takes no prisoners and doesn't like to lose.

Some have branded him a "vulture capitalist" because his fund hovers like that named bird over the dead carcasses of roadkill. His

---

4    The *Free Beacon*. http://freebeacon.com/about/

model is to buy up sovereign bonds on the cheap and then go after those countries in court and in the press for unpaid debt.

Argentina, Peru, Congo, and other desperate third-world countries have found themselves in his sights.

And he has cashed in. Boy has he cashed in.

Singer originally picked up the bill for Fusion GPS's research, which was done for the *Free Beacon*.

Singer is connected all over established Washington and in the halls of power. One of his best pals is the neocon idol, William Kristol.

Kristol himself is editor in chief of the *Weekly Standard*, a Rupert Murdoch-backed neoconservative weekly, and was the font of all Never Trumpism.

William Kristol's daughter, Anne, is married to Matthew Continetti, the editor of, what else, the *Washington Free Beacon*.

Must have been a family affair.

So, Fusion GPS agrees to pay Christopher Steele and his firm a grand total of $168,000 to create the special dossiers on Trump's alleged ties to Russia.

Fusion GPS was founded in 2011 by Glenn R. Simpson, a former investigative reporter who worked on Capitol Hill for *Roll Call* and the *Wall Street Journal*.

Simpson rarely makes appearances or gives interviews, preferring to be clandestine.

He co-authored the book *Dirty Little Secrets* with the University of Virginia political TV pundit, Larry Sabato. In the book they addressed things like "street money" and voter fraud.

A longtime Democrat, Simpson used to write stories for the Capital Hill rag, *Roll Call,* where he broke the story on GOPAC, which implicated Newt Gingrich.

He likes to "catch" Republicans. While Simpson claims to be bipartisan, he is nothing of the sort.

Simpson's firm had been accused of having purported connections with Russia and may have acted as an unregistered foreign agent for

Russia. Unsurprisingly, Simpson and his colleagues deny they were ever involved in lobbying or violating the Foreign Agents Registration Act (FARA).

Prior to founding Fusion GPS, Simpson did equally questionable work for a sheik in the UAE who sought to overthrow his uncle. Simpson and company did the same again in support of the leftist Maduro regime in Venezuela. In fact, he does this for questionable business entities quite often. For instance, he did this for Planned Parenthood to discredit its main opponents. And, most interestingly, he did similar research for the nefarious Russian clients on the Magnitsky Act—an American law that blacklists suspected human rights abusers.

For a company whose founder has such a checkered past, it begs the question, is Fusion GPS's opposition research standard procedure, or is there something more here? Is it misinformation? Disinformation? Sold to the highest bidder, or favoring establishment politics over an upstart like Trump?

Could Steele be operating as a double agent? Could he be receiving money not just from the Americans but also from Russian sources? Is it collusion between Fusion GPS, Orbis Business Intelligence, and other Russian entities?

Whatever it may be, with each passing month in 2016, Fusion GPS continues to gather information on Trump, mostly centered around his business and entertainment activities. On May 3, 2016, Trump is named the presumptive nominee for president, so *The Free Beacon* stops funding research on him. But just as the Republicans in Washington DC wrap up their opposition research on Trump, across the country in Seattle, the Democrats have been busy conducting their own.

# 7

# PERKINS COIE:
# THE INTERMEDIARY

IN APRIL 2016 THE LAW FIRM Perkins Coie, on behalf of the Clinton campaign and the Democratic National Committee, retains Fusion GPS to complete opposition research on Donald Trump.

Headquartered in Seattle, Washington, and founded in 1912, Perkins Coie LLP is the oldest and largest law firm in the Pacific Northwest. While it serves corporate clients, Perkins Coie is perhaps best known for representing political clients.

The chair of its prestigious Political Law Group is one Marc Elias. His focus is on representing public officials, candidates, parties, Political Action Committees (PACs), and tax-exempt organizations.

As a lawyer, Elias advertises himself as knowledgeable in campaign finance, government ethics, lobbying disclosure, and white-collar criminal defense. Elias is an avowed expert on the Foreign Agents Registration Act and the Lobbying Disclosure Act. He focuses on government gift rules, pay-to-play rules, and advises on voting rights. He has represented numerous clients in political corruption charges.

As general counsel to Hillary Clinton for America, he is responsible for the presidential campaign of Hillary Rodham Clinton.

He did the same for John Kerry in 2004. We would later learn from Michael Isikoff and David Corn's book titled *Russian Roulette*, released in March 2018, that Barack Obama's 2012 re-election campaign hired

Fusion GPS to dig up "dirt" on his rival Mitt Romney. According to Isikoff and Corn, the campaign's payments to Fusion GPS, which were not disclosed to the public, were reported as legal bills to the campaign's law firm, Perkins Coie.[5]

Elias's major clients include the Democratic National Committee, Democratic Senatorial Campaign Committee, Democratic Congressional Campaign Committee, Democratic Governors Association, and dozens and dozens of Democrat US senators, governors, and representatives and their campaigns.

He is in other words, Mr. Democrat.

Following the 2014 election, Elias was appointed by the DNC chair, Representative Debbie Wasserman Schultz, a Democrat from Florida, to review all key components of the role of the Democratic Party in elections.

In April 2016 Hillary makes Marc Elias the attorney of record for the 2016 presidential campaign. The Clinton campaign and the DNC pay Perkins Coie $5.6 million and $3.6 million, respectively, for their services.

Elias admits he helped to orchestrate funding from the Clinton campaign to the research firm Fusion GPS that paid for the anti-Trump dossier.

All of the dossiers and other material were passed from Steele himself to Fusion GPS, who provided them to Marc Elias at Perkins Coie. They were then given to both the Democratic National Committee and to the Clinton campaign.

Elias was what is called the "go-between." A bagman. He has long been the Democrats go-to super lawyer and is known as a "fixer" who gets things done.

In late October 2016 Perkins Coie released its client, Fusion GPS, from its client confidentiality obligation.

---

5    Isikoff, Michael; Corn, David. Russian Roulette. Twelve. 13 Mar 2018.

# 8

# MEET THE OHRS: BRUCE AND NELLIE

AT A PRESS CONFERENCE DURING HIS campaign for presidency, Trump once joked to the crowd that he could shoot somebody on Fifth Avenue and he wouldn't lose any voters. Though in jest, there's truth behind Trump's joke, and the Democrats knew this. So, Fusion GPS, working on behalf of the Clinton campaign, knows that to dig up dirt on a man nicknamed "Teflon Don"—to whom no scandal or dirt seems to stick—they'll need more than just one man on the job. They task FBI agent Bruce Ohr with the impossible . . .

In June 2016 Bruce Ohr is an Associate Deputy General at the US Department of Justice. His office is just four doors down from that of his boss, Rod Rosenstein, the Deputy Attorney General and the number two justice officer in America.

Ohr's career is going along swimmingly: for the past decade or so he has been climbing up the political ladder and accruing power. Digging up dirt on Trump will surely bring him one rung higher to the top of the ladder. And Fusion GPS, hedging their bets, contracts another agent for the job. In a clear case of nepotism and the Deep State at work, Fusion hires Bruce's wife, Nellie, to conduct oppo on Trump and any connections to Russia and similar matters.

Nellie is a well-known expert in Russian affairs with an extensive network in that country. She holds a degree in history and Russian literature from Radcliffe/Harvard and an MA and PhD in Russian Affairs from Stanford University. Throughout her career, Nellie has published extensively on the subject in peer-reviewed journals and worked for the CIA as an open source analyst. In short, she knows all things Russia-related.

Nellie not only speaks the language but also knows the turf inside out and is an experienced Russia hand. Perhaps more curiously, her PhD thesis, titled "Collective farms and Russian peasant society, 1933-1937: the stabilization of the kolkhoz order," blurs the "revisionist" line as she attempts to defend the millions killed by Stalin as "excesses," which, according to Ohr, "sometimes represented desperate measures taken by a government that had little real control over the country."

Is Nellie a Stalin sympathizer? Seems like Steele, a confirmed socialist since his days in Cambridge, has found the perfect woman to carry out his socialist agenda nearly thirty years in the making. He knows Nellie's the perfect woman for a crooked mission like this.

And interestingly, only a few months prior, Nellie obtained her ham radio license, which begs the question, why? Could it be to have secure and confidential contact with Christopher Steele?

Could Nellie be more than just an agent conducting research? Could she be a co-author of the Steele files? And more peculiarly, when prompted by the FBI down the line, why does Bruce hide the fact that his wife is involved? Is this a conflict of interest? What else is Bruce hiding?

Over the next few months, Bruce Ohr meets not only with Christopher Steele himself but also with Glenn Simpson, the founder of Fusion GPS, who hired Steele. Simpson is the operative behind this whole saga. Why exactly does Ohr meet with Steele? And how often?

# 9

# DIGITAL WARS

ANY GOOD POLITICIAN WORTH THEIR WEIGHT in salt knows that you can't win an election using oppo alone, only by attacking your opponent. You need to also know and understand the very people who are going to vote for you—what makes them tick and what they value in you as a candidate—so you can calibrate your approach to win the votes of those still sitting on the fence. So how do you tip the scale in your favor?

In the early days of presidential campaigning, that meant holding town hall discussions to meet face-to-face with the public to learn what issues matter to them most and how you can be of better service to them. Then, you'd travel across the country and repeat this process—the shaking of countless hands, kissing babies for photo ops, and delivering the same stump speech ad nauseam.

Politicians still do these motions to this very day, but with the rise of the internet, social media, and other advanced forms of technology, politicians have had to adjust their approach to account for these twenty-first-century changes. For instance, in just 140 characters, Trump and his tweets have upended decorum in the political realm and how politicians interact with the public.

So, in June 2016, the Trump campaign hires Cambridge Analytica to take over its "data operations." What a nebulous term. What exactly does that mean? In short, Trump and his team want to collect data on their supporters as well as their potential voters—those on the fence.

Sometimes referred to as data mining or analytics, companies like Google and Amazon rely on this type of technological research all the time. To be sure, all campaigns hire voter analytic firms. And just like every other campaign, Trump did the same when hiring Cambridge Analytica. He likely chose the firm because he was already familiar with some members of their administration, like Steve Bannon, who had been the vice president of their board in prior years.

Any time you search for something online, these companies are collecting valuable "psychographic" data on you. For instance, if you search for a waffle-maker on Amazon, but don't end up purchasing it, you can be certain that for the next week as you surf the web and check your email you'll see ads for a waffle-maker. This is undoubtedly a mildly annoying new trend, but there's no going back at this point. This type of data collection will only continue to become part of our lives.

And to be sure, throughout the campaign season, both sides are using digital technologies to advance their research, but you can be certain that the Democrats, specifically the Clinton campaign, are using it to directly smear and derail the Trump campaign. For example, when Hillary Clinton puts out a press release, Google marks it as "Update." But whenever the Trump campaign puts out a press release it is marked as "Promotion."

Coincidence or conspiracy?

If this isn't a clear instance of obvious media manipulation and bias then I don't know what is. This right here is the makings of a digital war.

Still, this type of metadata (as it is known) doesn't have to be as Orwellian as the media wants you to believe. For instance, Netflix uses this type of research on its users to better cater to each individual's preference, making each user's movie-watching experience that much better. This type of collection is more in line with what the Trump campaign is looking for when they hire Cambridge Analytica to better understand their supporters.

Sean Illing for *Vox* explains just what the Trump campaign is using their services for:

> The benefit of this kind of data is that it allows data companies like Cambridge Analytica to develop more sophisticated psychological profiles of internet users (more data points means more predictive power). Cambridge Analytica was also able to use this real-time information to determine which messages were resonating where and then shape Trump's travel schedule around it. So, if there was a spike in clicks on an article about immigration in a county in Pennsylvania or Wisconsin, Trump would go there and give an immigration-focused speech.[6]

This type of research is just the twenty-first-century form of traveling around the country, shaking hands, and then adjusting your schedule according to shifts and trends.

A bit of tech savvy, enough funding, personnel, contacts, and data can go a long way. Completely legal and aboveboard, and without need of any assistance from the Russians, an effective digital campaign can be launched. Jared Kushner made sure to maximize all the tools at his disposal. In an interview with Steven Bertoni at *Forbes*, he explains that he called "some friends from Silicon Valley, some of the best digital marketers in the world, and asked how you scale this stuff, they gave me their subcontractors."[7]

Before Trump's nomination, Kushner used Facebook micro-targeting to sell Trump hats to expand the branding and raise more funds, and created policy videos with Trump speaking into the camera, reaching over 74 million viewers. After securing the nomination, Kushner

---

6    Illing, Sean. "Cambridge Analytica, the shady firm that might be a key Trump-Russia link, explained." *Vox.* 18 Dec 2017. https://www.vox.com/policy-and-politics/2017/10/16/15657512/mueller-fbi-cambridge-analytica-trump-russia

7    Bertoni, Steven. "Exclusive Interview: How Jared Kushner Won Trump The White House." *Forbes.* 22 November 2016. https://www.forbes.com/sites/stevenbertoni/2016/11/22/exclusive-interview-how-jared-kushner-won-trump-the-white-house/#38e78cde3af6

dove into a data-driven approach to unify fundraising, messaging, and targeting.

Kushner tells Bertoni, "We played Moneyball, asking ourselves which states will get the best ROI for the electoral vote. I asked, How can we get Trump's message to that consumer for the least amount of cost?"[8] Tapping into the Republican National Committee's database, and with the help of Cambridge Analytica to map voter preferences, and plotting location density of nearly twenty voter types using a live Google Maps interface to create a customized geo-location tool, Kushner could zero in with precisely tailored TV ads, last-minute rallies, and armies of volunteers to call and knock on doors at exactly the most critical points and times in the campaign.

Illing continues:

> These online ads were spread primarily through bots on social media platforms. The ads that got liked, shared, and retweeted the most were reproduced and redistributed based on where they were popular and who they appealed to.[9]

And when you consider how close elections can typically be, even a few thousand votes can tip the scale in your favor. Any modern politician knows that to secure the vote, you need to use all the available resources.

---

8   Ibid.
9   Illing, Sean. "Cambridge Analytica, the shady firm that might be a key Trump-Russia link, explained." *Vox*. 18 Dec 2017. https://www.vox.com/policy-and-politics/2017/10/16/15657512/mueller-fbi-cambridge-analytica-trump-russia

# 10

# SMOKE BUT NO FIRE

WHILE BOTH THE TRUMP AND CLINTON campaigns are delving into data mining, FBI Director James Comey begins his investigation into his suspicions that Trump and his camp are colluding with Russians to tip the election in his favor.

But just who is this Comey character?

Standing six feet eight inches, James Comey towers over his peers and colleagues, using his size to intimidate his opponents and friends alike. A powerful US attorney for the Southern District of New York, he served as the Deputy Attorney General until former President Obama appointed Comey to become the FBI director in 2012.

Comey is no foreigner to the bright lights of the American media. He worked on the prosecution of the infamous Gambino family. Then, he served as counsel on the Senate Whitewater Committee on Bill Clinton's shady land deals. Comey supported the use of enhanced interrogation techniques for terrorists, including waterboarding, until this position fell out of political fashion. In the political world, Comey has a reputation of being a leaker, using the press as an outlet to broadcast his own opinions. So what was it that pushed Comey to be so adversarial against Trump? Who owns him? Or is it all about oversized ego and to get more face time in the American limelight?

While Comey might have good reason to suspect that there might be some sort of evidence for meddling, by no means is there evidence of collusion. Looks like a lot of smoke but no fire. Again, what we have here is Comey and the American media attempting to connect dots where there is no connection.

Meanwhile, US Army Lieutenant General Michael Flynn is working with the Trump campaign as an advisor. Unsurprisingly, Comey hones in on Flynn and his involvement with Cambridge Analytica. Comey wants to know what Flynn is doing with the information collected on voters.

Does Flynn have any real connection to the Russians? Did he pass any information along to them? Or is this just another feeble attempt of Comey and the Deep State in their collective witch hunt against Trump? Just how deep and wide does this state permeate? To better understand just how far back this Red November tale goes, we need to rewind even further to a business deal that took place a few years back. Its importance cannot be understated.

# 11

# THE HUNT FOR RED NOVEMBER

In 2010, A DEAL IS IN the works to allow Rosatom, the Russian nuclear energy agency, to acquire a controlling stake in Uranium One, a Canadian-based company with mining stakes in the United States. As the company's name suggests, they mine uranium, the same material used to make nuclear bombs and weapons.

However, for a multinational deal of this size and complexity to go through, there are multiple levels of approval from international players that need to be met—not to mention approval from the Nuclear Regulatory Commission and from the Committee on Foreign Investments in the US (CFIUS), on which the US Secretary of State sits—before it is finalized.

As secretary of state, Hillary Clinton plays an integral role in the success of such a deal. While she isn't the only member on CFIUS on whom the deal's approval hinges, Clinton undoubtedly holds plenty of clout and bargaining power to ensure its success. Through her heavy political hand and leverage, the deal goes through, and just like that, 20 percent of US uranium deposits are transferred to this Russian company.

Why then does Hillary Clinton approve this deal to give American uranium to the Russians, and what does she want in return? Could this be about more than just uranium?

Enter Frank Giustra, Canadian businessman, accomplished in finance and mining, and founder of the Hollywood and Vancouver-based film studio Lionsgate.

Formerly the chairman of a merchant-banking firm called Endeavor Finance, he helped build the company that would become Goldcorp Inc., which, having purchased a gold firm during a drop in the price of gold, became the fourth-largest producer of gold in the world. Giustra is currently CEO of Fiore Group of Companies.

In 2004, Giustra put together UrAsia Energy with his contacts in Kazakhstan and with the help of a very prominent US politician—one Bill Clinton.

In 2007, Giustra merged UrAsia with a company called Uranium One, chaired by an old friend, Ian Telfer. Giustra, who had retained stock in the company, sold nearly all of his interests shortly after that.

Several years later, in 2013, Uranium One was sold to a Russian state-owned company. The sale gave the Russians control of uranium deposits around the world, including several mines in the United States. That sale was reviewed by the State Department and other agencies at the time that Hillary Clinton was secretary of state.

Some Republicans have charged that this was a conflict of interest, though aides to Clinton have said she did not *personally* intervene in the approval process and showed no favoritism toward foundation donors. Did she? Records show otherwise.

Involved in philanthropy, Giustra has chaired his Radcliffe Foundation, giving support to disaster relief, economic development, and homelessness. These activities so captivated Giustra that he contributed $30 million to the Clinton HIV/AIDS initiative and later became a board member of the Clinton Foundation. Well, he became its largest donor, giving well over $100 million in gifts.

Touring seven African countries with former President Clinton aboard his MD-87 private jet, they were able to see the extent of global poverty firsthand.

We know that Giustra bonded with the Clintons and supported them in more than one way. They seemingly used each other. His relationship to them as regards the Uranium One transaction opens many questions and leads many to believe it involved extensive kickbacks, wrongdoing, and collusion.

The question arises—did Giustra and his Russian and Central Asia partners unduly benefit from a US government relationship, and is this in fact a real Russian collusion that Clinton wanted to cover up?

Did she create the Trump-Russia collusion and its dossier as a narrative and as a way to hide her own Russia storyline?

Is Red November a Clinton fiction?

# 12

# PAY-TO-PLAY:
# THE URANIUM ONE DEAL

OVER THE COURSE OF THREE SEPARATE transactions between 2009 and 2013, the Russian state-owned atomic energy giant and uranium monopoly Rosatom, through its subsidiary, ARMZ Uranium Holding, acquired Uranium One. The purchase of the company by Russian interests is now under investigation by the US Congress.

In 2009, ARMZ took control of 16.6 percent of shares in Uranium One in exchange for a 50 percent interest in the Karatau uranium mining project in southern Kazakhstan, in a joint venture with the country's national import and export operator of uranium, Kazatomprom. In 2010, Uranium One acquired 50 percent and 49 percent respective interests in southern Kazakhstan-based Akbastau and Zarechnoye uranium mines from ARMZ. In exchange, ARMZ increased its stake in Uranium One to 51 percent.[10]

The deal was subject to antitrust and other conditions and was not finalized until the companies received Kazakh regulatory approvals, approval under Canadian investment law, clearance by the US Committee on Foreign Investments, and approvals from both the Toronto and Johannesburg stock exchanges.

---

10 "CFIUS Investigations Currently Ongoing." Committee of Foreign Investment in The United States (CFIUS). Investigations. 31 Dec 2017. https://americandig italnews.com/2017/12/31/committee-foreign-investments-us-investigations/#.WqFSiYJG3OQ

In June 2010 the deal was finalized, and ARMZ took complete control of Uranium One in January 2013 by buying all shares it did not already own. Later, Uranium One Inc. became a private company and a wholly owned indirect subsidiary of Rosatom.

There appears to be a quid-pro-quo around the approval of the deal to transfer 20 percent of uranium to the company in exchange for donations to the Clinton Foundation. The donation of $145 million from those linked to Uranium One and UrAsia came largely from one person: Frank Giustra.

Was this a pay-for-play scheme? Did Hillary Clinton give American uranium to the Russians, and what did she get in return?

As the image of Hillary Clinton appeared across all of social media during the 2016 presidential election the ads asked, "So Hillary, if Russia is such a threat, why did you sell them 20 percent of our uranium? Are you a liar, or a traitor, or both?"

Complicating all these coincidental facts is one more.

In addition to the Clinton Foundation donations, former President William Jefferson Clinton booked a $500,000 speaking fee from a Russian investment bank in June 2010, just before the Uranium One deal was approved.

That fee, Clinton's highest ever, came from Renaissance Capital, the Russia investment bank tied to the Kremlin. Its analysts talked up the Uranium One deal, assigning it a BUY rating, saying it was the "best play" in all the uranium markets.

We later discover that not all the donations made to the Clinton Foundation were disclosed. There were donations from the Uranium One Chairman, Ian Telfer, a Canadian, from 2009-2012, that were not disclosed to the public. They were actually distributed through a subsidiary of the Clinton Foundation called CGSCI, which did not reveal its donors.

Is this an awkward collusion or just a slight oversight?

*The Hill*, a Washington newspaper, reported receiving documents and eyewitness testimony "indicating Russian nuclear officials had routed millions of dollars to the US designed to benefit former President Bill Clinton's charitable foundation during the time Secretary of State Hillary Clinton served on a government body that provided a favorable decision to Moscow,"[11] although no specifics about who those Russian nuclear officials were or how the money was allegedly routed to the Clinton Foundation were given.

The US House Intelligence and Oversight Committee recently announced the launch of a joint investigation into the circumstances surrounding the Russian purchase of Uranium One. There appears to be considerable Russia meddling not around Trump, but instead around the Clintons and their notoriously corrupt foundation.

11  Solomon, John; Spann, Alison. "FBI uncovered Russian bribery plot before Obama administration approved controversial nuclear deal with Moscow." *The Hill*. 17 Oct 17. http://thehill.com/policy/national-security/355749-fbi-uncovered-russian-brib-ery-plot-before-obama-administration

# 13

# THE CLINTON FOUNDATION

FOUNDED IN 1997 AS THE WILLIAM J. Clinton Foundation with a focus on raising funds for the future Clinton Presidential Center in Little Rock, Arkansas, the Clinton Foundation evolved to become a philanthropic empire, having raised more than $2 billion over its lifetime.

As an operating foundation, requiring that it raise money on an ongoing basis to fund its projects, the Clinton Foundation does not give much money to other nonprofits, instead focusing itself on global health and wellness, climate change, economic development, and improving opportunities for girls and women in the US and abroad. Within the foundation is the Clinton Global Initiative (CGI), started by and centering around Bill Clinton in 2005, which doesn't involve itself in funding or managing projects, but rather acting as a go-between to match funders with good causes.

Yes, all good, but transparency issues prevail.

During the 2016 election, Donald Trump called for a special prosecutor to investigation the foundation, charging that Hillary Clinton engaged in criminality for connections between the organization's donations from rich foreign power brokers and her activities as secretary of state. The establishment of CGI was an attempt to separate the secretary's official business with world leaders from Bill's interactions with those same people.

Who were those people, how much did they give, and what did they expect in return?

When the Hillary became secretary of state in 2008, she promised President Obama that the foundation would publish all its donors every year. It didn't.

Trump's concerns and calls for an investigation into conflict of interest and pay-for-play allegations are reasonable.

As Hillary campaigned for the presidency, donations to the Clinton Foundation by wealthy donors and foreign governments continued. And as soon as she lost the election, criticism directed toward the foundation was reaffirmed as foreign governments, such as Australia and Norway, began reducing and pulling out of annual donations. A clear sign that influence was predicated on donor access to the Clintons, rather than the foundation's philanthropic work.

# 14

# CASH FOR TRASH

Christopher Steele, who is now retired from MI6 and under far less scrutiny and pressure from government and regulatory superiors to produce informed research and properly documented information, is busy creating a series of documents, which the world would soon come to know as the Trump-Russia Dossier. This dossier is the very core of our tale in the hunt for Red November. Investigative journalist Joe Lauria confirms this:

> It's important to realize that Steele was no longer working for an official intelligence agency, which would have imposed strict standards on his work and possibly disciplined him for injecting false information into the government's decision-making. Instead, he was working for a political party and a presidential candidate looking for dirt that would hurt their opponent, what the Clintons used to call "cash for trash" when they were targets.[12]

Surely Steele would have taken a far different approach had he been doing legitimate intelligence. Instead, he gives his bosses what he knows they want to hear—the same way the media spins news stories to cater to their viewers. Lauria continues:

---

12 Lauria, Joe. "The Democratic Money Behind Russia-Gate." *Consortium News*. 29 Oct 2017. https://consortiumnews.com/2017/10/29/the-democratic-money-behind -russia-gate/

Instead Steele was producing a piece of purely political research and had different motivations. The first might well have been money, as he was being paid specifically for this project, not as part of his work on a government salary presumably serving all of society. Secondly, to continue being paid for each subsequent memo that he produced he would have been incentivized to please his clients or at least give them enough so they would come back for more.[13]

Still, questions linger: If Steele is tasked with the mission to uncover dirt on Trump—which would ultimately affect the outcome of the 2016 election and, in a wider sense, the history of the world—why would he agree to this task for only $168,000? On paper, this looks like a large sum, but why would Steele, who is financially secure from his MI6 days, accept such a potentially dangerous mission for such a grossly low price? Is there another motive for Steele? Is this more than just money? Or is it part of a larger plot: a personal attack to destroy Trump?

13  Ibid.

# 15

# CLASH OF CULTURES: GLOBALISM VERSUS NATIONALISM

IN ORDER TO BETTER UNDERSTAND THE stakes at play in this election, and the impact it would inevitably have on changing the course of history, let's zoom out a bit and take a bird's-eye view of the two ideologies at war here: globalism and nationalism, two polar opposites.

Globalism is Clinton's core belief: Open borders, diminished sovereignty, multilateralism—anything and everything defined as "worldwide" or global in scope. World government is Clinton's ultimate end goal.

Nationalism is the antithesis to Clinton's global government. For Trump, the nation-state is supreme: sovereign borders matter above all. The man plans to build a wall on the Mexico border. Bilateralism is ideal. National and ethnic identities are rooted in tradition. And these institutions of society come first: family, church, and civic duty.

Truth is, globalization has been ebbing while economic and political populism is surging. Globalists no longer provide the accepted set of rules for the political and economic order. Transnational, multilateral, and supranational organizations and their networks, experts, and regulators are everywhere on the defense. Cosmopolitan and globalist values are not ascendant. This is what made Trump's candidacy viable.

As a matter of fact, national sovereignty has soared back and is growing stronger, week by week and month by month. We saw it most clearly in President Trump's principled realism, which he called "America First."

With the battle lines set like never before, each candidate's ideology was pitted against the other—one set of beliefs against the other that, ultimately, will result in a drastic cultural shift. This was war. 2016 would be a watershed, historic year. The Clinton globalists did not want to lose to the Trump nationalists. They did not want their world or their ambitions for globalism disrupted. Clinton is willing to do anything in her power to stop Trump and his nationalistic views in order to further her global reach.

# 16

# TRUMP TOWER MEETING

MEANWHILE, BACK IN NEW YORK CITY, a meeting is scheduled at Trump Tower on June 9, 2016. Just days prior, Natalia Veselnitskaya, a powerful Russian attorney, reaches out to Donald Trump Jr., ostensibly to discuss the adoption of Russian children by US citizens, halted due to Russian government backlash against the Magnitsky Act.

However, Trump Jr. had also received a tip that she might have some dirt on Clinton. Trump Jr. accepts the meeting likely because he thinks the information could be helpful for his team conducting opposition research on Clinton. Jared Kushner, son-in-law to Trump, will be at the meeting. So will Paul Manafort, the political consultant and chairman of Trump's primary election campaign.

What else is on Veselnitskaya's agenda? Does she want the Act to go away? Why would she want to see Donald J. Trump, Jr.? And what exactly is the Magnitsky Act?

In 2009, a Russian tax account, Sergei Magnitsky, died in a Moscow prison after his investigation of fraud involving Russian tax officials. With severe medical conditions, Magnitsky was refused medical treatment while imprisoned and was later beaten to death. Formally known as the "Russia and Moldova Jackson-Vanik Repeal and Sergei Magnitsky Rule of Law Accountability Act of 2012," the bill was passed on a bipartisan basis by the US Congress and signed by then President Obama.

The act had one intention: to punish Russian officials responsible for the death of Sergei Magnitsky. The Magnitsky Act prohibits certain entrants into the US from Russia and their use of the US banking system. As a result of its enactment, the Russian government denied the adoption of Russian children and prohibited a list of Americans from entering Russia.

The *Los Angeles Times* writes, "The adoption ban was part of a tit-for-tat law which also blacklisted US citizens considered by Russia to have violated human rights. The Russian government also instigated a lobby campaign and media effort in the US against the legislation. They sought its repeal in Congress and in the Executive Office."[14]

In December 2016, Congress enlarged the scope of the Magnitsky Act to address human rights abuses on a global scale. The current Global Magnitsky Act (GMA) allows the US government to sanction corrupt government officials implicated in abuses anywhere in the world.

So, based on Veselnitskaya's original request days prior to the actual meeting, Kushner, Trump Jr., and Manafort assumed that the meeting would be in regard to the adoption policy.

During the meeting Veselnitskaya, who claimed to have damaging information about Clinton and her Foundation, dishes the dirt to the Trump camp.

Trump Jr. says he ultimately finds that the information is useless, so they continue to discuss adoption policy and the Magnitsky Act.

A seemingly ordinary meeting, yes? Or will this meeting become the subject of microscopic scrutiny once Steele finishes and release his dossier?

A few months later, when Trump Jr. learns that the *New York Times* is planning to publish a series of email exchanges between him and Veselnitskaya, Trump Jr., in true Trump fashion, exposes the *Times* and publishes them himself on his Twitter account, explaining that the meeting was about opposition research and, ultimately, "such a nothing . . . a wasted 20 minutes."

---

14 Loiko, Sergei. "18 Americans barred from Russia in tit-for-tat sanctions." *Los Angeles Times.* 13 April 2013. http://articles.latimes.com/2013/apr/13/world/la-fg-wn -18-americans-barred-from-russia-in-titfortat-sanctions-20130413

And more curiously, after this meeting, as it would become known, Veselnitskaya meets with Glenn Simpson himself. Why? What exactly was the purpose of that meeting?

# 17

# THE PROFESSOR, THE DIPLOMAT, AND THE EAGER BEAVER

GEORGE PAPADOPOULOS IS A FORMER MEMBER of the Trump for President foreign policy panel that met formally only once. While his Italian girlfriend disputes this, he is a nobody.

From Chicago, his Greek family was very involved in local politics. Graduating from DePaul University in 2009, Papadopoulos later received an MSc degree in security studies from University College London.

He directed international energy issues at the London Center of International Law Practice.

Landing an internship that turned into a job at the Hudson Institute, Papadopoulos listed himself as "an oil, gas, and policy consultant."

He served as an advisor on candidate Ben Carson's failed presidential bid, and then the policy advisor went on to associate with Trump.

Papadopoulos was called, by one publication, a "little known, little qualified 30-year-old."

In March 2016, he is approached by Professor Joseph Mifsud in London, who brags about his connections to high-level Russian officials and to Putin's niece, Olga Polonskaya (which turned out to be false). Papadopoulos is told Russia has "dirt" on Hillary Clinton.

Papadopoulos makes repeated requests of the Trump campaign to set up a meeting between the leaders, Putin and Trump. He also suggests various meetings with Russians in Russia.

These never occur, and he is repeatedly told "no" by more senior campaign officials.

As reported in the *New York Times*, in May 2016, Papadopoulos sits at an upscale bar, the Kensington Wine Rooms, in London, for a drink, and there he meets Australia's High Commissioner to the UK, Alexander Downer. Maybe it was the wine, but Papadopoulos goes on to reveal that Russia has "dirt" on Hillary Clinton.

Downer, the diplomat, tips off the FBI, and thus begins the Bureau's investigation into, not Hillary Clinton, but into possible ties between the Trump campaign and Russia.

Papadopolous will go on to be arrested at Dulles International Airport on July 27, 2017, and will plead guilty to making false statements to FBI agents.

# 18

# CARTER PAGE: RUSSIAN PLANT?

A FEW WEEKS FOLLOWING THE TRUMP Tower meeting, in July 2016 Trump selects Carter Page as his foreign policy advisor. Page is founder and managing partner at Global Energy Capital, a New York investment fund that specializes in Russia and Central Asia oil and gas markets.

Page served in the Navy for five years, including a tour as an intelligence officer. With a master's degree in national security from Georgetown University and an MBA from New York University, Page quickly found work as an investment banker for Merrill Lynch in its New York and London offices and then headed its Moscow office. He later earned his PhD from the University of London.

In 1998, he joined Eurasia Group as a strategy consultant but left after only three months as it was "not a good fit." The CEO claimed his views were too pro-Russia.

Expressing positive views about Russia, Putin, and energy developments there, Page was labeled as a Russia expert on the RT television network and in various journals where he stated his positive views.

On July 7, 2016, Page travels to Moscow to speak at the New Economic School. At the school he gives a speech that is heavily critical of current US foreign policy. He stays in Russia for three days in total . . .

Could Page possibly be a plant dropped by the Russians into the Trump campaign? Page has been the subject of a FISA court warrant since 2014 due to his connections to certain Russian officials.

In September, US intelligence officials begin investigating alleged contacts between Page and Russian officials, including Igor Sechin, the "de facto deputy" of Vladimir Putin. In other words, he is Putin's number two guy. Sechin's aide is a man named Oleg Erovinkin. He is a former general in the KGB. US intelligence officials suspect that Erovinkin might be in contact with Christopher Steele. If this delicate information were to make its way back to the Kremlin, this could be fatal for the former KGB general . . .

And once word spreads across media outlets connecting Page with Russia and Putin's government, Page steps down as Trump's campaign advisor.

The US intelligence community, however, continues investigating emails and conversations between Page and Russian officials subject to US sanctions.

# 19

# CYBER WARFARE

WHILE THE REDS AND BLUES ARE each busy with their own forms of opposition research, John Podesta, the chairman of Clinton's campaign, falls victim to an email phishing scam in March 2016. Podesta turns to expert cybersecurity firm CrowdStrike.

In 2011, George Kurtz and Dmitri Alperovitch founded CrowdStrike, a private cybersecurity firm. Both Kurtz and Alperovitch have long histories and experience in the cybersecurity field, and in 2015 when CapitalG (formerly Google Capital) backs them, CrowdStrike becomes the go-to team for all digital inquiries of the sensitive sort. So, on May 4, 2016, when Podesta and the Democratic National Committee want to investigate a possible intrusion into their servers, they look to CrowdStrike. The DNC was not unfamiliar with CrowdStrike, having used their services in December 2015 to investigate a security breach involving their party-administered voter file system known as VoteBuilder. After a systems forensic examination, including examining the system used by the Bernie Sanders campaign, CrowdStrike released their findings. Curiously, it was on the same day, April 29, 2016, that the DNC server breach was detected.

Following their hiring, CrowdStrike works surprisingly fast. In fact, on May 5, CrowdStrike's FalconHost software finds indicators such as malware and operating and behavioral techniques that point to Russians being behind the cyber intrusion. Naturally, the DNC and its figureheads take CrowdStrike's word and findings as gospel—why wouldn't they?

After all, Kurtz and Alperovitch are the experts, not the DNC. And when the DNC spreads this news to the media outlets, journalists across the board report on what they had been told—like in a game of telephone.

Did any of these journalists read CrowdStrike's findings? Did they conduct any form of firsthand research?

Instead, these reporters abandon their basic journalist duties and release unverified articles with headline-grabbing titles like this one in *Forbes*, "CrowdStrike Helped Trace the DNC Hack to Russia: Now Business is Booming." Once the CrowdStrike word spreads like wildfire throughout the Democratic political arena on this alleged interference, one headline dominates the mainstream media: The Russians Hacked America.

This story has an eerily familiar ring to it, doesn't it?

Sounds just like what Christopher Steele is busy doing for Fusion GPS: fabricating information that he knows his client wants to hear. This type of dirty work isn't just murky for those directly involved in this chain of communication exchange; it's even more dangerous for those at the receiving end of this information: the general public.

In her article for the *Baffler*, "From Russia, With Panic," journalist Yasha Levine writes about the potential danger here:

> CrowdStrike stuck to its guns, and other cybersecurity firms and experts likewise clamored to confirm its findings: Russia was behind the attack. Most journalists took these security savants at their word, not bothering to investigate or vet their forensic methods or look at the way CrowdStrike arrived at its conclusions. And how could they? They were the experts. If you couldn't trust CrowdStrike and company, who could you trust?[15]

Perhaps it's naïve to think that the DNC—like many other institutions and pillars of American government—is simply ignorant of the idea

---

15   Levine, Yasha. "From Russia, With Panic." *The Baffler*. March 2017. https://thebaffler
.com/salvos/from-russia-with-panic-levine

that their actions might have negative outward consequences that fall on the public, the very people they are there to serve and protect. Or is it too cynical to think that perhaps this is exactly what the DNC wanted: to hire a firm that they know will produce exactly what they want to hear—the Russians did it—so they can report this unverified information to the public to further their agenda of subverting the presidential campaign of Donald Trump?

While the media feverishly continues running a story it hasn't corroborated, Trump releases a statement: "We believe it was the DNC that did the 'hacking' as a way to distract the many issues facing their deeply flawed candidate and a failed party leader."[16]

Unsurprisingly, the media responds harshly, criticizing Trump and his campaign for being out of touch and way off base—that this supposed inside job is all in Trump's head.

And, should the word get out that this information was false, will the public point blame at the DNC or even CrowdStrike? Will they call out these institutions out for what they are—liars and manipulators of the truth? Or will this misinformation become buried by the national headlines claiming there is Russian interference, so a great, orchestrated lie becomes spun into truth?

Perhaps in time and once more evidence comes into question about the legitimacy of CrowdStrike's analysis, the tides of opinion will begin to turn in favor of Trump's position that this is all a hoax, concocted from within the belly of the beast.

---

16  Nelson, Louis. "Trump Accuses DNC of 'hacking' its own oppo research on him." *Politico*. 15 June 2016. https://www.politico.com/story/2016/06/donald-trump-opposition -224397

# 20

# THE CROWD MENTALITY

In the days that follow CrowdStrike's findings, the *Washington Post* is the first to publish the results. And on their own website, the CrowdStrike team provides further details in regard to their findings in a post titled "Bears in the Midst." In the post, Alperovitch attributes the DNC hack to two "distinct and very nefarious 'Russian espionage' groups: Cozy Bear and Fancy Bear."[17] Alperovitch writes that these two groups, known as "advanced persistent threats" or APTs, whose traits were known from past nefarious activities, are some of the most advanced cyber-operators he and his team have yet come across: "In fact, our team considers them some of the best adversaries out of all the numerous nation-state, criminal and hacktivist/terrorist groups we encounter on a daily basis."[18]

He continues: "Their tradecraft is superb, operational security second to none and the extensive usage of 'living-off-the-land' techniques enables them to easily bypass many security solutions they encounter."[19]

Why would anyone consider questioning Alperovitch and his team's findings? He's the expert, not us—the general public, the layman.

---

17 Alperovitch, Dmitri. "Bears in the Midst: Intrusion into the Democratic National Committee." *CrowdStrike Blog.* 16 June 2016. https://www.crowdstrike.com/blog/bears-midst-intrusion-democratic-national-committee/
18 Ibid.
19 Ibid.

A dangerous game of telephone we're playing here, especially considering how high the stakes are.

The CrowdStrike team then explains how these two groups were allegedly behind a string of recent attacks on American corporations and think tanks. In addition to those attacks, these groups are responsible for the recent penetrations of the unclassified networks of the State Department, the White House, and the US Joint Chiefs of Staff. According to CrowdStrike, Cozy Bear was most likely the FSB, while Fancy Bear was linked to the "GRU, Russia's premier military intelligence service."

Pointing out cybersecurity author Jeffrey Carr's questioning of the credibility of CrowdStrike's methodology, former Marine Corps intelligence officer and UN weapons inspector and author Scott Ritter writes, "Within elements of the cybercommunity, the credibility of CrowdStrike has been shattered by its involvement in the DNC hack. Its two premier product platforms—Falcon and Overwatch—have been exposed as being fundamentally (and perhaps fatally) flawed. The attributions derived from Falcon are little more than false positives generated by algorithms pre-programmed to deliver an outcome—CrowdStrike was looking for Russia, and therefore found it."[20]

Therefore, we must consider, is this complicated, overly detailed explanation—replete with names like Cozy Bear and Fancy Bear—of this email intrusion designed to distract the public from the truth? A story that sounds just convincing enough that no one thinks to question its credibility? Is this yet another prime example of the Deep State at work? Is this a Red November fabrication to subvert the president?

---

20 Ritter, Scott. "Crowdstrike: Making it up as they go along?" *Homefront Rising*. 31 Aug 2017. https://medium.com/homefront-rising/dumbstruck-how-crowdstrike -conned-america-on-the-hack-of-the-dnc-ecfa522ff44f

# 21

# FAUX RUSSIAN:
# A HOAX EMAIL LEAK

THIS STORY TAKES ANOTHER SHARP, INCENDIARY turn after a hacker who calls himself Guccifer 2.0 emerges from the woodwork and takes credit for the DNC hack. He calls CrowdStrike's investigation a fraud and begins leaking classified documents from the DNC, including the Democratic Party's 200-page opposition research report on Donald Trump.

On June 15, 2016, the day after the Democrats go public about two bears breaching their computers, Guccifer 2.0 introduces himself to the world with an email and attached documents marked "CONFIDENTIAL" to William Bastone, editor-in-chief of the investigative news site the *Smoking Gun*: "Hi. This is Guccifer 2.0 and this is me who hacked Democratic National Committee."[21]

"The main part of the papers, thousands of files and mails (about 100GB of data) I gave to WikiLeaks. They will publish them soon," Guccifer 2.0 writes in a blog post.[22]

Who exactly is this Guccifer 2.0, whose namesake Guccifer happens to be that of a Romanian hacker, arrested in 2014 and sentenced in May 2016 to four and a half years in prison after stealing the emails

---

21 Satter, Raphael. "Inside Story: How the Russians hacked the Democrats' emails." Associated Press. 4 Nov 2017. https://www.apnews.com/dea73efc01594839957c3c9a6c962b8a
22 Unknown. "Gufficer 2.0 Hacked the Clinton Foundation." 4 Oct 2016. https://guccifer2 .wordpress.com/2016/10/04/clinton-foundation/C

of famous celebrities. Is it an actual person? Or just a persona—a collective group working under the same name and cause?

Once WikiLeaks manages to get their hands on the entire DNC email archive, they slowly begin releasing it out to the public, coordinating their leak for July 22, 2016—one day before the Democratic National Convention is to begin—to ensure maximum exposure.

What exactly is in these classified emails? Could there be evidence of orchestrated political sabotage or smearing?

Within these leaks are the emails of John Podesta, the head of that campaign, which causes significant embarrassment to Hillary Clinton and the Democrat Party.

The US Intelligence Community says the source of the leaks is, of course, Russia. WikiLeaks, however, denies this accusation, claiming it is not a state source.

What then is WikiLeaks' role, if any, in the outcome of the election?

Once the media examines the emails of top DNC officials, a trend appears: an orchestrated attack on their own candidates, namely Senator Sanders.

On July 25, the FBI says it will investigate the hack. That same day, in attempt for damage control and to plug the leak, the DNC issues a statement:

"On behalf of everyone at the DNC, we want to offer a deep and sincere apology to Senator Sanders, his supporters, and the entire Democratic Party for the inexcusable remarks made over email."[23]

They then explain how the emails do not reflect the DNC's "steadfast commitment to neutrality during the nominating process."

What a sorry excuse for an apology. Even worse, the Democratic public accepts it. Here we have concrete evidence of sabotage against one of their own candidates and in favor of Hillary Clinton.

Joe Lauria poses a stark reminder on the Democrats' supposed neutral approach to politics: "The two sources that originated the

---

23  Drabold, Will. "DNC Apologizes to Bernie Sanders and Supporters Over Leaked Emails." *Time*. 25 July 2016. http://time.com/4422715/bernie-sanders-dnc-apology -leaked-emails/

allegations claiming that Russia meddled in the 2016 election—without providing convincing evidence—were both *paid for* by the Democratic National Committee, and in one instance also by the Clinton Campaign: the Steele dossier and the CrowdStrike analysis of the DNC servers. Think about that for a minute."

Clearly, the DNC abandons their so-called stance on neutrality. In fact, they are responsible for creating this entire notion of collusion.

Will these leaks change the course of the US election?

Is a foreign government really the culprit? Or is this an inside job?

# 22

# WILLIAM BINNEY WEIGHS IN

WHILE THIS HE-SAID-SHE-SAID GAME IS UNFOLDING live for the world to see, former NSA technical director William Binney is busy conducting experiments to dismiss this whole Russian hack claim. Binney is the same high-level NSA intelligence official who, following his 2001 retirement from the agency, blew the whistle on the extraordinary extent of NSA surveillance programs.

This time, his experiments show that "the known download speed of one batch of DNC emails could not have occurred over the internet but matched what was possible for a USB-connected thumb drive—an indication that a Democratic insider likely downloaded the emails and thus there was no 'hack.'"[24] Unsurprisingly, the mainstream media mocks Binney, calling him a "conspiracy theorist."

So if it wasn't Russia, but a Democratic insider, the question remains: who? And why?

In an interview for *Consortium News*, investigative journalist Dennis J. Bernstein bluntly asks Binney, "So was this a leak by somebody at the Democratic headquarters?" To which Binney replies, "We don't know that for sure, either. All we know was that it was a local

---

24  Parry, Robert. "Protecting the Shaky Russia-gate Narrative." *Consortium News*. 15 Dec 2017. https://consortiumnews.com/2017/12/15/protecting-the-shaky-russia-gate -narrative/

download. We can likely attribute it to a USB device that was physically passed along."[25]

Bernstein then asks, "So if, in fact, the Russians were tapping into DNC headquarters, the NSA would absolutely know about it."

"Yes, and they would also have the trace routes on where they went specifically, in Russia or anywhere else," Binney says.

Again, this begs the same question we've been searching for this whole time: where is the evidence? If there is some sort of Russian collusion, there should be a tangible form of proof. And yet, here we are, with nothing—no answers, just more questions.

With the world caught up with the drama unfolding on stage, Steele is continuing to create his report behind the drawn curtains.

25  Bernstein, Dennis J. "The Still Missing Evidence of Russiagate" *Consortium News*. 01 Jan 2018. https://consortiumnews.com/2018/01/01/the-still-missing-evidence -of-russia-gate/?print=print

# 23

# SPY GAMES

MEANWHILE IN CLEVELAND, AT THE REPUBLICAN National Convention, Sergey Kislyak is holding a "diplomacy conference." Kislyak, a stodgy Russian diplomat, served as Russia's ambassador to the US from 2008 to 2017. Before that he was Deputy Minister of Foreign Affairs and Russia's ambassador to Belgium from 1998 to 2003.

His nine-year tenure in the US established him as the ranking interlocutor on Russian affairs. Many referred to him as a "diplomat's diplomat."

In attendance at Kislyak's conference are J. D. Gordon and Carter Page. Is this coincidence that Page, a suspected Russian plant, is meeting with Kislyak? Or is it something more?

Later during the convention, on July 21, Senator Jeff Sessions, policy advisor on national security matters to Trump's campaign, Gordon, and Page have a meeting with Kislyak, in which, according to delegate Victor Ashe, "Much of the discussion focused on Russia's incursion into Ukraine and Georgia."[26] Surely, Jeff Sessions's attendance at this meeting will lead to intense media scrutiny and criticism.

Kislyak soon finds himself in the American media's spotlight, taking up plenty of airtime on CNN as a major player behind this so-called Russian interference with the election and the source of DNC's email

---

26 Yglesias, Matthew. "A Timeline of Jeff Sessions and Michael Flynn's Talk with the Russian Ambassador." *Vox*. 3 March 2017. https://www.vox.com/policy-and -politics/2017/3/3/14792942/sessions-flynn-kislyak-timeline

leak. US intelligence officials claim he is some sort of Russian spy and spy recruiter.

According to *Newsweek*, however, "People who have worked closely with Kislyak doubt the ambassador was up to anything more than just doing his job."[27] Kislyak, rightfully so, vehemently refutes this conjecture and denies that there was any sort of interference. John Beyrle, a former US ambassador to Russia, comes to his defense, saying that Kislyak is "a professional diplomat, not a politician. I'm sure he's surprised to have acquired such notoriety recently. I'm sure he's probably not enjoying his time in the limelight."

As an ambassador in Washington, DC, Kislyak did what all ambassadors do—namely, meet with people. He met with both Republican and Democratic senators and congressmen and various businesspeople and policy officials.

Michael McFaul, a former US ambassador to Russia, weighs in on the meeting: "On political involvement, I personally don't think [Kislyak] crossed any lines."[28] And Maria Zakharova, the spokeswoman for the Russian Foreign Ministry, calls the unwarranted speculation on Kislyak "the low professional standards of the American news media."[29]

Will this meeting, like the Trump Tower meeting, be of great focus in Steele's nebulous dossier?

This meeting with Sergey Kislyak is just another example in the line of many of how the mainstream media warps and distorts a story, spinning it into a web of lies that it knows will cater to its audience's already set-in-concrete views on Russia. It's a distortion manipulated by this Deep State in our hunt for Red November.

Maybe Putin had an opinion?

With an 80 percent approval rating in Russia and a seemingly

---

27  Cooper, Matthew; Matthews, Owen. "Spy or Diplomat? Meet Russian Ambassador Sergey Kislyak, The Most Radioactive Man in Washington." *Newsweek*. 22 June 2017. http://www.newsweek.com/2017/06/30/spy-diplomat-sergey-kislyak-russia-ambas sador-russia-probe-washington-627982.html

28  Ibid.

29  MacFarquhar, Neil; Baker, Peter. "Sergey Kislyak, Russian Envoy, Cultivated Powerful Network in US" *New York Times*. 2 March 2017. https://www.nytimes .com/2017/03/02/world/europe/sergey-kislyak-russian-ambassador.html

endless elected cycle as putative leader of that country, Putin is a bona fide world leader, even if Russia is not a true superpower. Russia is largely what it is today because of Putin and his nationalistic, hyperstrong relations and of course the natural resource wealth on which its economy (and Putin's reign and personal wealth) depends.

Whether Russia is in or out of the G7/G8, whether it is sanctioned or not, and whether it is seen as a regional or global power, Putin's imprint sticks.

And Russia via Putin has been known to endorse and coddle certain political leaders in places like the Middle East, Central Asia (former Republics in the USSR), Central America, Africa, and elsewhere. He likes to take center stage and flex his muscles—literally and figuratively.

In Syria, he backed Assad and put his troops and planes in to keep him in power. In Turkey, he appears to have a new détente with Erdogan and has sold him defensive missiles. Allegedly, he has helped to fund both political parties on the left and on the right, sowing discord and chaos in places like Georgia, Ukraine, and Western Europe. And yes, he has invaded Crimea.

The degree of Russian meddling in past elections is up for debate and the US Congress has multiple committees of senators and representatives "looking into" all that activity or in some cases less than overt activity. The US Intelligence Community has said Russia is a nefarious player with definite ambitions and inordinate power to do harm.

At any rate, what Putin thinks matters. What Putin does has consequences. Who Putin favors can result in support and influence.

In the 2016 US election between Clinton and Trump, undoubtedly Putin saw an opportunity.

Could he get one person elected over the other? No. Could he throw around his weight and affect the election? It seems not, except that he could indirectly pull some strings and show favoritism. Could he steal an election using cyber to control the voting machines? No. Did he control WikiLeaks? No. Did he try and use trolls to effect social media? Probably. Did Russia buy ads on Facebook and the like? It seems so, but at insignificant amounts.

So how precisely did Putin's opinion play a role in the US election?

Putin himself has called stories of his "meddling" both "nonsense" and "spy hysteria." He has said that there was no way he could damage the American political system.

But did Russia act to promote Trump over Clinton?

Truthfully, Putin hated Clinton because as Secretary of State she was behind the mass protests in Moscow in 2013.

He believed she had tried to undermine *his* power and prestige. Putin is known to seek revenge.

Was there a budding "bromance" between Putin and Trump? This may be more theory than fact but Trump has voiced admiring words for Putin as a leader and the favor has been returned. Each has called for improved relations between the two countries, something Clinton did not deem plausible or remotely possible.

Clinton has never concealed her disdain for Putin.

As a senator in 2008, she joked about President George W. Bush's famous line that he'd gotten a sense of Putin's "soul," suggesting that because Putin was a KGB agent, "by definition he doesn't have a soul."

Putin was logically and emotionally hostile to Clinton, as he felt personally stung by her words and actions.

He was angry.

She took a hard line and was even a proponent of regime change. That was a threat to him and his very survival.

Does this lead to speculation of payback? It does, but within a limited sense of what could be accomplished.

Certainly, Clinton was unloved by the Kremlin and they were skeptical of any "reset" under her future watch.

Putin therefore, like just about every other world leader, expected Clinton to win the election.

But at minimum the Russians wanted to send her a message that they were a power to be reckoned with.

# 24

# JAMES "DIRTY HANDS" BAKER

WITH THE DNC EMAIL LEAK CLOGGING up airtime on the media, the FBI is tasked with figuring out who let their finger off the plug. They tasked one man with the job: James Baker, the FBI's General Counsel. Baker has a very close friend: James Comey.

The two have a long history together, and in January 2014 Comey tapped Baker to become the FBI's top lawyer. They had been longtime colleagues at both the DOJ and for a spell at the private Bridgewater Associates.

Could Baker be a pawn working for Comey? Does Comey pick Baker for the job because he knows he'll say just what Comey wants to hear—the same way Steele knows just what the people funding his mission want to hear?

In the past, Baker has also been involved with a number of serious matters involving the DOJ and its past investigations, like his 2015 handling of the sensitive issues regarding Hillary Clinton's use of a private email server. It was Baker and his gang who failed to recommend criminal charges.

Baker had always been involved in FISA warrant requests. He was the FBI "go-to" on FISA. In 2007, Baker appeared on the PBS *Frontline* episode "Spying on the Home Front," where the show's producer, in the *Washington Post* online, referred to Baker as "Mr. FISA himself."[30]

---

30  Young, Rick (Producer). "Spying on the Home Front." *PBS Frontline*. 16 May 2017. http://www.washingtonpost.com/wp-dyn/content/discussion/2007/05/03 /DI2007050301142.html

Could Baker be a part of an effort to make sure Trump will never make it into the White House? Is he in the middle of the dump-Trump schemes? Is he a resister? Or worse?

Could he be in collaboration to keep this Russia-gate story alive and to support the candidacy of Hillary Clinton?

Did he have help, an ally—high up? Perhaps it was a certain Andy McCabe?

McCabe joined the FBI in 1996 and became what is known as a "lifer." He knew nothing else.

He started his long career in New York City with the FBI SWAT field office and moved next to become a special agent at the Eurasia Organized Crime Task Force. Promoted, he managed counterterrorism efforts and the National Security Branch of the entire FBI in Washington DC.

In 2009 McCabe directed the office on high-value detainees. He led the investigation on the Boston Marathon bombing and also the arrest of the Benghazi attackers.

McCabe was a dedicated FBIer and he became very attached to James Comey. Comey appointed him to many lead placements and eventually made him his deputy.

McCabe should have recused himself from the Hillary Clinton investigations and those of the Clinton Foundation because of political conflict of interest, given the fact that Clinton's Democrat cronies (Terry McAuliffe) had given almost $700,000 dollars in contributions to McCabe's wife in her campaign for Democratic state senate in Virginia. He didn't.

# 25

# PARAMOURS: PETER STRZOK & LISA PAGE

WHILE HILLARY IS BUSY HIDING EMAILS, FBI agent Peter Strzok (pronounced "struck") begins his investigation into her use of private emails. In August 2016, Strzok is in Virginia on FBI business, but he is sending amorous text messages to Lisa Page, a fellow FBI colleague. Page is married, but that doesn't stop her from falling for Strzok. Most couples in the early honeymoon phases of love talk about each other and their futures, but Strzok and Page, it seems, mostly discussed Trump—or more accurately, they were plotting against him.

Strzok is no ordinary FBI agent. He is Chief of Counterespionage during the investigation of Hillary Clinton's leaked emails and server intrusion. He would later become Deputy Assistant Director of the whole FBI counterintelligence office. He is the one who will edit the letter by James Comey reducing the liability of Clinton from extreme and punishable to a slap on the wrist by changing the description of Clinton's actions as "grossly negligent," which would be a criminal offense, to "extremely careless." A draft of the letter is then reviewed and corrected by several people until it reaches its final form. In this final statement, Comey says that "no reasonable prosecutor" would bring charges based on available evidence.

One thing remains clear about FBI agent Strzok: he certainly has a way with words . . .

In one text message, Strzok writes, "Just went to a southern Virginia Walmart. I could SMELL the Trump support. . . . it's scary real down here."[31] From this message alone, Strzok's deep-seated contempt for those working-class Trump voters is palpable.

Page responds to her knight in shining armor, writing: "Maybe you're meant to stay where you are because you're meant to protect the country from that menace [Trump]."[32]

In another text, Strzok warns of the need for an "insurance policy" to thwart Trump on the off chance that his poll numbers closed in on those of Mrs. Clinton, writing, "that there's no way he [Trump] gets elected—but I'm afraid we can't take that risk." Strzok adds, "It's like an insurance policy in the unlikely event that you die before you're 40."[33] Is Strzok referencing Steele here, as the insurance policy?

Why then would Strzok and Page, both FBI agents more than familiar with heightened surveillance, be so careless with text messages broadcasting their blatant opposition to Trump? Is this simply having a personal opinion? Or is this something more sinister and calculated?

This is people working together in a calculated plot against Trump. *This* is the Deep State.

---

31  Fox News. "Read FBIs Strzok, Page Texts About Trump." *Fox News*. 21 January 2018. http://www.foxnews.com/politics/2018/01/21/ex-mueller-aides-texts-revealed-read-them-here.html

32  Ibid.

33  Ibid.

# 26

# SOURCES AND METHODS

In order to better understand how intelligence professionals compile their research, it's important to define a few technical terms to have a clearer sense of the stages involved to produce accurate data and reports. *Intelligence and Information Policy for National Security: Key Terms and Concepts* by Jan Goldman and Susan Maret defines these as follows:

Sources: Persons, images, signals, documents, databases, and communications media capable of providing intelligence information through collection and analysis programs (e.g., Human Intelligence (HUMINT), Imagery Intelligence (IMINT), Signals Intelligence (SIGINT), Geospatial Intelligence (GEOINT), and Measurement and Signature Intelligence (MASINT)).

Methods: Information collection and analysis strategies, tactics, operations, and technologies employed to produce intelligence products. If intelligence sources or methods are disclosed without authorization, their effectiveness may be substantially negated or impaired.

And from the *Oxford Handbook of National Security Intelligence*, edited by Loch K. Johnson, we learn that "sources and methods," usually used together, describe the practice of intelligence collection and analysis.

Sources range from information obtained through espionage, satellite imagery, and intercepted communications, to media reports and personal contacts. Methods are the tradecraft—the techniques employed by operations agents and officers to obtain their valuable information. Methodologies can range from sociological and psychological profiling to live and predictive computer-based analytical tools.

Ensuring maintenance of communications while safeguarding sources and methods is also critical, since revealing these, and how information is analyzed, could give adversaries and competitors a means of evaluating a rival's capabilities and intentions.

Thus, for successful operations and analysis to continue into the future, a cloak of secrecy must be maintained by intelligence agencies.

A compilation based on sound sources and methods is highly valued; one based on anything less is worthless.

There is no source validation and no information on "chain of acquisition" of the material Steele collected. What was his vetting process to cross-check and corroborate sources and information? How can Steele stand by the credibility of his information when there is no validation of his sources and methods?

Not being privy to Steele's sources and methods, we must then analyze the veracity of his information, which we find not only suspect, but outrageous.

That's right, it is worthless.

Still, even though technically worthless, it could still be used if foisted off as the "real" thing . . .

# 27

# DISINFORMATION

USED FOR THE FIRST TIME IN 1939 to describe the actions of Soviet leader Josef Stalin, "disinformation" is defined as follows: "false information deliberately and often covertly spread (as by the planting of rumors) in order to influence public opinion or obscure the truth."[34]

As a form of deliberate deception, or so-called "black propaganda," the whole idea originated in Russia's darkest secret organization—the Soviets used it for everything and in every way possible.

They used it to advertise that the US had invented AIDS, to suggest the US backed apartheid, and to bribe officials. There was nothing they did not try to use it on. Anyone in their net was subject to being blackmailed. From forged documents to fake photos to bogus manuscripts, they employed disinformation with one intention: to spread dangerous and fabricated intelligence.

All of this came to light in the interrogations of numerous Soviet defectors from the late 1960s to the end of the 1980s.

Is the Trump-Russia dossier another package of such disinformation? Did it originate in the Russian FSB? Was it planted there to affect an American election? Did they want to destabilize the West?

What we do know is that Christopher Steele was an expert on the use and effect of disinformation.

Is he a dupe himself or perhaps an agent for such material, for a price?

---

34 https://www.merriam-webster.com/dictionary/disinformation

# 28

# THE FINISHED, FILTHY PRODUCT

JUST WEEKS AWAY FROM ELECTION DAY, Christopher Steele finishes his compilation, which is just what it suggests: You take all your sources and combine them into a finished, compiled product. Raw intelligence comes from human, electronic, and satellite sources that need to be fitted into a whole.

This combined effect does not include analysis. That last step is left to the analyst; any actions to be taken or decisions to be made are performed by the end user of the intelligence.

In today's world, where intelligence and journalism meet, you see a new linkage. The power brokers, whether corporate or political, want not just more data points, or more streams of information. They want sensational, high tone, actionable judgments that they can trust and act on.

Information of this kind is called knowledge.

The funding of this new business model, called "business intelligence," is critical in the case of the Trump-Russia dossier. It involves spies for hire and a journalistic tendency to go for the jugular. The two are not natural allies. Good intelligence is factual and proven, *not* invented or headline-grabbing.

Hiring former secret agents and their networks that supposedly know where all the bodies are buried, and who buried some themselves, sounds like a novel idea. With years and years' worth of assets, all with ears and eyes on the ground, in such distant and nefarious places as Moscow, it just made sense.

When Christopher Steele finishes his peculiar compilation, which as we know is funded in a scheme that made more and more sordid stuff likely, since he paid informants to make it up, he doesn't know what to do with the product.

That product was, remember, done for Fusion GPS and its clients: the DNC and the Clinton campaign.

These players, however, don't seem to be using it, and the news cycle is focused elsewhere: Anthony Weiner sexting, John Podesta lying, and WikiLeaks.

What is Steele to do with his valuable if not overly salacious compilation?

Finally, Steele rediscovers an old mate from the FBI who is now stationed in Rome. Steele flies there to meet with him and hands him a copy of his compilation. Will the FBI act quickly on Steele's dirty compilation, or will they drag their feet? Or will Steele have to find another outlet to get his dossier some attention?

# 29

# THE HAIL MARY
# FROM *MOTHER JONES*

JAMES BAKER, THE FBI'S GENERAL COUNSEL, who has now caught wind of Steele's dossier and read through its salacious details, meets with David Corn, a reporter from ultra liberal magazine *Mother Jones*, to discuss the contents of Steele's dossier. Corn gained a mild degree of media attention for his harsh criticism of George W. Bush in his book with the highly original title *Lies of George W. Bush,* in which Corn claims that Bush had "mugged the truth."[35]

Corn had also been involved in the coverage and controversy surrounding leaks to the media of former CIA officer Valerie Plame. Corn loved the limelight. He discovered that going to the edge and then one step farther brought him into the national light.

It was Corn who broke the story of the Mitt Romney "47 percent video"—a story that helped defeat the Republican candidate in 2012.

Frustrated and desperate that no one will publish his unverified dossier, Steele takes his compilation on a plane to New York, where he meets with David Corn—a meeting that is set up by none other than James Baker, who knows that the left-wing scandalmonger Corn will love what he's about to see: filthy dirt. Naturally, Corn promises to keep it secret.

---

35 Corn, David. *The Lies of George W. Bush: Mastering the Politics of Deception.* Penguin Random House. 2004.

Clearly, Baker has dirty hands and indeed appears to be a key figure working alongside this Deep State in the Red November plot to destroy Trump.

On October 31, 2016, Corn decides to run with the compilation—it's just too juicy not to. He calls it his "Hail Mary" pass to stop Trump, and runs a version of the story on the spy and the FBI. The compilation is now out in the open.

Mission accomplished.

# 30

# THE BRITISH CONNECTION

SIR ANDREW WOOD IS PART OF what they refer to as "the good and great" in Great Britain. He quite looks the part. The former British diplomat had a most distinguished career in foreign relations, culminating as ambassador to Russia and then Moldova before retiring from service.

Born in 1940, in Gibraltar, Wood was properly educated at upper crust Ardingly College and King's College, Cambridge University. He immediately entered into the Foreign and Commonwealth Office after graduation and was posted to Moscow. Following a number of other postings he was made ambassador to Yugoslavia from 1985 through 1989.

As a Russia expert, he has served on a number of boards, commercial and educational, and advised Prime Minister Tony Blair on Russia on various investments there. Wood was made GCMG, which translates as a high order, after having been knighted earlier. This is the most distinguished British Order of St. Michael and St. George. He is also the Russia advisor to Chatham House, a London think tank on international affairs.

As a highly distinguished man with a reputation and resume to match, how does Sir Andrew Wood fit into this puzzle?

He is an advisor to Orbis Intelligence.

On November 8, 2016, after Christopher Steele has passed his Trump-Russia dossier on to both his own MI6 intelligence service in the UK and to the FBI, Sir Andrew Wood attends the annual International Security Forum in Halifax, Canada, where Senator John

McCain is also in attendance. The ambassador confidentially discusses a report that has compromising information about the incoming president. He has McCain's full attention.

McCain is no fan of Donald Trump. He did not back Trump in either his primary or general campaign. He saw him as a dangerous isolationist, a challenge to the entire Establishment and to his neocon views.

After the meeting, McCain dispatches an associate, David Kramer, former State Department official and current senior fellow at the McCain Institute, to London to meet with Christopher Steele to be briefed on its contents. Kramer is given a partial copy of the dossier and in twenty-four hours, he returns it to Washington, DC—to McCain.

The following day, Glenn Simpson of Fusion GPS meets with McCain and gives him a full copy of the dossier. Senator McCain doesn't like what he reads, so he sets up a meeting with FBI Director James Comey, writing in a prepared statement that "Upon examination of the contents, and unable to make a judgment about their accuracy, I delivered the information to the Director of the FBI. That has been the extent of my contact with the FBI or any other government agency regarding this issue."[36]

Sure . . .

---

36 Greenwood, Max. "McCain gave dossier containing 'sensitive material' to FBI." *The Hill*. 11 Jan 2017. http://thehill.com/blogs/blog-briefing-room/news/313716 -mccain-gave-dossier-containing-sensitive-information-to-fbi

# 31

# THE TRUMP CARD

At this point in the race toward presidency Clinton is a shoo-in. In all the polls, she's projected to defeat Trump by a landslide. The question isn't will she win—it's by how much.

Her surrogates are legion and there isn't anybody in the media, save for one or two people at Fox News, who think she isn't a shoo-in to win.

All the newspapers endorse her. All the pundits kowtow to her. And all the pollsters are predicting her inevitable victory. The odds are 8-to-1 she will win in Las Vegas betting.

With the "woman card" up her sleeve, Clinton is a sure bet.

And in the highly unlikely scenario that Clinton loses to Trump, would she be willing to use Steele's phony intel to blackmail Trump to the Russians with incriminating evidence? But like a reserve parachute that you hope to never have to pull that cord, it's nice knowing it's there.

On the morning of November 8, 2016, with the election already underway and votes coming in, the *New York Times* posts an article online titled, "Who Will Be President?" The *Times*, using estimates based on pre-election polls, reports that Hillary Clinton is predicted to be the next president, with a staggering 85 percent chance to win. Trump, according to the *Times*, only has a 15 percent chance . . . [37]

---

37  Katz, Josh. "Who Will Be President?" *New York Times*. 8 Nov 2016. https://www.nytimes.com/interactive/2016/upshot/presidential-polls-forecast.html

By 6 p.m., the numbers are in Clinton's favor.

Around 8 p.m., Trump wins the vote in Michigan—a state that should have been a sure victory for the Clinton campaign. With Michigan falling, the scales begin to tip in Trump's favor.

Like dominoes falling in succession, each state that should have gone to Clinton goes to Trump instead. The world watches with bated breath, as the once impossible is about to be inevitable. An orchestrated hush falls over the Clinton campaign.

By midnight, it's still too early to call it, but the numbers continue in Trump's favor. With each passing minute, Americans remain glued to the television, watching it all unfold live. Others turn in for the night, hoping that if they close their eyes and to go to sleep, maybe when they wake up in the morning the election will somehow miraculously have corrected itself and Hillary Clinton will be the forty-fifth president.

At 2:30 a.m. on November 9, Donald Trump addresses the American public in his victory speech: "I pledge to every citizen of our land that I will be president for all Americans." And as those very words rolled off his tongue, the entire world—or those who were still awake—is in shock. But none more so than Hillary herself.

The offense of blackmail is ensconced in the US legal code by 18 USC. § 873:

*"Whoever, under a threat of informing, or as a consideration for not informing, against any violation of any law of the United States, demands or receives any money or other valuable thing, shall be fined under this title or imprisoned not more than one year, or both."*

Will Hillary concede gracefully and accept her defeat? Or will she go nuclear: cashing in on her "insurance policy"—Steele's dossier—in feeble attempt to blackmail and subvert Trump?

# PART II

# ELECTION AFTERMATH:
# THE FALLOUT
# NOVEMBER 9, 2016—FEBRUARY 2018

# 32

# HILLARY IN HIDING

IN THE DAYS THAT FOLLOW THE election results, Hillary is a hermit—shying away from the media attention she so craved and thrived on for the last six months. Behind drawn curtains of her Westchester mansion, Hillary begins scheming ways to "correct" the outcome—ways to explain her loss to herself and to the American public and to the world. How had she lost? What went wrong? She was a shoo-in, right?

Surely there must be an explanation.

Could it have been the fact that she mistakenly assumed that traditionally blue states like Michigan would continue to blindly vote for her because she is a Democrat? When was the last time she had even gone to Michigan to meet its citizens? Did she even bother visiting these potentially volatile swing states or had she spent too much of her time in states where her vote was unchallenged? Had she been truly bested by Trump, who had actually visited these states and gained the vote?

No, that couldn't be it. Nor of course, could it be that a large number of people were not happy with the use of the term "deplorable" to describe them. That's too simple and logical. Surely there must be some other more complicated and nefarious explanation. Not wanting to assume any personal responsibility for her defeat, Clinton looks for a scapegoat.

And who better than Russia—a natural sworn enemy—to point her crooked finger at? Russia, with their long-standing ideological feud with America, is the perfect choice to lay the blame.

"It was them! Those sneaky Russians meddling in our election, toying with our democracy . . . " Hillary surely wants to shout aloud from the steps of Capitol Hill for all the televised world to hear. And like their second-place hero, many Americans, too, are left searching for a collective salve to heal their shared wounds.

Joe Lauria, an independent journalist and correspondent for the United Nations for over twenty-five years, captures just how this hive mind mentality spread throughout America like wildfire in the immediate days after the election:

> Part of this Russia-gate groupthink stems from the outrage—and even shame—that many Americans feel about Trump's election. They want to find an explanation that doesn't lay the blame on the US citizenry or America's current dysfunctional political/media process. It's much more reassuring, in a way, to blame some foreign adversary while also discrediting Trump's legitimacy as the elected president. That leaves open some hope that this election might somehow be negated.[38]

With the President-elect Trump's inauguration just around the New Year's bend, it's time for Hillary to cash in the check on her insurance policy—her so-called failsafe. It's time to go nuclear and open the floodgates to Russia. This would be the perfect moment to get Christopher Steele's dossier in heavy rotation on all of America's mainstream media to blackmail Trump.

---

38   Lauria, Joe. "How Russia-gate Rationalizes Censorship." *ConsortiumNews*. 4 Dec 2017. https://consortiumnews.com/2017/12/04/how-russia-gate-rationalizes-censorship/

# 33

# HOUSE OF CARDS: THE COLLAPSE OF THE CLINTON FOUNDATION

As if things couldn't get any worse for poor Hillary, now it seems inevitable that her Clinton Foundation is beginning to topple like a house of cards in a hurricane. And as if the world needed more proof that her previous business transactions like the Uranium One deal were, in fact, pay-to-play schemes, countries like Norway and Australia, who had both donated heavily to the foundation during Hillary's run for the presidency, have now backed out of their financial agreements since they know that there will be no return on their original investments.

It will be reported later that documents show that the Australian diplomat Alexander Downer, who sat down for a drink with George Papadopolous in London, learning that the Russians had "dirt" on Hillary, and whose tip to the FBI prompted the Russia-Trump investigation, previously arranged one of the largest foreign donations to Bill and Hillary Clinton's charitable efforts. Downer, a Clintonista, signed over $25 million in Australian government funds to the Clinton Foundation to fight AIDS in Southeast Asia.[39]

---

39  "Russia Scandal: Did Hillary Clinton Run FBI's Trump Investigation?" *Investor's Business Daily*. 7 Mar 2018 . https://www.investors.com/politics/editorials/russia -scandal-did-hillary-clinton-run-fbis-trump-investigation/

All Hillary has to offer now is her disgraced name and reputation. The question now isn't if, but when the Clinton Foundation will run dry and close up shop.

While the Clinton Foundation continues to reel, the circus-like spectacle that was the 2016 election is also finally winding down, and Washington, DC readies itself for a brief hiatus going into the Christmas season. But over in Russia, a plot for murder is set into motion in our Red November tale.

# 34

# THE PECULIAR DEATH
# OF OLEG EROVINKIN

REMEMBER THE EX-KGB CHIEF, OLEG EROVINKIN, who was suspected of helping Christopher Steele draft his dossier? The same Erovinkin who was the aide to Igor Sechin, former Russian Deputy Prime Minister. The same man who, if word got out that he was commiserating and possibly supplying information to a British spy, his fate would be sealed.

On December 26, 2016, Oleg Erovinkin is found dead in the back of his car in Moscow.

Was Oleg more than just an aide? Turns out he was called Putin's Treasurer, and for good reason: Oleg knew where all the bodies were buried. He knew all the secrets, and just about every last asset. He was the one who had to account for them.

When his body is found the police say they suspect "foul play." As Igor Sechin's right hand man, his death is very suspicious. And, as the possible source for the Trump-Russia dossier, it looks even more suspicious.

And yet Christopher Steele adamantly insists that Erovinkin was not one of his sources. "Not one of ours," he says to reporters, adding that, "Sometimes people just die."[40]

Who killed Oleg Erovinkin? What else might have he known?

---

40  Harding, Luke. *Collusion: Secret Meetings, Dirty Money, and How Russia Helped Donald Trump Win.* Penguin Random House. 2017.

Could it have been Igor Sechin—Russia's "second most powerful person"?

Just who is Sechin? Born in 1960 in what was Leningrad, USSR. He is Putin's foremost ally and started his Putinesque career long ago. He was deputy to Putin already in the late 1980s. Sechin is considered Putin's literal right-hand man, his most conservative partner and leader of the Kremlin's Siloviki faction, which consists only of former high-ranking security agents.

Sechin served as Deputy Prime Minister of Russia, serving in Putin's innermost cabinet, until May 2012, when Putin made him Executive Chairman of Rosneft, the state-owned Russian oil company.

Sechin went on to serve his trusted friend Putin everywhere he went. He became Chief of the Russian presidential administration. When Medvedev came to power he was demoted to Deputy Prime Minister, but even then he protected the interests of Putin. According to open intelligence sources, Sechin had inordinate power. He represented the FSB in all dealings in oil and gas. He was all-powerful. His face was all over deals with BP, Gazprom, with Cuba and offshore drilling, and with Venezuela.

In 2014, Sechin was sanctioned by the US government in response to the unrest in Ukraine. He had a travel ban to the US imposed and his assets were frozen. He has been banned from all business transactions between US citizens and corporations. Sechin has been harmed but retains all his influence and all his considerable power and wealth as the foremost Putin crony.

What does he know about the Trump-Russia dossier and why would such a powerful Putin crony with so much to lose be implicated? Is there another line to follow?

Is it coincidence that soon after Erovinkin's murder, Christopher Steele goes into hiding?

To this day, Steele has been sighted, but won't travel or give interviews.

# 35

# DÉJÀ VU: IRAQ AND
# THE MISSING WEAPONS
# OF MASS DESTRUCTION

ONCE WASHINGTON RESUMES ITS GOVERNMENTAL OFFICES following the holiday break, the mainstream media—desperately trying to maintain its previously peaking ratings during the race—needs a new story to capture the attention of the American public. Like a broken record stuck in the same groove, the media focuses solely on new reports emerging about Russian interference in the election. The public wants answers in their whodunit mystery of Clinton's surprise upset, and the media is more than happy to offer a suspect.

This isn't anything new—this idea of a foreign enemy either meddling in our American affairs, attacking our freedom and democracy, or posing as a grave threat to the world, even if this sworn enemy is thousands of miles and an ocean away from American soil. Like the yin to our yang, America's intelligence community and the Deep State work together to establish this often-imaginary bogeyman, so to say, to blame for all of our own problems and shortcomings, to justify our ever-increasing defense budget, as we've seen with the 2016 election.

Political analyst Gilbert Doctorow reinforces this very idea:

While the Iraq deception was driven by the neoconservatives in the Bush-Cheney administration, the Russia paranoia was started by the nominally left-of-center administration of Barack Obama in the closing months of his presidency. It has been fanned ever since by liberals and centrists in the Democratic Party and the never-Trump contingent in the Republican Party as well as the mainstream media—with the goal of either removing Trump from office or politically crippling him and his administration, i.e., to reverse the results of the 2016 election or, as some might say, reverse the "mistake" of the 2016 election.[41]

And to be sure, this isn't the first time Russia is our enemy. This is just the beginning of a new Cold War. Before this recycling of animosity toward Russia and pointing our collective finger at Putin, we did the same to Saddam Hussein and Iraq. Dan Kovalik, in his book *The Plot to Scapegoat Russia*, writes on this very idea:

> As with the CIA's claims about WMDs, the US media has been all too willing to accept and regurgitate the CIA's claims about Russian hacking and Trump's alleged conspiracy with Russia to steal the election. A journalist I trust, Pulitzer Prize winner Seymour Hersh, who has properly condemned the media for accepting these claims at face value. I join Hersh, if he would allow me to, in asking, where is the evidence for this? Indeed, we may have to continue asking this pointed question, as even a number of Democratic leaders are now warning their base.[42]

What a seemingly savvy move on behalf of the US intelligence agencies: tell the American public that Saddam and his cronies are hiding weapons of mass destruction that could obliterate and destroy the world with the potential to wipe out the entire human race. And just like that, you have almost unilateral, unconditional support from the American media and public. Kovalik continues:

---

41  Doctorow, Gilbert. "Questioning the Russia-gate 'motive'." *Consortium News*. 18 Dec 2017.
42  Kovalik, Dan. *The Plot to Scapegoat Russia*. Skyhorse Publishing. 16 May 2017.

Thus, as Glenn Greenwald wrote in *The Intercept* on March 16, 2017, in the face of the Russia conspiracy frenzy, which has now become a "fixation" of the Democratic rank 'n file, "former acting CIA chief Michael Morell . . . one of Clinton's most vocal CIA surrogates . . . appeared at an intelligence community forum to 'cast doubt' on 'allegations that members of the Trump campaign colluded with Russia.'"[43]

With a majority of the American public seeking some form of retribution after the devastating loss to Trump, the US intelligence agencies are preparing to discuss the contents of Steele's dossier being passed around like wildfire in DC.

James Clapper, the former Director of National Intelligence and the same man behind the phony WMD claims, is selected to serve on the Advisory Board of the Committee to Investigate Russia—a nonpartisan, nonprofit group formed to help "Americans understand and recognize the scope and scale of Russia's continuing attacks on our democracy." The rhetoric of Clapper's advisory board sounds strikingly similar, almost verbatim . . . is it déjà vu?

---

43  Ibid.

# 36

# GROUPTHINK: THE HIVE MENTALITY OF THE INTEL COMMUNITY

On January 6, 2017, James Clapper releases the findings from his investigation, the Intelligence Community Assessment (ICA), assessing Russian activities and intentions in recent US elections [See Appendix A]. There are seventeen American intelligence agencies that work in tandem to supposedly govern and protect our borders and ensure our nation's security—the same intelligence agencies that make up the Deep State. As lead on the investigation, Clapper handpicks three analysts from three separate departments—FBI, CIA, and NSA—of those seventeen, including James Comey and CIA Director John Brennan, both known anti-Trumpers.

Brennan always seems angry.

He was the Director of the Central Intelligence Agency from 2013 until 2017 under then President Barack Obama, where he briefed Obama daily as his chief counterterrorism advisor. With twenty-five years at "The Agency," Brennan was what is called "a lifer." He was part of the Deep State.

His work focused over that long career on the Near East, and he served as CIA station chief to Saudi Arabia. Brennan is a fluent Arabic speaker and, most interestingly, a rumored convert to Islam.

Brennan is a known hothead and is closely tied to the Democrat Party and the Clintons. His rise to power came during their reign and he was a controversial CIA Director to say the least.

Many thought him to be less than objective, if not entirely politicized.

He would later tell *Fox News*'s Chris Wallace that he doesn't think President-elect Donald Trump has "a full appreciation of Russian capabilities, Russia's intentions," and that Trump's public displays of contempt for the US intelligence community could undermine national security.

His remarks were made after Trump rejected intelligence agencies' reports of claims that Russia had compromising information on the president-elect.

Clearly, Brennan is a big fan of the Trump-Russia dossier.

He is behind Red November.

Yasha Levine confirms that this isn't the first time Clapper has claimed unanimity without disclosing proper evidence for this conclusion:

> In a frustratingly vague statement to Congress on the report, then-DNI director James Clapper hinted at deeper and more definitive findings that proved serious and rampant Russian interference in America's presidential balloting—but insisted that all this underlying proof must remain classified. For observers of the D.C. intelligence scene, Clapper's performance harkened back to his role in touting definitive proof of the imminent threat of Saddam Hussein's WMD arsenal in the run-up to the US invasion of Iraq.[44]

After his investigation, Clapper claims that the decision is unanimous across American intelligence agencies that this information is accurate and even describes the leaks as damaging to US national security. How

---

44  Levine, Yasha. "From Russia, With Panic." *The Baffler*. March 2017. https://thebaffler .com/salvos/from-russia-with-panic-levine

could Clapper then only choose three investigators—three left-leaning analysts to be exact—whom he knew would support his claim and his already-laid plot against Trump? How could he announce that this is a general consensus when fourteen agencies hadn't even been contacted or read through the dossier itself?

Former CIA officer Ray McGovern explains just how transparently this Deep State operates: "In other words, not only did the full intelligence community not participate in the ICA but only analysts 'handpicked' by Obama's intelligence chiefs conducted the analysis—and as we intelligence veterans know well, if you handpick the analysts, you are handpicking the conclusions."[45] Through this supposedly "unanimous" decision, we're beginning to see just how this Deep State operates and exercises its unilateral reach by a carefully calculated design. In doing so, our basic tenets of democracy are tested and strained.

Trump, rightfully, goes on the offensive during a press conference on November 11, 2017, aboard Air Force One while speaking to the press on his way to Hanoi, Vietnam, saying, "You hear it's seventeen agencies. Well it's three. And one is Brennan . . . give me a break. They're political hacks . . . I mean, you have Brennan, you have Clapper, you have Comey. Comey is proven to be a liar and he's proven to be a leaker."[46]

And in some odd, ominous warning three days prior to Clapper's release of his findings, Senator Chuck Schumer, leader of the Democratic Party, publicly warns President-elect Trump, saying that when you "mess with the intel community they have six ways from Sunday to get back at you." Why would Schumer suggest such a thing? Is there truth behind this, or is it just an intimidation tactic? What else does Schumer know about the Deep State and its capabilities?

---

45  McGovern, Ray. "Mocking Trump Doesn't Prove Russia's Guilt." *Consortium News.* 13 Nov 2017. https://consortiumnews.com/2017/11/13/mocking-trump-doesnt-prove-russias-guilt/

46  Shelbourne, Molly. "Brennan: Trump called us hacks to delegitimize intelligence report." *The Hill.* 12 Nov 2017. http://thehill.com/homenews/sunday-talk-shows/359982-brennan-trump-called-us-hacks-to-delegitimize-intelligence-report

And just who is this John Brennan that Trump calls a political hack?

During Trump's campaign toward the presidency, John Brennan, the director of the CIA, had gone out of his way to attack Trump, even saying publicly he would refuse to employ waterboarding in some extreme cases. "I can say that as long as I'm director of the CIA, irrespective of what the president says, I'm not going to be the director of a CIA that gives that order. They'll have to find another director,"[47] said the preemptively insubordinate Brennan.

Former CIA field operations officer Gene Coyle once said that Brennan was "known as the greatest sycophant in the history of the CIA, and a supporter of Hillary Clinton before the election. I find it hard to put any real credence in anything that man says."

William Binney has this to say about Clapper's character and tendency to make sweeping claims on tenuous assumptions:

> Mr. Clapper was a key player in facilitating the fraudulent intelligence. Defense Secretary Donald Rumsfeld put Mr. Clapper in charge of the analysis of satellite imagery, the best source for pinpointing the locations of weapons of mass destruction—if any. When Pentagon favorites like Iraqi emigre Ahmed Chalabi plied the US intelligence with spurious "evidence" on WMD in Iraq, Mr. Clapper was in a position to suppress the findings of any imagery analyst who might have the temerity to report, for example, that the Iraqi "chemical weapons facility" for which Mr. Chalabi provided the geographic coordinates was nothing of the kind. Mr. Clapper preferred to go by the Rumsfeldian dictum: "The absence of evidence is not evidence of absence."

Despite the fact that Clapper and his cronies think they're pulling the wool over the public's eyes, Trump calls him and his crew out, citing

---

47  Landay, Jonathan. "CIA director says he would resign if ordered to resume waterboarding." *Reuters*. 13 July 2016. https://www.reuters.com/article/us-usa-cia-waterboarding/cia-director-says-he-would-resign-if-ordered-to-resume-waterboarding-idUSKCN0ZT2T3

yet another clear example of how top officials in Washington, like the director of the CIA, are working in orchestration in a plot to subvert his presidency. What we have here is the same cast of characters who championed the Iraq war are now, with the help of mainstream media, stirring up anti-Russia hysteria.

And with all the hearsay and spreading of misinformation, Scott Shane, a longtime journalist for the *New York Times* captures the glaring flaw in the dossier's logic:

> What is missing from the public report is what many Americans most eagerly anticipated: hard evidence to back up the agencies' claims that the Russian government engineered the election attack . . . Instead, the message from the agencies amounts to "trust us."[48]

Finally, someone speaking some truth, and from the *New York Times*, no less. Had anyone from the media actually read the dossier? Had anyone fact-checked it? Was there any substance to the wild claims? Again what we have here is a blatant disregard for basic journalistic duties being shelved in favor of gossip.

Despite the dossier having been thoroughly challenged as unrealistic and unsubstantiated by real experts like Professor Cohen, one of the premier Kremlinologists in the whole world, it remains the core of all the proponents of the Russia gate storyline.

Cohen, who has served at the top ranks of the US government and taught Russian history at Princeton, has written a mountain of books and professional articles about Russia. He knows it inside out and upside down—and you can't fool him. In his February 2018 article "Russiagate or Intelgate?" which he wrote for *The Nation*, Cohen proposes that the Russia-gate brouhaha would be better termed "Intelgate," and he's right; the world should listen to him.

This could be the makings of a new cold war. Russia-gate is,

---

48   Shane, Scott. "Russian Intervention in American Election Was No One-Off." *New York Times*. 6 Jan 2017. https://www.nytimes.com/2017/01/06/us/politics/russian -hacking-election-intelligence.html

however, without Russia in this case: it is something much darker and more sinister.

The collusion was not between the White House and the Kremlin but between the US Intelligence Community and the Democrats.

Cohen asks pointed questions on this Intel-gate saga: when, and with whom, did this opposition to Trump begin? When did Christopher Steele get his information and who gave it to him? The investigation was not instigated by drunken remarks by George Papadopoulos to some anti-Trump Australian ambassador late at night in a London pub.[49]

No, Cohen refutes. It was John Brennan and the CIA who started the whole thing.

Brennan played a crucial role in promoting Russia gate from the get-go. He briefed members of Congress and President Obama as early as July and August of 2016, using Steele's dossier. He shared information with James Clapper and FBI Director, James Comey.

Still, the question remains: when did Brennan start his (CIA-based) investigation of Trump? Could have been in late 2015? His own testimony demonstrates he, not the FBI, was the godfather of Russia-gate.

It was Brennan who provided information to Christopher Steele—he spoon-fed it to him. Steele did not have deep contacts in Russia since he had not been there for about twenty years. He was badly out of touch.

Steele's sources are incredible. He doesn't and won't name them.

Would Russian insiders really collaborate with an old former MI6 operative under the eyes of the former KGB chief, Vladimir Putin? Would they risk their positions, incomes, and their lives, for that?[50]

Cohen rightly asks these questions. He also points out all the glaring and telling mistakes in the dossier—mistakes that real, current Kremlin experts do not make.

Christopher Steele's source is John Brennan and the FBI, who as we now know, was already collaborating with Steele. Nellie Ohr,

---

49  Cohen, Stephen. "Russiagate or Intelgate?" *The Nation*. 7 Feb 2018.
50  Ibid.

of Fusion GPS, provided CIA research and also funneled it into the Steele dossier. She was his co-author. Convenient.

If the information did not so much come from Russian sources, where did it come from? Is Russia-gate the product of the US Intel Community, specifically of, John Brennan, the political appointee sitting at the helm of the CIA?

Is this not perilous to democracy? Does it pale to Watergate by comparison? Why was it done?

Loathing Trump is one thing; opposing any connection or better relations with Russia is another. Could there also be ambition at play here, since it was no secret that Brennan badly wanted to become Secretary of State to future President Hillary Clinton?

Should Brennan not come under the bright light? And, what was Obama's role in all this? What did he know and when did he know it?

And furthermore, why did the intelligence community wait two months after the election to brief President-elect Trump on the dossier?

Why is James Comey, Brennan's number two, selected to do the briefing?

By broadcasting their findings into the national spotlight, is Comey's investigation an attempt to legitimize the dossier? If enough people believe a lie, is it still a lie? Can an untruth suddenly become a truth?

Russia-gate is in reality Intelgate. The Red November plot thickens.

# 37

# BLIND FAITH

PERHAPS ONE OF THE GREATEST UNTRUTHS that had been spun into gospel was the conclusion reached by George Kurtz and Dmitri Alperovitch from their investigation into the DNC email leak. Remember those reports from CrowdStrike, the cybersecurity intelligence firm who claimed they had definitive proof of Russian intrusion into DNC emails and how the Russians were directly responsible for the hack and, therefore, the outcome of the 2016 election? And how the American public blindly believed what these so-called cyber experts told the DNC?

And how James Clapper claimed to have good reason to believe Saddam had WMDs, but like Geraldo Rivera opening Al Capone's vault, there were no WMDs? In the same conniving vein, the CrowdStrike team, as it turns out, completely falsified their results to match what their client wanted to hear. It didn't matter to the DNC what the results were as long as it pointed back to the Russians. And it didn't matter to Clapper *what* his analysts would find; to Clapper all that mattered was *who* was doing the finding—because he knew they supported his foregone conclusion.

Yasha Levine reports on just how quickly this mentality spread following Trump's victory:

> After Donald Trump's surprise victory in November, these four words reverberated across the nation: The Russians Hacked America.

Democratic Party insiders, liberal pundits, economists, members of Congress, spies, Hollywood celebrities, and neocons of every stripe and classification level—all these worthy souls reeled in horror at the horribly compromised new American electoral order. In unison, the centers of responsible opinion concurred that Vladimir Putin carried off a brazen and successful plan to throw the most important election in the most powerful democracy in the world to a candidate of his choosing.[51]

This is a dangerous game to play—a game that harkens back to the Orwellian false dogma: 2+2=5. When you already have the answer but the numbers don't add up, you're left with but one logical option: change the conclusion. But if you're willing to play by Orwellian logic, you have another option: change the data to make it match your conclusion. And just like that, no longer does 2+2=4.

Clapper's and the Deep State's pre-selected conclusion appealed to a core American psychology, an already-established American dichotomy: a good versus evil, us versus them mentality—and at the center of the evil is one man: Vladimir Putin.

Stephen F. Cohen, professor emeritus of Russian studies and politics at NYU and Princeton, captures this false vilification of Russia and Putin:

> This too is unprecedented. No Soviet or post-Soviet leader was ever so wildly, baselessly vilified as Putin has increasingly been for more than a decade—and even more since a few selected members of a few US intelligence agencies claimed in January 2017, without making known any evidence whatsoever, that he personally ordered the "attack on America" in 2016. Demonizing Putin has become so maniacal that leading "opinion-makers" seem to think he is a Communist.[52]

---

51   Levine, Yasha. "From Russia, With Panic." *The Baffler.* March 2017. https://thebaffler.com/salvos/from-russia-with-panic-levine

52   Cohen, Stephen. "Russia Is Not the 'No. 1 Threat'—or Even Among the Top 5." *The Nation.* 27 Nov 2017. https://www.thenation.com/article/russia-is-not-the-no-1-threat-or-even-among-the-top-5/

In a game of Russian roulette played according to Orwellian dogma, the numbers, the data, and the research no longer matter—only the outcome.

With the DNC, the so-called seventeen intelligence agencies (actually three), and the majority of news outlets all agreeing that Christopher Steele's dossier was the truth—and deemed a threat to America's national security and democracy (how ironic!)—it didn't matter to the public where the information came from so long as it confirmed their suspicions. Each headline was the salve that these wounded Americans were so desperately looking for—a topical solution to all their issues with democracy, the very proof that confirmed their already set-in-stone conclusion: the Russians hacked America.

Following Trump's inauguration, these intelligence agencies work together in calculated orchestration to connect Trump with Russia. But since they know they'll be unable to find a direct line of collusion between Trump and Russia, they widen their net, beginning with his National Security Advisor Michael Flynn. Flynn, as we know, had met with Sergey Kislyak, the Russian ambassador to the US, on December 29, 2016, during Trump's campaign.

Meanwhile, anti-Russia hysteria is brewing within the Capitol and throughout America, so when pressed by the FBI on January 24, 2017, regarding his contact with Russia, Flynn, perhaps in an attempt to minimize his interaction with Kislyak, downplays what occurred during these meetings and withholds pertinent information. However, once word spreads that Flynn did in fact have contact with the Russians and met with Kislyak, Michael Flynn, under intense pressure and public scrutiny, is forced to resign from his position on February 13.

Donald Trump would later chime in on Flynn's forced resignation through Twitter, writing, "I had to fire General Flynn because he lied to the Vice President and the FBI. He has pled guilty to those lies. It is a shame because his actions during the transition were lawful. There was nothing to hide!"

And during a press conference, Trump adds, "I feel badly for Gen.

Flynn. I feel very badly. He's led a very strong life, and I feel very badly about it. I will say this. Hillary Clinton lied many times to the FBI and nothing happened to her. Flynn lied, and it destroyed his life, and I think it's a shame."[53]

Trump is spot-on here. While Flynn did perhaps mislead the FBI and the public, it wanes in comparison to the lies told by Hillary Clinton to the FBI.

53  Wilkie, Christina. "Trump: 'I feel very badly for General Flynn.'" *CNBC*. 4 Dec 2017.
     https://www.cnbc.com/2017/12/04/trump-i-feel-very-badly-for-general-flynn.html

# 38

# REFUTING THE DOSSIER

WITH CLAPPER CLAIMING HIS INVESTIGATION THOROUGHLY examined, he then turns to the American press and media outlets to spin his untruth into a truth—an announcement that is heard across the world. As a direct result of his unsubstantiated claims, a majority of the American public, which is now clamoring for an explanation to correct the outcome of the election, blindly believes the so-called unanimous decision from Clapper and other intelligence agencies regarding the accuracy of Steele's dossier. And just like that, Steele's dossier becomes the Democratic gospel.

For any discerning reader (not any member of the CIA, FBI, or NSA), the Christopher Steele dossier should be read in its entirety and read closely to better understand its gravity. The document, as released by *Buzzfeed* on January 10, 2017, is available in Appendix B at the end of this book.

Many reporters, in the US and abroad, received the dossier months before its public exposure, but let this hot potato sit as they hadn't been able to verify its contents.

Also, Alfa, the name of Russia's largest privately owned commercial bank, mentioned on page 25 of the dossier, was misspelled, not once, not twice, but multiple times. One would think that a professionally compiled dossier by a "credible" source would dot all of its i's and cross all of its t's.

The document can be distilled down into six main takeaways, as identified by Matthew Yglesias and Andrew Prokop in their February 2, 2018, *Vox* article.[54] Six egregious claims that are entirely unverified, and can be refuted with simple logic.

### Claim #1: Trump had an ongoing cooperative relationship with Russian authorities for years.

In his dossier, Steele claims that Russia "had been feeding Trump and his team valuable intelligence on his opponents," including Clinton, for "several years" before 2016, and that in exchange, Trump's team fed the Kremlin intelligence on Russian oligarchs and their families.

It is now public knowledge that the Russians had been attempting to "sow discord" in the 2016 election nearly two years prior to the election, in 2014—almost a year before Trump announced his run for candidacy. Using this basic math, Steele's claim just isn't logical. It seems that Steele is attempting to draw connections based on Trump's previous business ties to Russia.

Dan Kovalik touches in on the Steele's flawed logic, using an example of Obama's previous relations with Ukraine:

> Moreover, even if Trump's friendliness with Russia may be motivated by his business interests—Obama's Ukraine policy may have been motivated at least in part by the Ukrainian business interests of Vice-President Biden's son Hunter . . . this does not in itself make it wrong.[55]

As Kovalik notes, there is nothing inherently illegal or corrupt with having friendly relations with Russia simply because Trump had previous business interests. Additionally, as any mildly informed civilian knows, international relationships are constantly and continually evolving, as witnessed with the collapse of the Soviet Union and the end of the Cold War. Following this dissolution, US-Russian relations

---

54  Yglesias, Matthew and Prokop, Andrew. "The Steele dossier, explained." *Vox*. 02 Feb 2018. https://www.vox.com/2018/1/5/16845704/steele-dossier-russia-trump
55  Kovalik, Dan. *The Plot to Scapegoat Russia*. Skyhorse Publishing. 2017.

slowly, over time, became less strained, especially during Boris Yeltsin's tenure as president. During this relaxed period, Trump worked closely with Russian entrepreneurs, further expanding his real estate empire. And now, as we enter a new Cold War, any previous ties or business connections with Russia are viewed unfavorably. Steele knows this, and he knows he is making a terribly loose connection between Russia and Trump. He also knows Clinton will love it and will use it as potential blackmail.

### Claim #2: Trump is compromised and vulnerable to Russian blackmail due to sexual escapades.

The most salacious of all the accusations in his dossier, Steele claims that during a trip to the Moscow Ritz-Carlton, Trump hired prostitutes to "perform a 'golden showers' [urination] show in front of him," "defiling" the presidential suite bed in which the Obamas had previously slept. In this wild claim, Steele also implies that Russian intelligence taped this sex act and that it is one of several forms of blackmail the Russians have on Trump.

Though it's the most egregious and potentially most character-damaging claim, its veracity is simple to refute: if there is an actual tape, where is it? And why not release it? Had Steele ever seen the tape? Surely, if he had, wouldn't he release it to support his claims with tangible evidence? Clearly, Steele never saw the tape because there is no tape because this never happened at the Moscow Ritz-Carlton.

President-elect Trump himself publicly refuted the story many times and even said at a press conference at Trump Tower on January 11, 2017, the day after *Buzzfeed's* story, " . . . I am extremely careful . . . Because in your hotel rooms and no matter where you go, you're gonna probably have cameras . . . cameras in the strangest places . . . that are so small with modern technology, you can't see them and you won't know. You better be careful, or you'll be watching yourself on the nightly television . . . I'm also very much of a germaphobe, by the way, believe me."

And yet, the question remains: why would Steele, who is likely working for the Russians, write such slanderous statements? Is it perhaps because it isn't the Russians blackmailing Trump, but members of the Deep State, the CIA?

Again, Kovalik writes about this likelihood:

> More disturbingly, there is in fact good reason to believe that it is not the Russians at all who are blackmailing Trump, but rather, the CIA itself. Thus, from what we have been given to know, it was not the Russians who came to Trump to tell him that they had incriminating evidence on him, as any blackmailer would do. No, it was the CIA—who we know wants to pressure Trump into staying on the path toward confrontation with Russia—that not only went to Trump to tell him about the allegedly incriminating evidence on him, but also went to a number of other government officials and the public to let them know about this "evidence."[56]

Knowing the lengths and depths the Deep State and CIA are willing to go to subvert Trump, it's no surprise that they would stoop so low as to blackmail him.

## Claim #3: An extensive conspiracy of cooperation existed between Trump's campaign and the Kremlin.

As claimed by Steele, Paul Manafort initially managed the Trump-Russia "conspiracy" with Carter Page as intermediary until Manafort was fired in August 2016.

After Manafort's firing, Trump's lawyer, Michael Cohen, played an increasingly large role in managing the so-called "Kremlin relationship."

Former CIA officer Ray McGovern exposes the glaring flaw in this accusation:

---

56  Kovalik, Dan. *The Plot to Scapegoat Russia*. Skyhorse Publishing. 2017

The Russia-gate narrative always hinged on the preposterous notion that Russian President Vladimir Putin foresaw years ago what no American political analyst considered even possible, the political ascendancy of Donald Trump. According to the narrative, the fortune-telling Putin then risked creating even worse tensions with a nuclear-armed America that would—by all odds—have been led by a vengeful President Hillary Clinton.[57]

And furthermore, yes, it's been established that Paul Manafort has connections to both the Ukraine and Russia. It is no secret that he served as an advisor for Viktor Yanukovych during his run in the Ukraine presidential election of 2010.

It has also been established that Carter Page lived in Moscow while he worked for Merrill Lynch.

Both Manafort and Page are businessmen who have connections to several Eastern European countries, which is to be expected from successful venturers of the sort.

Again, what Steele and the intelligence agencies are attempting to do here is draw lines where there is no larger picture. Furthermore, Carter Page is still the subject of nebulous investigations, and perhaps we'll never know exactly whom he is working for. One thing remains clear: the FBI was illegally surveilling Page and used the dossier to continue their investigation on Page and then Trump.

## Claim #4: Trump's team had full knowledge of Russian plans to deliver emails to WikiLeaks, offering policy concessions in exchange.

Despite all this media speculation and attention regarding this completely unsubstantiated claim that Trump's team somehow knew and approved the Russian delivery of emails to WikiLeaks, we know this from several sources that this is false. Even Julian Assange continues

---

57  McGovern, Ray. "The FBI Hand behind Russia-gate." *Consortium News*. https://con sortiumnews.com/2018/01/11/the-fbi-hand-behind-russia-gate/

to maintain his position that Russia is not the source for the leaks. If Russia is not the source, then why or how would Trump's team know? Could Assange himself be lying? Doubtful. The man's sole purpose in life is to expose the truth, all while living in secrecy.

And as previously noted, William Binney, the former NSA analyst turned whistleblower, explained that the leaks were from within due to the known speed of the downloads, which matched a USB-connected thumb drive and not an outside source using the internet. Binney explains that had there been outside interference, the NSA would easily have been able to recognize it. So, if there was any external interference—which there was not, but for argument's sake, we'll pretend there was—why wouldn't the NSA release such findings? This would be the very proof they need, right? Or did they choose not to share their findings because they know it will be self-incriminating, pointing inward to someone within the Deep State?

## Claim #5: Carter Page was heavily involved in the conspiracy.

The dossier says claims that Carter Page had "conceived and promoted" the idea that the DNC emails to WikiLeaks should be leaked during the Democratic convention, "aimed at switching Sanders (protest) voters away from Clinton and over to Trump."

The hacking began in 2015, when Page was not part of the Trump campaign. How could Page conceive this idea before his involvement with the campaign? It makes no logical sense. How then, for even a second, could the FBI even consider this claim as truth? After all, they were wiretapping and surveilling Page. They would know best.

## Claim #6: Michael Cohen was a major player in the conspiracy.

In the fabricated Christopher Steele Trump-Russia dossier, the claim was repeatedly made that Donald Trump's corporate lawyer, Michael Cohen, a rough-and-tumble corporate lawyer from New York, had traveled to Prague.

He was allegedly there to meet with Russian agents on interference in the 2016 US elections.

The core allegation is that Cohen traveled to Prague and was allegedly said by Czech intelligence to have met with known Russian agents to elaborate a scheme and funding to interfere on behalf of his boss, Donald J. Trump, to secure the US election. The sourcing suggested it was coming from the Czech BIS.

Not only do they deny it, but it also turns out that Cohen has never been to Prague, or anywhere else in the Czech Republic for that matter. As his passport shows, there is no record of his going there. And he has only one passport.

On the day Steele and his bogus sources say he was in Prague, Cohen, it turns out, was actually in Los Angeles with his son, playing baseball during college tryouts. USC and its coaching staff have confirmed this fact.

Now that dossier has, according to Cohen's sworn Congressional testimony, been "riddled with fabrications" and uses unnamed and unverified sources. It also contains "blatant lies."

# 39

# THE FAULTINESS
# OF STEELE'S LOGIC

CLEARLY, AS WE'VE JUST SEEN, IT takes basic logic, using simple chronological timelines, to disprove the claims put forth by Steele in his dossier, which raises the question: how did he arrive at such misinformation?

It turns out Steele himself has not been in Russia for seventeen years and used third-hand, former KGB sources, and paid them to make up good stories. The problem is he never verified any of them, nor did his employer Fusion GPS and the Democratic National Committee, who funded the opposition research.

Since its release, Steele now claims that some 70 percent of what he reported in the dossier is true. The question is, plainly, which 70 percent?

Since he did not verify the details, does he even know? He never went to Russia to collect the material himself and depended on his old networks of FSB agents in country.

Michael Cohen weighs in on Steele's methods: "In my opinion, the hired spy didn't find anything factual, so he threw together a shoddily written and totally fabricated report filled with lies and rumors."[58]

Cohen's sentiment leads us to our next question: how, or more accurately why, would the FBI ever approve of such a clearly falsified

---

58 Lucas, Ryan. "Senate Calls Trump Attorney In For Open Session After Reports About Closed One." *NPR*. 19 Sep 2017. https://www.npr.org/2017/09/19/552041493 /trump-confidante-rejects-any-collusion-in-russia-election-interference

document—a document that can be disproven with simple logic? Is it perhaps because the FBI was offering payment to Christopher Steele to corroborate his Trump-Russia connection?

On March 6, 2017, Chairman of the Senate Committee on the Judiciary Charles Grassley sends a memo to James Comey with twelve pointed questions on the FBI's handling, involvement, and contact with Steele and his dossier [See Appendix C].

Grassley is demanding answers, but will Comey have any?

# 40

# THE FALSE DOGMA OF THE FBI

SINCE ANY RATIONAL, DISCERNING READER OF Steele's dossier would immediately recognize its flawed logic, why then does the FBI find it to be accurate? Clearly, the FBI—along with the other Deep State constituents—already had their collective minds made up: Trump must go. It is now known that the FBI used the dossier to bolster its Foreign Intelligence Surveillance Act (FISA) warrant targeting the early Trump campaign advisor Carter Page and others.

Trump threatens this Deep State. This is a mutual understanding. And we saw through Senator Schumer's ominous warning to Trump about what will happen if he attempts to stand in their way. But, as he's said so many times throughout his campaign, Trump's plan is to drain this swamp. Knowing this, the FBI understands that in order to take down a man with this much gumption, they'll need to dig deep, collecting as much dirt on him as possible, even if it is phony intel, while they steady their aim and place him in their crosshairs.

So, when the contents of the dossier were shared across the intelligence communities and given to both President Obama and his key lieutenants, these bodies knew that they had some potentially heavy arsenal in their hands to work with—they just had to package, manipulate, and execute it carefully. President-elect Trump was also later briefed on them, albeit two months later, which is questionable and disconcerting in its own right.

In an attempt to save face, the CIA comments on its delay in relaying the sensitive information to Trump: "Rather, after consider-able thought and discussion, DNI Clapper and the heads of the FBI, CIA, and NSA decided that because the dossier was circulating among Members of Congress and the media, it was important to warn the President-elect of its existence."[59]

And yet, more curiously, the CIA Deputy Robert Morell, who would have become head of the agency had Clinton won the election, says, "On the question of the Trump campaign conspiring with the Russians here, there is smoke, but there is no fire, at all. There's no lit-tle campfire, there's no little candle, and there's no spark. And there's a lot of people looking for it."

Morell points out that during an interview on *Meet the Press,* former Director of National Intelligence James Clapper said that he had seen no evidence of a conspiracy when he left office January 20.

"That's a pretty strong statement by General Clapper,"[60] Morell concluded.

Despite this, the story continues to run on no legs, being propped up precariously by the mainstream media, especially CNN, whose attention remains fixated on Steele and his juicy dossier.

And in regard to the dossier itself and any information of the like, Morell pointedly says, "Unless you know the sources, and unless you know how a particular source acquired a particular piece of informa-tion, you can't judge the information—you just can't."

Had anyone at CNN read the dossier to verify Steele's audacious claims? Doubtful.

59  Bertrand, Natasha. "Former intel official: Trump-Russia dossier 'played no role' in our analysis of Russian meddling." *Business Insider.* 27 Oct 2017. http://www.business insider.com/robert-litt-says-dossier-played-no-role-in-intel-community-russia-assess ment-2017-10

60  Dilanian, Ken. "Clinton Ally Says Smoke, But No Fire: No Russia-Trump Coll-usion." *NBC News.* 16 Mar 2017. https://www.nbcnews.com/news/us-news/clinton -ally-says-smoke-no-fire-no-russia-trump-collusion-n734176

# 41

# WIDENING THE NET: PAUL MANAFORT AND RICK GATES

IN ATTEMPT TO RILE UP MORE anti-Russia hysteria and to prove their already drawn conclusion, Special Counsel Robert Mueller widens his investigation in attempt to connect Trump to Russia. Since he knows he can't reel in the biggest catch, he goes after others caught in his dragnet: Paul Manafort and Rick Gates.

Manafort, the lobbyist and political consultant, served as Trump's campaign manager from June through August of 2016. Manafort was a lead partner and co-founder of the renowned Washington, DC, lobbying firm of Black, Manafort & Stone (BMS). He is tasked with getting Trump the delegates needed to secure the Republican nomination. Manafort had served almost every other Republican presidential campaign in recent memory and was most familiar with the processes and rules to get over the top.

Most of Manafort's clients were what are called "pariahs."

He lobbied and worked for Victor Yankovych of Ukraine, Ferdinand Marcos of the Philippines, DRC dictator Mobutu, Angolan guerilla leader Jonas Savimbi, and the Kashmiri Council, which was funded by Pakistan.

Under investigation by numerous federal agencies for his dealings in Ukraine, the FBI counterintelligence probe into Russia's influence on the 2016 election indicted Manafort.

He surrendered to the FBI on October 30, 2017, and was released from house arrest with a gag order, after the grand jury on thirty-two counts found him a person of interest. His longtime business associate and deputy when Manafort was Trump's campaign manager, Rick Gates, was also indicted and arrested.

Manafort is charged with laundering money, failure to report foreign bank accounts, being an unregistered agent of a foreign principal or government, false and misleading testimony, and filing false FARA (Foreign Agent Registration Act) statements.

Noticeably missing from the long list of charges is any "collusion" with the Russian government or influencing in any fashion the 2016 election.

Again, what we have here is Mueller attempting to take down peripheral people who come in contact with Trump in an attempt to prove guilt by association. But his logic is deeply flawed and, surely, Mueller will continue on his fool's errand attempting to find collusion where there is none. Despite this, the media and public eat this story up. But with a taste for this Russian connection, Mueller knows they'll be asking for seconds in no time. What will he have to offer them?

# 42

# ROD ROSENSTEIN: FRIEND OR FOE?

MUELLER'S INVESTIGATION WAS MADE POSSIBLE BY one man who ultimately greenlit the project and gave Mueller carte blanche: Rod Rosenstein, the Deputy Attorney General of the United States Department of Justice. He is its Number Two.

Though a relatively unknown figure until recently, he is not unimportant. Rather timid and mild-mannered, Rosenstein does not look authoritative in either appearance or tone. A longtime DOJ employee, Rosenstein was previously US Attorney for the District of Maryland—where he in fact served in the position longer than any of his predecessors. President Trump appointed him as deputy to Attorney General Sessions and the US Senate confirmed him only in April of 2017.

Rosenstein came into the public's eye quickly after Jeff Sessions recused himself on all Russia matters.

Rosenstein authored the memo which Trump used to dismiss FBI Director James Comey, in which he asserts that the FBI must have "a Director who understands the gravity of the mistakes and pledges never to repeat them." He ends with an argument against keeping Comey as FBI director, on the grounds that he was given an opportunity to "admit his errors" but that there is no hope that he will "implement the necessary corrective actions." [See Appendix D]

Most critically, however, Rosenstein was the one who appointed

Robert Mueller as Special Counsel to investigate the Trump campaign interaction and possible collusion with Russia during the 2016 election. [See Appendix E]

Rosenstein has come under close scrutiny and is now in the crosshairs.

Did he cover up malfeasance in the Department? We know he extended the notorious FISA Court warrants used to perform surveillance on the Trump team.

Curiously, in December 2017, Rosenstein testifies before the House Judiciary Committee for an oversight hearing on Capitol Hill. During the testimony, Representative Ron DeSantis asks Rosenstein if the FBI paid for the Russia dossier, to which he replies, "I'm not in a position to answer that question." DeSantis follows up: "Do you know the answer to the question?" To which Rosenstein replies, "I believe I know the answer, but the Intelligence Committee is the appropriate committee. . . ."

Rosenstein's dodging during the line of questioning makes us wonder: whose team is he on?

In the same House committee hearing, Rosenstein, a registered Republican, said "Nobody has asked me to take a loyalty pledge, other than the oath of office."

Called a prosecutor not a persecutor, by a lawyer friend, is Rosenstein a "by the book" kind of lawyer?

He did think that Comey "broke the rules."

Was he used by Trump or is Trump frustrated by him now that the goods are out on him?

Does he protect his pals in the Deep State because he is really one of them?

# 43

# RETRACING STEELE'S STEPS

WE KNOW THAT THE DEMOCRATIC NATIONAL Committee and the Clinton campaign—using Fusion GPS and the law firm Perkins Coie to funnel the money—financed the dossier. This money eventually went to Christopher Steele in the UK and his intelligence firm, Orbis Business, which made repeated payments to his Russian sources to dish out material on Trump.

The whole process, as we know, was polluted and involved a pay-to-play scheme wherein the "sources" knowingly made up stories to simply get paid more. The more they made up the more they got paid. And the FBI itself allegedly paid Steele, who they knew well and had paid before as an informant. In his dossier, Steele lists his sources as "A, B, C, D, and E." So, exactly who are these sources? A tragic incident and revelation would soon add a dark twist to Steele's organization. On March 4, 2018, former Russian agent Sergei Skripal and his daughter Yulia were found slumped on a bench in Salisbury, England —the apparent victims of poisoning by an extremely deadly nerve agent called Novichok. Allegations abound that Skripal was close to an unnamed person at Orbis.[61] Who is this unnamed person, and how close might they have been?

Might Skripal have been a source?

---

61 Martin, Séamus. "Unlikely that Vladimir Putin behind Skripal poisoning." *The Irish Times*. 14 Mar 2018. https://www.irishtimes.com/opinion/unlikely-that-vladimir-putin-behind-skripal-poisoning-1.3425736)

Steele vaguely suggests his sources' backgrounds, but provides no way to ascertain their complete identities or motivations.

So, how then did the FBI use this skimpy, unverified dossier to request secret court authorization to spy on Americans and Carter Page?

# 44

# FISA WARRANT

OBTAINING A FISA WARRANT TO SURVEIL or wiretap a person is by no means easy to obtain. An agent needs to go to the Foreign Intelligence Surveillance Court (FISC) or FISA court, which consists of a tribunal of eleven members, all federal judges, whose actions are carried out in secret. So, in order to obtain a warrant of this nature, it needs to be approved by this community of eleven, which further begs the question, who was working inside this Deep State to convince them to get a FISA warrant on Carter Page based on Steele's dossier? No rational judge would do this who actually read Steele's compilation.

FISA is the acronym for Foreign Intelligence Surveillance Act, which went into force in 1979.

This federal law provides procedures for the surveillance, both physical and electronic, of foreign intelligence information by foreign powers suspected of espionage or terrorism.

The Act utilizes special courts to request such surveillance warrants.

Growing out of President Nixon's tendency to spy on his enemies—political and activist groups—the Act was created to bring judicial and congressional oversight over the government's covert surveillance of foreign entities and individuals in the United States.

The Act is fashioned to allow both secrecy and security.

Understanding how the FISA application runs on secrecy, and the fact that FBI agents like Peter Strzok have a knack for falsifying reports and letters for investigation, is it possible that he worked on the application to insure approval of the warrant? Could his secret lover, Lisa Page, be involved? And what about the Ohrs? Just who was behind all this nefarious activity in the Deep State?

Falsifying documents and warrant approvals is no small infraction, and is reason for great concern for the American public.

# 45

# FISA-GATE

IN HIS *TOWNHALL* ARTICLE, "WHY FISA-GATE Is Scarier Than Watergate," Victor Hanson writes, "We are now in the midst of a third great modern scandal. Members of the Obama administration's Department of Justice sought court approval for the surveillance of Carter Page, allegedly for colluding with Russian interests, and extended the surveillance three times."[62]

Hanson then explains how none of these government officials told FISC that their warrant requests were based on Steele's dossier, which was clearly a "hit piece" on Trump, directly funded by the Clinton campaign. And how these same officials failed to mention the fact that Steele and his dossier had been dismissed by the FBI for obvious lack of credibility as a source. These same officials also failed to mention that DOJ official Bruce Ohr had personally met with Steele and that his wife Nellie was hired by Fusion GPS to work on the dossier.

This pattern of recklessness and blatant disregard for standard government procedure is exactly how this Deep State functions. And to be sure, like many tactics and operations in American government, this isn't new—it's simply a heightened version of a Deep State past, a collective group armed with more technological warfare. And with the rise of instant messaging and broadcast, everything is caught on tape, able to be shared with all the world—the same way David Corn broke

---

62 Hanson, Victor Davis. "Why FISA-gate Is Scarier Than Watergate." *TownHall*. 8 Feb 2018. https://townhall.com/columnists/victordavishanson/2018/02/08/why-fisagate -is-scarier-than-watergate-n2445740

the Mitt Romney "47 percent" video. Nothing is off limits now. And this dangerous game is played by both sides, internally and externally.

James Baker, the FBI's General Counsel, leaked the Steele dossier to David Corn, knowing full well that the dossier was pure smut. What we have here are government officials engaging in dirty tricks and politicizing their own agendas in favor of one candidate and against another.

And yet, when a former or even current government employee speaks out against this machine, they're immediately branded as whistleblowers—disloyal and treasonous citizens who ought to be shamed, not lauded for their courage and outspoken actions. Just look at William Binney, the former NSA analyst of twenty-five years, who spoke out about the breadth and illegality of the NSA's surveillance of the American public. Or Edward Snowden, who lives in hiding just like Julian Assange. What led to this shift in the way we view whistleblowers?

# 46

# THE DECLINE OF THE FOURTH ESTATE

ENSHRINED IN THE FIRST AMENDMENT IS a principle that protects what Thomas Jefferson meant when he said, "Where the press is free and every man able to read, all is safe." However, depending on the survey, an average of only 35 percent of Americans can name the three branches of government, and only around four in ten can name a right protected by the First Amendment. There should be no surprise then that although "Congress shall make no law . . . abridging the freedom of speech, or of the press," our press today is somewhat compromised.

The concept of the Fourth Estate suggests that beyond the checks and balances of those three branches of government, there exists an unhindered sentinel against chaos and tyranny, guarding truth and democracy and keeping watch over those who might abuse power.

Have our media ever been fully unhindered or untethered from influence or manipulation? We'd like to believe so, but reality throughout history has proven otherwise as national priorities and security interests have at times supplanted full media independence. However, the sentinel remained vigilant and tried its best to speak truth to power.

The Radio Act of 1927 established that the Federal Radio Commission and its FCC successor should only issue broadcast licenses when ensured that the public interest is served. In 1949 the FCC expanded the mandate to mean that licensees should include discussions of matters of public importance in their broadcasts and should do so in a fair manner.

TV and radio stations with FCC-issued broadcast licenses were required to devote some of their programming to issues of public importance and allow airing of opposing views on those issues.

Enter the present day and a media atmosphere where the truth is relative and subject to financial interests, power agendas, and manipulation. What happened?

In 1987, under the Clinton administration, the FCC revoked the Fairness Doctrine. With revocation came not only less regulation and more broadcaster freedom, but also more and more opportunities to fix programming to a particular ideological perspective.

Going one step further, the Obama administration opened the door to a genie that might be difficult to contain as opportunities for abuse by future presidents are plenty. Using the 1917 Espionage Act to prosecute more whistleblowers and leakers than all prior administrations combined, the administration was able to go after phone records and emails of a mix of reporters, including James Risen from the *New York Times*, who faced a jail sentence if he didn't reveal a government source—he didn't.

Whistleblowers like Thomas Drake, a senior executive at the National Security Agency, who was prosecuted when he decided to take his allegations to the press after efforts to alert superiors and Congress to what he saw as illegal activities, waste, and mismanagement at the NSA led nowhere.

Upon entering office, Barack Obama took the position that whistleblowing by government employees was an act "of courage and patriotism" that "should be encouraged rather than stifled." However, by the end of his administration, he brought more leak prosecutions than all previous presidential administrations combined.

Freedom of speech and of the press is taking on a capricious nature.

# 47

# DEEP STATE 2.0

WITH THIS NEW DEEP STATE 2.0, there is a strange cultural shift that occurred almost overnight within the government and in the mentality of many Americans. Steele's dossier, which we know was false, was released to the public without any verification. Now, as other memos and information are slated to be released, all of a sudden, the FBI and other intelligence agencies, a majority of the media—and of course, liberals—are now opposed to the disclosure of public documents. These governmental bodies and media heads are, as Victor Hanson notes, "siding with those in the government who disingenuously sought surveillance to facilitate the efforts of a political campaign."

And it is Dennis Bernstein who best points out the paradoxical nature of this shift in ideological stance from the left:

> A changing-places moment brought about by Russia-gate is that liberals who are usually more skeptical of US intelligence agencies, especially their evidence-free claims, now question the patriotism of Americans who insist that the intelligence community supply proof to support the dangerous claims about Russian "hacking" of Democratic emails especially when some veteran US government experts say the data would be easily available if the Russians indeed were guilty.[63]

---

63   Bernstein, Dennis. "The Still-Missing Evidence of Russia-Gate." *Consortium News*. 01 Jan 2018. https://consortiumnews.com/2018/01/01/the-still-missing-evidence-of-russia -gate/

This shift likely was able to occur because of the Deep State's calculated agenda to subvert Trump and minimize his character. In doing so, a majority of the public, through the media's warped projection of Trump, thinks he is this buffoon clowning around the White House, a trigger-happy tweeter with one hand on his phone and the other on his nuclear red button. And his so-called peers, too, are working against him to perpetuate this myth and weaken his character.

When Obama was in office, he expressed a distrust toward the Deep State and yet his administration weaponized the IRS and surveilled the Associated Press communications.

So what accounts for this change in ethos?

Is it because Obama, the progressive constitutional lawyer, didn't fit this right-wing authoritarian bill attempting to subvert the DOJ and other agencies? Is this why Comey, an Obama appointee, is so unwilling to conduct a proper investigation into Hillary Clinton's hard drives that she wiped? Or the fact that she paid Steele to produce opposition research on Trump that was unverified?

Does Comey know that Hillary is simply untouchable?

Ultimately, without verification, what is the worth of so-called "intelligence"? Why would the FBI be so interested? Why would they run with it?

Who was running the FBI? Could there be a cabal in the FBI?

# 48

# THE STRZOK-PAGE TEXT MESSAGES

On february 7, 2018, president trump tweets in all caps: "NEW FBI TEXTS ARE BOMBSHELLS!" His tweet refers to the release of Peter Strzok's messages and correspondences with his lover, fellow FBI agent Lisa Page. The text messages are the tangible proof that Trump had been looking for—evidence that Strzok and Page, two FBI agents, two government officials were working together, as an extension of this Deep State, in a coordinated plot to keep him from winning the presidency. Though Trump had great cause for celebration, one still has to question the motivation of the FBI's release. Typically, during an ongoing investigation of this sort, there is no reason to make such information public. Trump and his team are elated they did; however, they certainly must be wary of what moves the FBI has planned down the line? Is this some sort of trap? Or a distraction?

And why did the FBI release only 375 of the 10,000 text messages? When can the American public see the remaining 9,625 messages?

Why does the FBI pick and choose who and what they will properly investigate? Is there a method to their madness?

# 49

# THE UNTOUCHABLES: HILLARY CLINTON AND BARACK OBAMA

WITH THE RECENT RELEASE OF THE Strzok-Page text messages, perhaps this helps us better understand why James Comey gives up on his investigation of Hillary Clinton and the 30,000 emails that she had scrubbed from her server. Is it because he knew that they were too big a fish to fry? Is that why he tasked FBI agent Peter Strzok to change the language and rhetoric of his initial draft letter in which Strzok relays his findings on his investigation into Clinton's use of personal emails?

Remember, Strzok had originally reported that Clinton's actions were "grossly negligent" and that this alone should warrant an investigation. However, upon receiving Strzok's report, Comey asks him to adjust the wording to "extremely careless." Clearly, Comey does this for two reasons: He knows that the political powerhouses like Hillary Clinton and Barack Obama are untouchable, with enough political clout to destroy and mow down anyone who stands in their path. Therefore, Comey wouldn't dare risk his reputation and career trying to take down such big fish. So, with his conclusion regarding the potential investigation already set in his mind, Comey tasks Strzok to change the language of his report so Comey can come back to the press and his other investigative bodies claiming that "no reasonable prosecutor" would bring charges based on available evidence.

Will Mueller's investigation on Trump and his alleged nefarious connection to Russia highlight the FBI's favoritism?

Victor Hanson comments on the paradoxes presented by Mueller's investigation:

> Investigating any possible crimes committed by members of the Clinton campaign or the Obama administration is taboo, given the exalted status of both. But every time Mueller seeks to find incidental wrongdoing by those around Trump, he only makes the case stronger that those involved in the Clinton campaign and the Obama administration should be investigated...If such matters are not treated in an unbiased manner, we are not a nation of equality under the law, but a banana republic masquerading as a democracy.[64]

Hanson is absolutely right. In playing favorites, the FBI threatens the sanctity of our democratic processes.

---

64  Hanson, Victor Davis. "The Paradoxes of the Mueller Investigation." *Townhall.* 22 Feb 2018. https://townhall.com/columnists/victordavishanson/2018/02/22/the -paradoxes-of-the-mueller-investigation-n2452240

# 50

# CABAL AT THE FBI

THE FBI, AS WE NOW KNOW, was given the first installment of the dossier as early as July 2016 and got additional chapters as they were developed. That timing suggests a long enough period for the FBI to verify and find the dossier either credible or not.

The FBI is supposed to be a safeguard of good government and the protector of the rule of law. It is the nation's federal police force, and therefore it should not be tainted, corruptible, or biased. It should be objective, fair, honest, and trustworthy. The public depends on it.

As a result of its politicization, however, the FBI itself has earned a tarnished reputation and has lost much of its former credibility.

The former Director of the FBI, James Comey, whom President Trump would later fire, stuck his foot in his mouth often and exercised so much bad judgment during his tenure in office that he brought down the agency with him.

He was swayed by politics and became a maligned figure in both Republican and Democratic circles. The President early in his tenure decided he "had to go" for poor judgment and because of bias and insubordination. At times, it appeared Comey had put his large figure above the law and had a higher esteem for his own notoriety than for the agency he ran. He most certainly was not the embodiment of "ethical leadership" he claimed.

Comey allowed leaks in his time at the FBI and admitted under oath that he himself leaked. The agency became a literal sieve during his directorship.

It also became a hotbed of utter and complete partisanship.

Indeed, there were many, perhaps a "society," of anti-Trump FBI agents coordinating against his election and against his very presidency. There also developed a cabal of pro-Clinton FBI agents, like worker bees protecting the queen, who sought to protect her at all costs and manipulated policy and inquiries to benefit her and her campaign.

This group sidelined evidence, frustrated investigations, and contrived to condemn Trump and his advisors while hiding, and perhaps destroying, emails and memos regarding Clinton's own emails and illegal server. They also destroyed or lost emails and texts of those agents who were working to support her, as evidenced in recently uncovered text messages.

The former Assistant Director of the FBI, James Kallstrom, said in a radio interview with John Catsimatidis that he believed behind the scenes there was a "fifth column conspiracy" in the bureau determined to defeat Trump.

Was there a felony involved? Was this small cabal inside the FBI a devious Deep State? Were they working of their own accord or tied to some higher power? Were they James Comey sycophants?

"This whole thing with Russia is just a farce," Kallstrom said, adding: "If we find out that that phony [Russian dossier] was brought to the US Foreign Intelligence Surveillance Court in the form of an affidavit for a judge's authority, and if we find out that the people signing that affidavit in the bureau knew that that was phony information, that is indeed a serious felony."[65]

Yet, in the words of one anonymous agent quoted by the left-wing UK *Guardian* newspaper, some FBI personnel see Clinton as "the anti-Christ," and "the reason why they're leaking is they're pro-Trump." The FBI, the agent said, "is Trumpland."

Which is it? Was the FBI pro-Trump? Or pro-Clinton?

And why is it that it was either?

---

65   James Kallstrom interviewed on radio by host, John Catsimatidis, on *Cat's Roundtable*. 10 Dec 2017. https://omny.fm/shows/cats-interviews/12-10-17-james-kallstrom

Was there truly a "secret society" of agents actively working to depose the elected president? This went beyond resistance and it involved proactive measures.

They call that treason.

# 51

# BRUCE & NELLIE OHR: TAKE 2

As NEW INFORMATION CONTINUES TO POUR in from the House Intelligence Committee about what exactly the FBI knew, what they claim they didn't know, and what they intentionally kept hidden from the public, consider these new revelations about FBI agent Nellie Ohr and her husband Bruce Ohr, the FBI agent contracted by Glenn Simpson of Fusion GPS. It turns out the Nellie was more than just an extra hand here, another point-of-contact for Fusion. In fact, it seems that she may have had a heavy hand in the creation of the dossier. In a memo released by the House Intelligence Committee, Nellie Ohr was "employed by Fusion GPS to assist in the cultivation of opposition research on Trump." The memo continues to detail how Bruce Ohr "later provided the FBI with all of his wife's opposition research." So, what exactly was Nellie's role? Is she no longer this peripheral figure as we previously assumed? Is she at the heart of our hunt for Red November? Could Nellie have been right in the middle, the one actually completing the research for Steele?

A larger question looms: when and how did the FBI learn that Nellie worked for Fusion GPS? And why did they stall to release this information?

More curiously, new information has been leaked regarding Bruce. As we know, he met with Glenn Simpson *before* the election, but now it seems he also met with Simpson *after* the election. Why? Was it to get their story straight after Clinton lost? Or was it to recalibrate their plot to subvert President Trump?

# 52

# MEDIA DISTRACTION

IN THE AFTERMATH OF STEELE'S DOSSIER going viral online around the world and becoming the centerpiece for water-cooler gossip in DC, one has to wonder, could this all be just a distraction from something more serious?

In a news analysis published in the *Guardian*, Cas Mudde, an associate professor at the University of Georgia, reports on the absurdity of Mueller's investigation and goes so far to call it all a "farce." Mudde writes that "the Russia-Trump collusion story might be the talk of the town in Washington, but this is not the case in much of the rest of the country."[66] As with most narcissistic politicians in DC, they like to bump their own gums and surround themselves with stories *about* themselves. But, as Daniel Lazare reports for *Consortium News*, "Out in flyover country, rather, Americans can't figure out why the political elite is more concerned with a nonexistent scandal than with things that really count, i.e. de-industrialization, infrastructure decay, the opioid epidemic, and school shootings."[67] Lazare is right: in the months following the 2016 election and Trump's upset, a major rift in America was exposed. All these pundits, polling officials, mainstream media talking heads—and even Hillary Clinton—all thought that what

---

66  Mudde, Cas. "Democrats beware: the Trump-Russia inquiry isn't the path to power." https://www.theguardian.com/commentisfree/2018/feb/21/trump-russia-mueller-investigation-democrats

67  Lazare, Daniel. "The Mueller Indictments. The Day the Music Died." *Consortium News*. 24 Feb 2018. https://consortiumnews.com/2018/02/24/the-mueller-indictments-the-day-the-music-died/?print=print

was important to them in DC and other major metropolitan areas was exactly what was important to the rest of the country—as if the minority spoke for the majority of America. And look how wrong they were with all their predictions for who would win the election. Now, look how out of touch they are assuming that the entire American population cares about this Russia-gate story. Sure, there is a large portion of people who do care about it—but they care about it because the media tells them to care about it.

Lazare explains the danger in this type of thinking: "As society disintegrates, the only thing the Democrats have accomplished with all their blathering about Russkis under the bed is to demonstrate just how cut off from the real world they are."[68]

Again, Lazare hits it right on the head. But who's to blame? The media, the public, or the intelligence committees? Perhaps it's a combination of all three.

---

68  Ibid.

# 53

# US MEDDLING IN ELECTIONS

PERHAPS THIS DISTRACTION IS TO SHIFT the blame away from ourselves to free ourselves from culpability. It seems the motto within these intelligence communities can be best summed up as "Do as we say, not as we do."

Did Russia intervene in the US election? Very plausible, and more and more apparent with each passing day that yes indeed, they did. Causing disruption and confusion aligns with their earlier noted agenda to encourage the demise of the West.

Americans are justified in their anger at alleged interference with the very bedrock of their democratic process. However, a mirror is called for. The reflection, not so pretty.

In a 2016 NPR interview with Carnegie Mellon University researcher Doc Levin, Ari Shapiro opens the conversation: "This is hardly the first time a country has tried to influence the outcome of another country's election. The US has done it, too, by [Doc Levin's] count, more than 80 times worldwide between 1946 and 2000."[69] This is not counting US orchestrated coups as in Iran in 1953 or in Guatemala in 1954. Levin estimates that Russia or the Soviet Union have tried to alter the outcome of elections around thirty-six times between those same years.

---

69 Doc Levin interviewed on radio by host, Ari Shapiro. "Database Tracks History of US Meddling in Foreign Elections." *All Things Considered*, NPR. 22 Dec. 2016. https://www.npr.org/2016/12/22/506625913/database-tracks-history-of-u-s-meddling -in-foreign-elections

Levin and Shapiro go on to discuss whether US promotion of democracy and democratic values conflicts with election intervention. They conclude that it depends on whether the objective is to help the pro-democratic side or the less-than-savory side.

Imperatives such as geopolitical and strategic national interests, for example during the Cold War, factor into the equation. Richard Nixon's national security advisor, Henry Kissinger, said about Chile in 1970, "I don't see why we need to stand by and watch a country go communist due to the irresponsibility of its own people."

Speaking with the *New York Times*, Loch K. Johnson, regents professor, author, and editor of the journal *Intelligence and National Security*, said, "We've been doing this kind of thing since the CIA was created in 1947. We've used posters, pamphlets, mailers, banners—you name it. We've planted false information in foreign newspapers. We've used what the British call 'King George's cavalry': suitcases of cash."[70]

The difference today is that new digital or cyber tools are employed along with the old-school espionage techniques and operations.

---

70  Shane, Scott. "Russia Isn't The Only One Meddling in Elections. We Do It, Too." The *New York Times*. 17 Feb 2018. https://www.nytimes.com/2018/02/17/sunday -review/russia-isnt-the-only-one-meddling-in-elections-we-do-it-too.html

# 54

# PERPETUATING MYTHS AND "FAKE NEWS"

NOT ONLY IS A MAJORITY OF the mainstream media out of touch with what the public cares about, but the journalists themselves are out of touch with what real journalism is. Following Trump's victory, media outlets across the political spectrum abandoned any semblance of journalistic integrity and engaged in a race to the bottom in an attempt to delegitimize his presidency even before it began.

And could we expect anything less from them? These are the same people who read Christopher Steele's dossier, likely saw it for what it was—pure trash, political smearing at its worst—and decided to forgo any basic firsthand research to verify its authenticity, accepted it as truth, and then passed this information along to the public, who, rightfully so, assumed it was truth. After all, as we've seen with the so-called experts at CrowdStrike, why shouldn't we believe them? They're the ones looking at the data, analyzing and interpreting the reports to synthesize for us, the laymen. The public shouldn't have to discern between fact and fiction, between technical jargon and governmental gobbledygook, or between real news and fake news.

These are the very reasons we have specialized experts like lawyers who can interpret the obfuscated language of the law, which is intentionally designed to prevent the layman from understanding it and simply representing themselves in the court of law. If we could decipher this judiciary code, this so-called legalese, then surely we wouldn't be subjected to the steep costs of hiring a lawyer for protection.

This same logic applies to government officials and representatives of the media. They are meant to serve as buffers, protectors of our democracy. They are the ones paid to sift through the information and weed out the fake news. Yet, in an ironic twist of fate, the ones who once protected us against fake news are now the ones perpetuating these myths and untruths. Which begs the question: do we even need them anymore?

With social networks becoming embedded into our everyday lives, where news travels not by ink on the page, but in 140 digital characters, political figureheads, the Donald Trumps of the world, can now reach the general public in an instant, cutting out the middleman journalist.

As we've seen with Trump's explosive Twitter account, these journalists have been upended and the efficacy of their practice has been questioned. They're angry, and rightfully so. Trump has threatened their very existence and the necessity of their profession. But Trump overrides them with the click of the button. This new form of instant-gratification news will likely be the only tool to challenge and correct this decline in journalism.

# 55

# CONGRESSIONAL WITCH HUNT

DURING HIS METEORIC RISE TO THE presidency, Trump became a prime target from all media, receiving unfair, biased treatment from journalists and reporters and members of Congress, but none more disparaging than from the left, particularly the *New York Times* and CNN, who already had their minds set on him and his plans for presidency. Ray McGovern captures the biased mindset of the mainstream media from the start:

> It didn't even seem to matter when new Russia-gate disclosures conflicted with the original narrative that Putin had somehow set Trump up as a Manchurian candidate. All normal journalistic skepticism was jettisoned. It was as if the Russia-gate advocates started with the conclusion that Trump must go and then made the facts fit into that mold, but anyone who noted the violations of normal investigative procedures was dismissed as a "Trump enabler" or a "Moscow stooge."[71]

It should be clear by now just how dangerous this type of hivemind thinking can be, especially when it begins with the media, the ones who are, by definition, meant to be unbiased and simply present the facts. But long gone are the days of neutrality. This groupthink mentality

---

71  McGovern, Ray. "The FBI Hand Behind Russia-gate." *Consortium News*. 11 Jan 2018.
    https://consortiumnews.com/2018/01/11/the-fbi-hand-behind-russia-gate/

doesn't end with the media; it reverberates outward to the American public, creating a further divide among individuals who exist in their own political echo chambers. On both sides we have talking heads simply projecting their opinions, which confirms their viewers' positions and reaffirms the protection of their echo chambers. And yet, if we step away from it, looking at a distance, we see two wildly different stories. The responsibility is now on the individual to decide what is real and what is fake, or to decide what they want to believe or deny. It's like a Rorschach test where the patient sees what they want to see. This is a dangerous exercise from the mainstream media that threatens American democracy and further exacerbates this rift between DC and the rest of the country.

# 56

# THE EVOLUTION OF FAKE NEWS

So how did we reach this point? Where journalism is no longer about presenting fact-checked news, but rather presenting ad hominem attacks on political figures. Surely the media hasn't always been this slanted, disregarding facts and truth for unverified gossip. For instance, CNN, or what many conservatives jokingly refer to as the "Clinton News Network," didn't start out that way.

Founded in 1980 by Ted Turner, the flamboyant entrepreneur with a pencil mustache resting above his upper lip and Jane Fonda clinging to his his arm, CNN originally was a mega-radio station based in sleepy Atlanta, labeled the "Mouth of the South."

Evolving over time and making the switch to television broadcasting, CNN's reputation took off during the Gulf War in 1990, through their extensive coverage and reporting from the scene with the live feed of troops in Baghdad.

Quickly, Turner gained raw media power and became the most powerful news outlet on cable television. CNN was on 24/7 worldwide, so you couldn't escape it. Though it had a reputation for flamboyance and in-your-face journalism, it was anything but phony.

However, during the Bush years, CNN drifted politically to the left as Turner was highly critical of US policy. As his personal politics began going beyond his person, Turner and his ego became increasingly more controversial.

When his parent company, Time Warner, made a deal with AOL,

Turner got squeezed out, losing his once-tight control over CNN and its direction.

Over the ensuing years, to recuperate from their losses, CNN commercialized and tried to extend its coverage, shows, and bureaus, but it was soon handicapped and faced new competitors, like Fox News, who had a much more conservative approach. Perhaps to overcompensate for their rival's conservative views, CNN took an even sharper turn left, to cater to their dwindling viewership.

CNN brought in Jeff Zucker to bend its programming even more to the left and to also compete with MSNBC, a subsidiary of the larger NBC, which was overtly leftist and exclusively Democrat in its outlook, favoring Obama and his entire thrust.

It was therefore inevitable that CNN would be one-sided in the 2016 election.

It had backed Clinton so strongly that claims of bias were abundant. It never took the Trump campaign seriously, instead ridiculing him and his followers on both the nightly news and all their various hosted programs and panel shows.

The panels were particularly biased with a normal four Clintonistas versus one Trump surrogate per show. And panelists themselves were outrageous and not only opinionated but bigoted and often mocking of Trump and his ideas, hair, color, and rallies.

But it wasn't just CNN attacking Trump. The majority of left-leaning outlets, following in the shadows of CNN, approached their so-called journalism in the same way: as a personal attack. The *Huffington Post* dragged Trump and his character through the mud. The *Washington Post* didn't hold back any personal punches, either. And, of course, the *New York Times* did the same. But it didn't stop at just the media outlets. Even search engines like Google and Yahoo were in on the muckraking. We see that for example at Google, when the Trump campaign put out a press release it was marked as "Promotion." When the Hillary Clinton campaign put out a press release it was marked as "Update."

An analysis of the mainstream networks and CNN during the

2016 election empirically showed what was self-evident. The bias was extraordinary: 95 percent of mainstream media was pro-Clinton and anti-Trump.

In true Trump fashion, however, he fought back in a comedic way. Armed with his explosive Twitter account, Trump created the "Fake News Awards" and, through tweets, awarded CNN with four out of his eleven awards. To date, undoubtedly, this is CNN's greatest accomplishment.

Though clearly in jest, there is a grave danger with all this new media and the degradation of journalism, which has evolved into what we now know as Fake News.

Like most trends, this isn't a new invention; it's a cyclical crutch that media and government rely on to advance an agenda, to perpetuate propaganda, and spread disinformation. Dating back to ancient times, fake news is just the modern reincarnation of what's previously been termed "misinformation" or "yellow journalism" to single out a few. Regardless of its nomenclature, this type of news is dangerous. Marc Antony, the Roman general, killed himself because of misinformation.

Though an extreme example, the danger of fake news is its increasingly difficult nature to spot and separate from real news.

Take for instance, the comedic routines featured on *Saturday Night Live*. SNL is not news, rather an attempt at funny political satire, even if most of it is anti-Trump in nature. Similarly, the *Onion* is a satirical political newspaper. These two media forms don't pretend to be true and factual representations of the news. Though they do project an agenda and opinion, it's easily discernible.

However, shows like Jake Tapper's *State of the Union* and Becky Anderson's *Connect the World* on CNN are not comedies. They parade, as do other shows like them, as real news. When in fact, they are not. They push their own opinions, and opinions are not facts. They push an agenda. That agenda is a globalist liberal agenda.

It's a dangerous, slippery slope we're sliding down, where opinion is being misconstrued as fact and disguised as news. The end result is undoubtedly dire. Yet, is there reason to remain hopeful? Hopeful that somehow we can correct and recalibrate this decline in journalism?

# 57

# SLEEPER AGENTS: RUSSIAN TROLLS

A MAJOR FOCUS OF THE MEDIA'S attention is on the use of Russian trolls that supposedly swung the election in favor of Trump. Had any decent journalist looked into these trolls and how they were operating? Or did they just assume they were negative forces because of the negative connotation associated with the name troll and the fact that it's the Russians behind them?

One can only imagine that Vladimir Putin is sitting in his office, legs kicked up on his desk, laughing at the television as he watches the media stir up hysteria across America, reporting on how Russian interference influenced the outcome of the election using electronic trolls and bots to skew and spew data online. Some reports even explain how Russians pretending to be Americans were used as plants to rally support for the election. Sounds calculated and nefarious, right? Like some evil plan concocted in a secret Russian lair. Let's look more closely at just what these trolls and bots were doing to better understand if and how they might have affected the outcome of the 2016 election.

A St. Petersburg based company called the Internet Research Agency (IRA) was sending trolls and bots across the internet and social media platforms for distortion and to generate support for both candidates. For instance, according to Sarah K. Burris for *Raw Story*, "they used the Facebook group 'Being Patriotic' to get Americans to organize small pro-Trump rallies that gave the illusion that Trump had volunteers all over the state."[72]

This doesn't exactly sound illegal, now does it? Seems like the people duped by these trolls should have been more savvy.

The *Washington Post* reports that these trolls "did not ask the Americans to do or say anything they were not already doing, a sign of how effectively the Russian effort learned to echo Trump's own campaign themes."[73]

Still, despite this instance of Trump-leaning support, Melissa Ryan, a Democratic social media marketing expert who tracks right-wing online activity, confirms this, saying, "The idea wasn't necessarily to help one political party over another, but to sow as much discord as possible."[74]

"I was supporting Donald Trump anyway. I didn't need persuading," said lawyer Max Christiansen, who had volunteered to host an event from that same "Being Patriotic" Facebook group.[75]

This attack does, however, highlight just how badly social media platforms like Facebook and Twitter were played by these Russian bots and trolls. It also shows that this wasn't an orchestrated attempt by the Russians to tip the voting scale in Trump's favor; it was merely an attempt to create chaos and add to the white noise on an already clogged media circuit. And despite social media execs like Mark

72  Burris, Sarah K. "Here's how the Russian government trained online trolls to infiltrate your favorite social media and websties." *RawStory*. 20 Feb 2018. https://www.rawstory.com/2018/02/heres-russian-government-trained-online-trolls-infiltrate-favorite-social-media-groups-websites/

73  Troianovski, Anton; Helderman, Rosalind S.; Nakashima, Ellen; Timberg, Craig. "The 21st-century Russian sleeper agent is a troll with an American accent." *Washington Post*. 17 Feb 2018. www.washingtonpost.com/amphtml/business/technology/the-21st-century-russian-sleeper-agent-is-a-troll-with-an-american-accent/2018/02/17/d024ead2-1404-11e8-8ea1-c1d91fcec3fe_story.html

74  Anderson, Mae. "Indictment says social media firms got played by Russian agents." PBS News Hour. 17 Feb 2018. https://www.pbs.org/newshour/politics/indictment-says-social-media-firms-got-played-by-russian-agents

75  Troianovski, Anton; Helderman, Rosalind S.; Nakashima, Ellen; Timberg, Craig. "The 21st-century Russian sleeper agent is a troll with an American accent." *Washington Post*. 17 Feb 2018. www.washingtonpost.com/amphtml/business/technology/the-21st-century-russian-sleeper-agent-is-a-troll-with-an-american-accent/2018/02/17/d024ead2-1404-11e8-8ea1-c1d91fcec3fe_story.html

Zuckerberg claiming that they'll somehow magically fix this issue and rid their sites of bots and trolls, David Gerzof Richard, a communications professor at Emerson College, explains that "This is the new norm. It's not going away."

And despite the media's tendency to project the use of trolls as just a tactic used by outsiders promoting a right-wing agenda, Paul Blumenthal reports on how the media startup company, Mic, cashed in on exploiting the social justice narrative: "The founders of Mic were trolls in the standard internet sense. They tapped into strong feelings and sentiments they didn't necessarily share, and thus they reverse-engineered a briefly successful media operation out of the algorithmic preferences of social media platforms like Facebook and Twitter."[76]

Blumenthal goes on to explain how the company's goals were like that of any other modern media startup: "to attract venture capital and advertising dollars."

Rob Goldman, Facebook's vice president of advertising, under intense scrutiny from his concerned users, defended his company on Twitter, writing, "The main goal of the Russian propaganda and misinformation effort is to divide America by using our institutions, like free speech and social media, against us. It has stoked fear and hatred amongst Americans. It is working incredibly well. We are quite divided as a nation."[77]

It's clear that America is undoubtedly divided. However, as Blumenthal notes, "Americans didn't need help from Russia to get there. What the Internet Research Agency did was enlist itself in the American culture war being waged across our social media platforms, with the platforms' complicity if not outright encouragement."[78]

---

76  Blumenthal, Paul. "Russian Trolls Used This One Weird Trick To Infiltrate Our Democracy. You'll Never Believe Where They Learned It." *HuffPost*. 28 Feb 2018. https://www.huffingtonpost.com/entry/russian-trolls-internet-research-agency _us_5a96f8cae4b07dffeb6f3434

77  Kuchler, Hannah. "Facebook says Russia's main goal is to divide US." *Financial Times*. 18 Feb 2018. https://www.ft.com/content/f681fed6-144f-11e8-9376-4a6390addb44

78  Blumenthal, Paul. "Russian Trolls Used This One Weird Trick To Infiltrate Our Democracy. You'll Never Believe Where They Learned It." *HuffPost*. 28 Feb 2018. https://www.huffingtonpost.com/entry/russian-trolls-internet-research-agency _us_5a96f8cae4b07dffeb6f3434

And considering that the Russians spent a total of $12 million on these trolls versus the nearly $2 billion combined budget of the campaigns, the term "interference" seems to be grossly misrepresented.

Again, what we have here are media platforms promoting agendas from both sides of the political spectrum to increase ad revenue and capital. This is nothing new.

The question now is how this tactic of trolling will affect upcoming elections.

And, knowing how benign these Russian bots and trolls turned out to be, does Mueller have anything to hinge his tenuous investigation on?

# 58

# THE SECOND DOSSIER

ALL OF A SUDDEN, AT THE height of the Trump-Russia fear factory, appears, out of nowhere, a *second* dossier.

Yes, another dossier, just like the first.

A hack journalist wrote this memo, Cody Shearer, and it sets out all the same allegations that were in the original Steele document.

The controversial leftist activist is actually no journalist and most certainly not a member of the Intelligence Community.

But he is a Clintonite.

With no background whatsoever in espionage or intelligence, Shearer's dossier was based on gathered gossip and inventions.

It was shared with the FBI in October 2016, it has been disclosed. They took it seriously. Seriously.

Who shared it with them?

This is too much—Christopher Steele did.

He handed it through an intermediary to the FBI because it corroborated his research on the seditious acts of Trump. Steele liked it because it reflected well on his own curious dossier. It did so because it was a ditto copy of everything he crammed into his false estimate.

Steele has now said that he "could not vouch for this new dossier's veracity." But he felt obligated to provide it to authorities as a copy and as an independent source.

Could he vouch for the veracity of his own concoction?

Is it likely that the second dossier came first? By that I mean was this Clinton political trick given to Steele who, using his MI6 hat, then made it to look like an intel product?

It was the same source. Steele himself—and his circle of informants—are the very sources.

The farcical "Golden Shower" in the Trump-Russia fantasy appears verbatim in both documents.

Shearer is a known hatchet man and a longtime part of the Clinton orbit. The DNC and the Clinton campaign both knew about the Shearer document and had a long appreciation for his "circle of private spies."

The primary actor among them is the longtime Clinton confidant, a controversial figure in his own right, one Sidney Blumenthal.

Was this a desperate act by the left-wing cabal given its entire hubbub about Libya? Was it an attempt at false information to corroborate the original false flag?

Does the complete Shearer dossier even really exist? Or was it the invention of the left-wing British newspaper the *Guardian,* in order to camouflage and obfuscate matters and to sell books of one of its correspondents?

The *National Review*, a conservative magazine, even called Mr. Shearer "the strangest character in Hillary's vast left-wing conspiracy." It is all rather strange.

Shearer has family connections to the Clintons, it turns out. His brother-in-law, Strobe Talbot, was very tight with Bill Clinton while at Oxford, where Clinton was a Rhodes scholar until he was supposedly quietly removed before completing his time because of a sexual allegation—the rape of a young woman at a town pub.

Talbot later served in a high-level position at Clinton's Department of State as a FOB (friend of Bill). He then became president of the Democratic-leaning Brookings Institution in Washington, DC. Shearer's own brother was Clinton's ambassador to Finland.

Shearer was not an official in the Hillary Clinton for President campaign in 2016. The campaign has said he worked "more indirectly."

The existence of an additional dossier by Christopher Steele or with his involvement that was not published by *Buzzfeed* in January 2017 raises new questions.

In a criminal referral it is established that coordination existed between Steele and Clinton aides. People in Clinton's innermost circles and in the Obama administration were in cahoots with Steele and both used his information and supplied him with raw intelligence. That package was delivered to the US Department of State through a Clinton conveyor. That unseen dossier relies nearly entirely on the original Steele work of art.

Christopher Steele was, it turns out, untruthful to the FBI and shared information and contacts obtained at the FBI with the press. It cost him—the FBI dropped him but continue to use his material.

Why a second dossier? Was one not enough?

Or was it too much?

# 59

# MEMO WARS:
# A POLITICAL PISSING CONTEST

FOLLOWING THE POLITICAL FALLOUT OF STEELE'S explosive dossier is a he-said-she-said, back-and-forth pissing contest from members of both the Republican and Democratic parties. Meanwhile, the whole world is watching, the media captures and reports all the drama unfolding live, and all the actors on stage directly in the limelight couldn't care less.

And perhaps the spark that led to this war is a letter written on January 4, 2018 by Charles Grassley and Lindsey Graham, both of the Senate Judiciary Committee, addressed to Deputy Attorney General Rod Rosenstein and FBI Director Christopher Wray, who replaced Comey after Trump fired him. In the letter, Grassley and Graham demand further answers on the FBI's approach to Steele's dossier and whether they used his memo to gain approval for a FISA warrant [See Appendix F].

The incendiary letter lights a political war. Artillery is in the form of paper memos, which are being drafted feverishly by each side in attempt to underscore and undercut their opponent. And to their divided audience, the American public, each memo serves as a Rorschach test—where each side chooses to see what they want to see.

### Nunes Memo

In mid-January 2018, Representative Devin Nunes compiles a four-page memo arguing that the FBI had abused its power in the investigation of

Trump's campaign. Nunes writes that investigators used Steele's dossier as the basis for gaining approval for a FISA warrant to further investigate Trump and other members of his campaign. Nunes's argument is logical, because as we now know, Steele's dossier is phony, and in his dossier he claims that the Russians have rather compromising information on Trump. Nunes is right when he claims that the FBI didn't do its job properly by verifying the accuracy of Steele's dossier before accepting it as gospel, the truth. Instead, they used it as a means to grant full access to investigate Trump. An investigation which, we are now seeing, was incredibly biased from the very start. Nunes also argues that the dossier, which is clearly falsified, should be of no importance, and that the warrant should never have been approved because of the dossier.

The document isn't yet made public. Meanwhile, the Democrats are busy compiling their own ten-page memo in rebuttal to Nunes's memo.

Despite never reading the memo, the Justice Department warns the House Intelligence Committee against releasing the memo, claiming that it would be "extraordinarily reckless" to do so before allowing the FBI to review it first. They worry that it could "risk sources and methods used to collect information."

How ironic!

The FBI, the very body of investigators who used a completely falsified dossier compiled by Christopher Steele who himself used shoddy sources and methods to collect his information—information that was then used as the basis for the FISA warrant used to investigate Trump—now, all of a sudden, has a moral compass and some semblance of basic investigative duties, is hesitant to release Nunes's memo.

The answer to the question why is obvious: Nunes's memo is proof that the FBI recklessly used Steele's dossier as a way to get a FISA warrant to investigate Trump, more specifically to monitor Carter Page, who reportedly has ties to Russian recruiters. Nunes's memo is proof of political targeting from the FBI.

By now, we know what happens when you take a stand against the

Deep State. This time is no different as the FBI and DOJ attempt to silence Nunes and his memo.

But Republicans and members of the conservative media begin to rally together to declassify the memo, saying that the public has a right to it. After all, Steele's unverified dossier was released without debate, why should this be any different?

Even Trump himself speaks out to get the memo to be released. He knows that he will finally have the inexorable truth to put an end to this congressional witch hunt in attempt to subvert his presidency.

On February 2, 2018, the memo is released. [See Appendix G]

The Nunes memo clearly elaborates and establishes improper surveillance techniques used by the DOJ and FBI in the Russia investigation. But it does more than that.

We now know that Christopher Steele confirmed to Bruce Ohr, Associate Deputy Attorney General, that he "was desperate that Donald Trump not get elected and was passionate about him not being President." This establishes motive and bias and discredits the entire campaign.

And, to get FISA court warrants to target Trump's team, Nunes's memo highlights how the FBI used the dossier in a central way. The warrants did not say who paid for the dossier (i.e., the Clinton campaign and the DNC), and the FBI knew such. This amounts to obstruction of justice, withholding or concealment of vital information, and misrepresentation of material information.

Also, this memo details that Bruce Ohr's wife, Nellie, worked for Fusion GPS, the ones who were contracted to produce the dossier and assist in opposition research on Trump. This information was likewise not included in any warrant. This is a failure to report prejudicial evidence that was knowingly withheld.

The warrant did use as corroboration an article that appeared in Yahoo written by left-wing investigative journalist Michael Isikoff. And his source in that article was Christopher Steele, who met him personally to brief him and others in Washington, DC. In real journalistic circles this is called "circular reporting," but the DOJ and FBI didn't work on such premises.

The warrant was actually reapproved numerous (four) times and such requests were signed by James Comey, Andrew McCabe, Sally Yates, and Rod Rosenstein. All of them knew that the warrants were based on faulty and unverified information. This amounts to lying, falsehood, and conspiracy to subvert the courts and the US government.

McCabe gave evidence to Congress in testimony under oath on December 2017 that a FISA warrant would not have been sought without the dossier and what it purportedly revealed.

But he knew what it revealed was a pile of lies.

So, what can we conclude?

The yearlong probe of Trump is polluted and politicized like no other in American history.

Beyond reasonable doubt the extreme abuses of authority and bad faith were instrumental in using the Deep State to spy on American citizens, thereby circumventing the Fourth Amendment. Weaponizing intelligence collection processes on behalf of a political party and for one political candidate over another during a presidential election is without precedent. It makes Watergate look like a minor crime by comparison.

Who will be held accountable? Who bears ultimate responsibility?

Do we not need a complete rethinking of the entire Russia collusion storyline because it is false? Is a second Special Counsel necessary now?

How can we recover from such abuse of power?

The FISA memo proves disingenuous acts. It is spurious. It is deceptive and blatantly corrupt. It is an utter and outright abomination.

On the days that follow the public release of the Nunes memo, the Democrats, led by US Representative Adam Schiff of California, work feverishly on their own memo in an attempt to refute and delegitimize the Republicans'.

Following the publication of his memo, a new target entered Nunes's crosshairs: Jonathan Winer.

On February 8, 2018, Jonathan Winer, the former US deputy assistant secretary of state and former Libya special envoy (and an Obama appointee), published an op-ed in the *Washington Post* titled "Devin Nunes is investigating me. Here's the truth." In his article, Winer unapologetically details that he had shared "more than 100 of Steele's reports with Russia experts at the State Department" over a period of two years.

He then details his connection with Cody Shearer, the Clinton-tied activist/hack journalist, and the reports he had received from him, which were later passed on directly to Steele. Winer writes, "Given that I had not worked with Shearer and knew that he was not a professional intelligence officer...I did not expect them to be shared with anyone in the US government." However, as we've come to learn, Steele did, in fact, share Shearer's notes with the FBI.

These revelations from Winer himself provide even more insights as to just how closely connected Steele was with top US intelligence officials. And, more importantly, how this unverified information was able to circulate throughout Washington thanks to Winer's involvement and carelessness.

Even more curious is that Winer acknowledged that he signed disclosure forms from his former firm to represent Oleg Deripaska, a Russian billionaire, known as Putin's "favorite oligarch." This raised even more questions: what relationship did Deripaska have with Steele himself? And, considering the oligarch's close ties to Putin and the fact that he has long since been viewed as pushing Russian national interests, could Deripaska be a source for Steele? Was Steele getting paid by Desipaska at the same time he was being paid by Fusion GPS?

### Schiff Memo
In the opening line of his memo, prepared on January 29, 2018, and released to the public on February 24, Representative Adam Schiff reports that "FBI and DOJ officials did not abuse the FISA process, omit material information, or subvert this vital tool to spy on the Trump campaign." In direct rebuttal to Devin Nunes's memo, Schiff's is one

clearly crafted and fabricated by Democrats in political attempt to override Nunes and the Republican charge. Like Steele's dossier, Schiff's is baseless—as you can see from that first line. [See Appendix H]

On February 25, Howard Dean, the former governor of Vermont and chair of the DNC, spoke about the release of Adam Schiff's memo during an interview on MSNBC, saying, "We wouldn't have put ours out it they hadn't put theirs out." To Dean, this is clearly just a pissing contest, a political back-and-forth waste of time.

One surely must wonder whether these memos are merely political instruments to simply undermine their opponent's agenda and ego, all while distracting the American public from issues that warrant real attention.

Even President Trump weighed in on this nonsense, calling into Jeanine Pirro's Fox News show *Justice with Judge Jeanine* and saying, "We shouldn't be fighting like that. We should all be on the same team. That includes Adam Schiff. Two sides fight all the time . . . fighting. We should all come together as a nation."[79]

On March 12, 2018, the House Committee on Intelligence, led by Representative Mike Conaway from Texas, released his committee's findings, stating, "We have found no evidence of collusion, coordination, or conspiracy between the Trump campaign and the Russians" [See Appendix J for House Committee on Intelligence's Memo].

President Trump immediately took to Twitter, writing in all caps:

THE HOUSE INTELLIGENCE COMMITTEE HAS, AFTER A 14 MONTH LONG IN-DEPTH INVESTIGATION, FOUND NO EVIDENCE OF COLLUSION OR COORDINATION BETWEEN THE TRUMP CAMPAIGN AND RUSSIA TO INFLUENCE THE 2016 PRESIDENTIAL ELECTION.

At a press conference that same day, Conaway says, "We found no

---

79 Trump-Pirro. *Justice with Judge Jeanine*. 24 Feb 2018. https://archive.org/details /FOXNEWSW_20180225_020000_Justice_With_Judge_Jeanine

evidence of collusion . . . we found perhaps some bad judgment...we found no evidence of any collusion of anything people were actually doing other than taking a meeting they shouldn't have taken or just inadvertently being in the same building."

Conaway concludes, "Bottom line: Russians did commit active measures against our elections in '16, and we think they'll do that in the future. It's clear they sowed discord in our elections...But we couldn't establish the same conclusions the CIA did that they specifically wanted to help Trump."

Undoubtedly, the Democrats, likely Adam Schiff, will respond with their own report in attempt to refute Conaway's; however, as we've seen, there is very little tangible evidence to hinge their collusion argument on.[80]

### Mystery Memo

To add yet more intrigue to the memo wars, Jane Mayer writes, in her March 12, 2018 feature profile in *The New Yorker* about Christopher Steele, that there existed another memo—this one hidden from public view, since it was not included in the release of the now widely known Steele dossier.

What is contained in that memo might be considered an extraordinary bombshell if it were not for the fact that its contents are outrageous and unsubstantiated hearsay upon circulated rumor.

Mayer notes that the memo was written by Steele in late November 2016, after his contract with Fusion GPS had ended, and that it was "based on one source, described as a 'senior Russian official.' [and] The official said that he was merely relaying talk circulating in the Russian Ministry of Foreign Affairs, [where] people were saying that the Kremlin had intervened to block Trump's initial choice for Secretary of State, Mitt Romney."[81]

---

80   Winer, Jonathan. "Devin Nunes is investigating me. Here is the truth." *Washington Post*. 8 Feb 2018.

81   Mayer, Jane. "Christopher Steele, The Man Behind the Trump Dossier." *The New Yorker*. 12 Mar 2018. https://www.newyorker.com/magazine/2018/03/12/christopher-steele-the-man-behind-the-trump-dossier

Mayer also reveals that the memo described how, through unspecified channels, the Kremlin "had asked Trump to appoint someone who would be prepared to lift Ukraine-related sanctions, and who would cooperate on security issues of interest to Russia, such as the conflict in Syria."

I guess his name was Rex Tillerson—slanderous.

# 60

# GUILTY BY OSMOSIS

With the media in a rabid frenzy claiming that they finally have verifiable proof that not only is Trump's character more questionable than that had originally thought, but also that he does in fact have shady connections to the Russians, the very people who supposedly helped get him elected.

And, as we know, Steele's dossier is a work of fiction. So when Robert Mueller is tasked to lead an investigation into the collusion between Trump and the Russians, he is placed on a fool's errand. How can he find collusion where there is none? And worse, the American media is only focusing on this story, so it runs rampant and causes national hysteria, only furthering the public's demand for Mueller to find proof. Mueller is, undoubtedly, now under enormous pressure to find collusion.

Let's get one thing clear about Trump and his connection to Russia. First and foremost, Trump is a businessman. The entire world knows this. He made his fortune as a real estate developer. Back in 2015, Trump planned to build a Trump Tower in Moscow. This isn't secret information. *This* is his connection to Russia. Despite the reports from CNN and others, there aren't some clandestine meetings happening underground in a secret lair, as though Trump and Putin are plotting some nefarious plan like in James Bond movies. Mueller knows this, but he's also tasked with the impossible: to find evidence of collusion where there is none.

Since there is no direct collusion to Trump, he turns to the smaller fish, the peripherals, in an attempt to prove Trump's guilt by association or osmosis. But this is a syllogism that doesn't work.

As Victor Hanson reports, the investigation hinges on a fundamental paradox: "Mueller's existential problem has been with him from the start. Due to the shenanigans of his discredited friend Comey and a rabid media, he was appointed to investigate crimes that did not exist. But if they did exist, collusion and obstruction were committed by those associated with the Clinton campaign and even members of the Obama administration."[82]

With both the media and public in a rabid feeding frenzy, like hungry dogs eyeing a steak on a table too high, Mueller knows he has to offer them something to quell their hunger, but all he has is scraps.

---

82   Hanson, Victor Davis. "The Paradoxes of the Mueller Investigation." *Townhall.* 22 Feb 2018. https://townhall.com/columnists/victordavishanson/2018/02/22/the-paradoxes -of-the-mueller-investigation-n2452240

# 61

# LOOSE CONNECTIONS

ON FEBRUARY 16, 2018, MUELLER THROWS his rabid public a bone and indicts thirteen Russian nationals and three Russian companies for allegedly conspiring to create confusion in the 2016 presidential election. So, after nine months of work, Mueller indicts them in a feeble attempt to prove his worth as an investigator and to show that he's making headway on finding Trump's collusion with the Russians.

One of those three companies in Mueller's indictment is the Internet Research Agency, the company often referred to as the "Russian troll farm." The two others are companies that helped finance their operation. Of the thirteen Russian nationals indicted, twelve of them were employees at the agency, and the other was agency's financier.

Any discerning viewer would see right past the misguided headlines and right through Mueller's cellophane ploy. We already know just what the Russians—through bots and trolls and troops on the ground—did to "sow discord" in the election. Americans were doing the same.

What no one seems to be focusing on is the fact that no Trump associates have been specifically charged with any crimes related to the Russian interference. Instead, Mueller is attempting to pin guilt on Trump through his prior associations with former advisors, like Michael Flynn, who had pleaded guilty to making false statements to the FBI back on January 24, 2017. [See Appendix I for Statement of the Offense]

In similar fashion, Mueller goes after George Papadopoulos, Paul Manafort, and Rick Gates. Manafort and Gates, both of whom worked for the Ukrainian government for a decade each, are alleged to have "acted as unregistered agents" for the Ukrainians, generating "tens of millions of dollars in income," which they then "laundered" through "scores of United States and foreign corporations, partnerships, and bank accounts."[83] In short, Manafort and Gates are being charged on their questionable financial histories—nothing related to the Russian interference in the 2016 election. Whereas, in October 2017, Papadopoulos pleads guilty to making false statements to the FBI about contacts he had had relating to his Russia-US relations and the Trump campaign.

Papadopoulos agreed to a plea bargain as part of the Mueller investigation.

Many suspect he was pressed to turn information on other Trump officials. It was alleged that he wore a wire as an FBI informant—but it yielded no goods.

Nothing.

While we can certainly tend to judge a person by the company they keep, we certainly can't prove one's guilt through that judgment. Yet, this is the false logic on which Mueller's investigation rests. But Mueller, just another pawn of the Deep State, runs his investigation according to Orwellian logic, and he already has his conclusion: Trump is guilty. Now, he needs to find an equation that fits his conclusion. But above all, he knows that the media and public, who too have their minds set, won't question or doubt his process.

In his article for *Consortium News*, Daniel Lazare reports on the three major failures of Mueller's indictments:[84]

1.  It failed to connect the Internet Research Agency, the alleged St. Petersburg troll factory accused of political meddling, with

83  Prokop, Andrew. "Robert Mueller just flipped his third fromer Trump aide." *Vox*. 23 Feb 2018. https://www.vox.com/2018/2/23/17045226/robert-mueller-flip-rick-gates -russia

84  Lazare, Daniel. "The Mueller Indictments. The Day the Music Died." *Consortium News*. 24 Feb 2018. https://consortiumnews.com/2018/02/24/the-mueller-indictments -the-day-the-music-died/?print=print

Vladimir Putin, the all-purpose evildoer who the corporate media say is out to destroy American democracy.

2. It similarly failed to establish a connection with the Trump campaign and indeed went out of its way to describe contacts with the Russians as "unwitting."

3. It described the meddling itself as even more inept and amateurish than many had expected.

# CONCLUSION

It should be transparently clear now just how this machine, the Deep State, operated in a calculated orchestration to subvert the presidency of Donald Trump. And the lengths and depths the media stooped to intentionally distort this story for ratings—whether through viewership, clicks, likes, or shares—which translated into more ad revenue. And yet, as we've seen through this complicated, tangled story—a story that is truly stranger than fiction, because much of it is—the media is just one of the many cogs in this machine that is capable of taking a seedling of information and, through a game of telephone, grow that seed into a great big redwood of a story: Red November.

In the time it takes to fire off 140 characters, a personal opinion can begin trending in the morning—with pundits and reporters across the globe quoting a tweet, using it as a crutch to prop up their story—and by nightfall we've spun an opinion, one person's perspective into a shared, collective stance. And like that, an untruth becomes a truth because the media knows it's what their audience wants to hear. It's become a mutual, symbiotic relationship that deepens our cultural and political echo chambers for the worse.

Replete with headlines that are about as subtle as a jackhammer and with advertisements longer than actual news clip, the media—like the hand that feeds the fish—treats us as such. With each flake they drop, we swarm to the surface like piranhas and ask for more. And like moths drawn to the light, the media and government use their head-lines and warped stories like torches to keep us distracted, when the real fire, a bigger blaze, is burning in the distance.

This game of telephone used to be a linear line of communication, a one-way conversation from supplier to consumer. Yet, with the rise of social media platforms, that linear line has spread laterally and another cog has been added to this machine: the public. Despite what these talking heads want us to believe, things haven't gotten worse, the tech-nology is just getting better. Now, the ones who once had the last word in this conversation no longer do.

We saw this with the #MeToo movement, which began out of the disturbing revelations centered around one Hollywood mogul: Harvey Weinstein. News spread quickly *because* of this heightened technology. Through social media platforms that allow the individual user to con-trol the direction of content and the news, a deeply hidden truth that had intentionally been buried was suddenly exposed.

And yet, as the movement grew, it became bloated once the media stuck its ugly, money-grubbing nose in when the feminist website Babe recklessly published an article with a headline that readied the reader for the worst: "I went out on a date with Aziz Ansari and it turned out to be the worst night of my life."[85]

Like everyone else in America, we clicked.

Unsurprisingly, the article was a cheap, failed attempt to compare unwanted sexual advances with an all-too-familiar bad date.

And just like that, the movement buckled under its own weight and became too big to support itself. The *New York Times* reported that the article was "Arguably the worst thing that has happened to the #MeToo movement since it began in October. It transforms what

---

85  Way, Katy. "I went out on a date with Aziz Anzari. It turned into the worst night of my life." *Babe*. 13 Jan 2018. https://babe.net/2018/01/13/aziz-ansari-28355

ought to be a movement for women's empowerment into an emblem for female helplessness."[86]

No one in their right mind would argue against the bravery of this movement and its importance for sparking social change. Yet it also speaks even louder on behalf of the media's overt desperation for our attention, so they sensationalize and exploit a seedling of an idea into a redwood that can't support itself.

This is exactly how Christopher Steele's dossier, a work of unverified salacious gossip, was able to spread like wildfire through Washington, DC, and with the orchestrated help of members of this Deep State, an untruth became a truth and one headline above them all blared across the nation: Trump was guilty of treason for collaborating with Russians. Yet we're missing one piece: the proof or even a whisper of truth.

Most recently, both Senator John McCain and David Kramer, the former State Department official who met with Christopher Steele to receive the dossier, pleaded the Fifth when questioned by the House Permanent Select Committee on Intelligence to avoid revealing Steele's sources. Their silence speaks volumes.

And yet, while this story continues to unfold and more layers are added, this whole Trump-Russia story will surely implode on itself as Robert Mueller widens his net and wildly misconstrues the definition of collusion. Through his misguided investigation, along with the media's blatant disregard for journalism, we see a carefully designed plot that begins with Christopher Steele and runs through the FBI, CIA, and NSA all in an attempt to subvert the Trump presidency.

To be sure, this isn't the sounding of the alarms. There is a silver lining here with all this misinformation being passed around: the credibility of the mainstream media and of our governmental agencies has been tested. Now, the public is becoming more attuned to the lies, manipulation, and distortion being pitched.

---

86  Weiss, Bari. "Aziz Anzari is Guilty. Of Not Being a Mind Reader." *The New York Times*. 15 Jan 2018. https://www.nytimes.com/2018/01/15/opinion/aziz-ansari-babe-sexual -harassment.html

An unintended consequence of the media's reckless abandonment of their journalist duties is a shift in autonomy: the onus is on us—the consumers of information. We are the ones who are now tasked to sift through the white noise and decide what is worth listening to. We are the ones who are now tasked to listen to wildly different perspectives on the same story. And we already are and will continue to become more savvy. We'll continue to become more astute listeners and discerners of the truth. We'll be able to look past the headlines that blare, the six-second soundbites that yell in our faces, and click-bait articles that masquerade as truth.

Yet, as we've witnessed in the past, the ones who are smart enough to listen aren't usually the ones doing the talking. In what has become the age of shouting, perhaps what we need most is a whisper of truth.

# POSTSCRIPT

On March 27, 2018, I flew on a long international flight into Boston's Logan International airport. I was to connect to a domestic flight en route to my in-laws' house, just outside of Cleveland, Ohio for the Easter holidays.

After exiting the plane, I was escorted to a special line for passport control. There, I was formally detained and asked to wait, along with my wife who was traveling with me. They would not say why, and I found it most curious as I am a frequent flier and go back and forth to the US and Europe and elsewhere many times a year. I never had had such treatment.

After about twenty minutes left waiting, we were taken by a TSA official and an FBI agent to a separate hall where they thoroughly checked my suitcase and asked about any electronic devices, phones, or computers I had in my possession.

This all seemed very foreboding and I have never experienced anything like this before, unless you include trips to communist China or in the old world to eastern bloc countries as a diplomat. What's going on, I thought?

When they found nothing suspicious and would not answer my questions about why they were detaining me, they separated me from my wife and told her to wait in a lounge, without explanation, while I was to be interviewed. That is all they said. Naturally, this left her in a state of total confusion and near panic.

What had I done? Why Ted Malloch?

I was then escorted to another building and into a secure conference room where two young FBI agents introduced themselves to me. They said I was being detained to answer questions regarding the Department of Justice Special Counsel probe and showed me their identification.

They seemed to know everything about me and had my color photograph and personal details and said in intimidating ways that it was a felony to lie to the FBI. I stated that I realized that, and I would readily, in fact gladly, cooperate with them.

I did, however, find it objectionable to treat me the way they had, as I was entering my home country, where I am a citizen and have served at the highest levels of government. They did not need to use such tactics or intimidation. I was a US patriot and would do anything and everything to assist the government and I had no information that I believed was relevant.

They asked for my cell phone and any laptop (I didn't have a computer on me) and produced a document to seize it and perform forensics on it. I gladly signed permission and asked if at least I could keep my driver's license and credit cards. They said yes and gave them back to me. One of the agents took the phone into another room and downloaded items but returned to say they would need to keep it and take it to Washington, DC for a full assessment. I asked when I could get it back. They assured me that in a few days they would definitely get it to me one way or another.

The other agent then proceeded for about an hour to interrogate me and involved himself in various disarming chitchat about my career, sterling academic credentials, top-secret code word government clearances in an earlier era, and my being a fan of the championship Philadelphia Eagles. All well and good, I presumed. What did they want? Why me? And why in this underhanded fashion? What had I done?

The questions got more detailed about my involvement in the Trump campaign (which was informal and unpaid); whom I communicated with; who I knew and how well—they had a long list of names.

They seemed to then focus more attention on Roger Stone (whom I have met a grand total of three times and with groups of people); Jerome Corsi, a journalist who edited a memoir I had written some years ago; and about Wikileaks, of which I knew nothing.

Had I ever visited the Ecuadorian embassy in London? they asked. No, I replied truthfully.

I was unfazed and very dubious about why they thought I knew anything. I couldn't help but wonder: had they read a copy of my soon-to-be-released book? The timing of this interrogation along with the nearing publication date seems to me to suggest yes: they *had* read it.

Then they served me with a subpoena, which I noticed had only been issued that very day in Boston to appear before the Mueller grand jury in Washington, DC that very Friday. They said I could telephone the lead attorney on that team and make necessary arrangements.

They shook my hand and had agents take me to my wife, who was very alarmed and in disbelief. They then escorted us to the adjoining terminal to catch our delayed domestic flight.

I called the Special Counsel's office the next morning and they said it would be better to appear later, which we agreed would be April 13th and they would pay for my travel. I told them I had legal representation and asked that they establish contact.

The Deep State is sending a signal and has no doubt read this book.

What could they want from me, a policy wonk and philosophical defender of Trump? I am not an operative, have no Russia contacts, and—aside from appearing on air and in print often to defend and congratulate our President—have done nothing wrong. What message does this send?

# AFTERWORD

*I WAS BORN IN A CROSSFIRE HURRICANE*, a lyric from a Rolling Stones hit, was an apt prediction of the political storm that has torn the shingles off the entire Establishment.

Ironically, it was also the name of the *coup* staged to take down Trump—that has now been exposed. We outlined the whole thing first and we put almost ALL of the pieces together of what had become a gigantic jigsaw puzzle.

President Trump needs to go "full animal" and insure a time of reckoning now that the allegations against him have been put to rest. He says he will. The Red November conspiracy was not the Trump-Russia collusion, which as the Mueller Report stated was a fiction, but as Trump himself called it a "collusion delusion."

He should take revenge as an act of vindication and a strong statement that the *real* conspiracy against America, and against himself, was formulated and executed by the Deep State.

Bring them all to justice, now.

Well, you ask whom does this include? We tell the whole story in this book and name all the characters.

Let's name names and start at the very top. They need to go under the bright light.

**Barack Hussein Obama** was clued into and orchestrated this *coup* attempt as is evident from the Lisa Page emails and testimony.

He needs to be investigated by a new Special Counsel, as do <u>all</u> the following members of his orbit for their gambit to destroy Trump in their treasonous Red November conspiracy.

We should presume innocence, but the facts speak to the truth.

### John Brennan

He is the kingpin who started and framed this whole plan. His hands are dirty and his vehement attacks on the President underscore his active role. Now he is caught.

### James Comey

He lied, leaked and covered up. He was a signatory of the FISA warrants to spy on Trump and his associates.

### Andrew McCabe

Liar and leaker extraordinaire, he was the FBI's man in this conspiracy.

### James Clapper

The DNI lied, leaked and furthered the whole Russia myth. He is the same person who brought us the Iraq WMD falsehoods.

### Sally Yates

She was key to the FISA process and was behind the horrible effort to frame General Flynn.

### Peter Strzok

He is the 'operator' who worked on behalf of Brennan to start the counter Intel operation and his actions are utterly despicable.

**Lisa Page**

The paramour of Strzok was implicated in every move and her anti-Trump emails are the evidence.

**Loretta Lynch**

We all know what happened on that tarmac in Phoenix. She got Hillary Clinton excused and ramped up the efforts against Trump.

**James Baker**

He was the FBI bagman on the FISA warrants and gave the salacious dossier to *Buzz Feed* to publish.

**Christopher Steele**

This is the foreign MI6 spy who paid Russians to provide fake gossip and dirt for a bogus dossier that is at the very center of the entire conspiracy.

**Glenn Simpson**

The Fusion GPS opposition research firm was the vehicle the DNC and Clinton used and paid to concoct the whole set of lies.

**Hillary Clinton**

She knew, approved and expanded the conspiracy after she lost badly in the 2016 election.

**Nellie and Bruce Ohr**

The wife was a CIA agent working with both Brennan and Fusion GPS to research and draft the dossier. Her husband was a top DOJ official who fronted it to the FBI and other outlets.

**John McCain**

So opposed to Trump was he that he and his staff took the fake dossier and ran with it.

### Susan Rice
Obama's NSA not only unmasked people illegitimately but had intimate knowledge of the entire operation.

### Samantha Power
Obama's UN Ambassador was intricately involved in the operation, politicizing the intelligence, and "unmasking" many American citizens, thus subjecting them to surveillance.

### Ben Rhodes
Hillary's flunkie was up to his eyeballs in the operation and implicated in its outputs.

As I have laid out in considerable detail, and everything I said has proven to be correct, this was a Red November conspiracy against the President, not Russiagate.

It was not so much about Russia meddling in US elections.

It is rather the conspiracy by anti-Trump forces from former MI6 agent, Christopher Steele and Fusion GPS to the FBI and DOJ to The CIA's John Brennan and the Deep State to subvert the President by inventing a narrative that was falsely fabricated and which they themselves concocted to delegitimize, subvert, and depose President Donald Trump.

Now it has been exposed for what it is.

These criminals and liars must be prosecuted to the full extent of the law.

Justice demands nothing less for the long-term health of our democratic republic.

Read backwards now and you will learn how this all started and what a hoax it was. It was nothing short of a *coup d'état*.

# APPENDICES

# APPENDIX A

## Intelligence Community Assessment into Russian Activities and Intentions in US Elections

## Background to "Assessing Russian Activities and Intentions in Recent US Elections": The Analytic Process and Cyber Incident Attribution

**6 January 2017**

# Background to "Assessing Russian Activities and Intentions in Recent US Elections": The Analytic Process and Cyber Incident Attribution

"Assessing Russian Activities and Intentions in Recent US Elections" is a declassified version of a highly classified assessment that has been provided to the President and to recipients approved by the President.

- The Intelligence Community rarely can publicly reveal the full extent of its knowledge or the precise bases for its assessments, as the release of such information would reveal sensitive sources or methods and imperil the ability to collect critical foreign intelligence in the future.

- Thus, while the conclusions in the report are all reflected in the classified assessment, the declassified report does not and cannot include the full supporting information, including specific intelligence and sources and methods.

## The Analytic Process

The mission of the Intelligence Community is to seek to reduce the uncertainty surrounding foreign activities, capabilities, or leaders' intentions. This objective is difficult to achieve when seeking to understand complex issues on which foreign actors go to extraordinary lengths to hide or obfuscate their activities.

- On these issues of great importance to US national security, the goal of intelligence analysis is to provide assessments to decisionmakers that are intellectually rigorous, objective, timely, and useful, and that adhere to tradecraft standards.

- The tradecraft standards for analytic products have been refined over the past ten years. These standards include describing sources (including their reliability and access to the information they provide), clearly expressing uncertainty, distinguishing between underlying information and analysts' judgments and assumptions, exploring alternatives, demonstrating relevance to the customer, using strong and transparent logic, and explaining change or consistency in judgments over time.

- Applying these standards helps ensure that the Intelligence Community provides US policymakers, warfighters, and operators with the best and most accurate insight, warning, and context, as well as potential opportunities to advance US national security.

Intelligence Community analysts integrate information from a wide range of sources, including human sources, technical collection, and open source information, and apply specialized skills and structured analytic tools to draw inferences informed by the data available, relevant past activity, and logic and reasoning to provide insight into what is happening and the prospects for the future.

- A critical part of the analyst's task is to explain uncertainties associated with major judgments based on the quantity and quality of the source material, information gaps, and the complexity of the issue.

- When Intelligence Community analysts use words such as "we assess" or "we judge," they are conveying an analytic assessment or judgment.

- Some analytic judgments are based directly on collected information; others rest on previous judgments, which serve as building blocks in rigorous analysis. In either type of judgment, the tradecraft standards outlined above ensure that analysts have an appropriate basis for the judgment.

- Intelligence Community judgments often include two important elements: judgments of how likely it is that something has happened or will happen (using terms such as "likely" or "unlikely") and confidence levels in those judgments (low, moderate, and high) that refer to the evidentiary basis, logic and reasoning, and precedents that underpin the judgments.

## Determining Attribution in Cyber Incidents

The nature of cyberspace makes attribution of cyber operations difficult but not impossible. Every kind of cyber operation—malicious or not—leaves a trail. US Intelligence Community analysts use this information, their constantly growing knowledge base of previous events and known malicious actors, and their knowledge of how these malicious actors work and the tools that they use, to attempt to trace these operations back to their source. In every case, they apply the same tradecraft standards described in the Analytic Process above.

- Analysts consider a series of questions to assess how the information compares with existing knowledge and adjust their confidence in their judgments as appropriate to account for any alternative hypotheses and ambiguities.

- An assessment of attribution usually is not a simple statement of who conducted an operation, but rather a series of judgments that describe whether it was an isolated incident, who was the likely perpetrator, that perpetrator's possible motivations, and whether a foreign government had a role in ordering or leading the operation.

*INTELLIGENCE COMMUNITY ASSESSMENT*

# Assessing Russian Activities and Intentions in Recent US Elections

ICA 2017-01D | 6 January 2017

This page intentionally left blank.

# Scope and Sourcing

Information available as of 29 December 2016 was used in the preparation of this product.

## Scope

This report includes an analytic assessment drafted and coordinated among The Central Intelligence Agency (CIA), The Federal Bureau of Investigation (FBI), and The National Security Agency (NSA), which draws on intelligence information collected and disseminated by those three agencies. It covers the motivation and scope of Moscow's intentions regarding US elections and Moscow's use of cyber tools and media campaigns to influence US public opinion. The assessment focuses on activities aimed at the 2016 US presidential election and draws on our understanding of previous Russian influence operations. When we use the term "we" it refers to an assessment by all three agencies.

- This report is a declassified version of a highly classified assessment. This document's conclusions are identical to the highly classified assessment, but this document does not include the full supporting information, including specific intelligence on key elements of the influence campaign. Given the redactions, we made minor edits purely for readability and flow.

We did not make an assessment of the impact that Russian activities had on the outcome of the 2016 election. The US Intelligence Community is charged with monitoring and assessing the intentions, capabilities, and actions of foreign actors; it does not analyze US political processes or US public opinion.

- New information continues to emerge, providing increased insight into Russian activities.

## Sourcing

Many of the key judgments in this assessment rely on a body of reporting from multiple sources that are consistent with our understanding of Russian behavior. Insights into Russian efforts—including specific cyber operations—and Russian views of key US players derive from multiple corroborating sources.

Some of our judgments about Kremlin preferences and intent are drawn from the behavior of Kremlin-loyal political figures, state media, and pro-Kremlin social media actors, all of whom the Kremlin either directly uses to convey messages or who are answerable to the Kremlin. The Russian leadership invests significant resources in both foreign and domestic propaganda and places a premium on transmitting what it views as consistent, self-reinforcing narratives regarding its desires and redlines, whether on Ukraine, Syria, or relations with the United States.

# Assessing Russian Activities and Intentions in Recent US Elections

ICA 2017-01D
6 January 2017

## Key Judgments

**Russian efforts to influence the 2016 US presidential election represent the most recent expression of Moscow's longstanding desire to undermine the US-led liberal democratic order, but these activities demonstrated a significant escalation in directness, level of activity, and scope of effort compared to previous operations.**

**We assess Russian President Vladimir Putin ordered an influence campaign in 2016 aimed at the US presidential election. Russia's goals were to undermine public faith in the US democratic process, denigrate Secretary Clinton, and harm her electability and potential presidency. We further assess Putin and the Russian Government developed a clear preference for President-elect Trump.** We have high confidence in these judgments.

- **We also assess Putin and the Russian Government aspired to help President-elect Trump's election chances when possible by discrediting Secretary Clinton and publicly contrasting her unfavorably to him.** All three agencies agree with this judgment. CIA and FBI have high confidence in this judgment; NSA has moderate confidence.

- Moscow's approach evolved over the course of the campaign based on Russia's understanding of the electoral prospects of the two main candidates. When it appeared to Moscow that Secretary Clinton was likely to win the election, the Russian influence campaign began to focus more on undermining her future presidency.

- Further information has come to light since Election Day that, when combined with Russian behavior since early November 2016, increases our confidence in our assessments of Russian motivations and goals.

**Moscow's influence campaign followed a Russian messaging strategy that blends covert intelligence operations—such as cyber activity—with overt efforts by Russian Government agencies, state-funded media, third-party intermediaries, and paid social media users or "trolls."** Russia, like its Soviet predecessor, has a history of conducting covert influence campaigns focused on US presidential elections that have used intelligence officers and agents and press placements to disparage candidates perceived as hostile to the Kremlin.

- Russia's intelligence services conducted cyber operations against targets associated with the 2016 US presidential election, including targets associated with both major US political parties.

- We assess with high confidence that Russian military intelligence (General Staff Main Intelligence Directorate or GRU) used the Guccifer 2.0 persona and DCLeaks.com to release US victim data obtained in cyber operations publicly and in exclusives to media outlets and relayed material to WikiLeaks.

- Russian intelligence obtained and maintained access to elements of multiple US state or local electoral boards. **DHS assesses that the types of systems Russian actors targeted or compromised were not involved in vote tallying.**

- Russia's state-run propaganda machine contributed to the influence campaign by serving as a platform for Kremlin messaging to Russian and international audiences.

**We assess Moscow will apply lessons learned from its Putin-ordered campaign aimed at the US presidential election to future influence efforts worldwide, including against US allies and their election processes.**

This report is a declassified version of a highly classified assessment; its conclusions are identical to those in the highly classified assessment but this version does not include the full supporting information on key elements of the influence campaign.

# Contents

## CIA/FBI/NSA Assessment: Russia's Influence Campaign Targeting the 2016 US Presidential Election

## Annexes

# Russia's Influence Campaign Targeting the 2016 US Presidential Election

# Russia's Influence Campaign Targeting the 2016 US Presidential Election

## Putin Ordered Campaign To Influence US Election

We assess with high confidence that Russian President Vladimir Putin ordered an influence campaign in 2016 aimed at the US presidential election, the consistent goals of which were to undermine public faith in the US democratic process, denigrate Secretary Clinton, and harm her electability and potential presidency. We further assess Putin and the Russian Government developed a clear preference for President-elect Trump. When it appeared to Moscow that Secretary Clinton was likely to win the election, the Russian influence campaign then focused on undermining her expected presidency.

- We also assess Putin and the Russian Government aspired to help President-elect Trump's election chances when possible by discrediting Secretary Clinton and publicly contrasting her unfavorably to him. All three agencies agree with this judgment. CIA and FBI have high confidence in this judgment; NSA has moderate confidence.

- In trying to influence the US election, we assess the Kremlin sought to advance its longstanding desire to undermine the US-led liberal democratic order, the promotion of which Putin and other senior Russian leaders view as a threat to Russia and Putin's regime.

- Putin publicly pointed to the Panama Papers disclosure and the Olympic doping scandal as US-directed efforts to defame Russia, suggesting he sought to use disclosures to discredit the image of the United States and cast it as hypocritical.

- Putin most likely wanted to discredit Secretary Clinton because he has publicly blamed her since 2011 for inciting mass protests against his regime in late 2011 and early 2012, and because he holds a grudge for comments he almost certainly saw as disparaging him.

We assess Putin, his advisers, and the Russian Government developed a clear preference for President-elect Trump over Secretary Clinton.

- Beginning in June, Putin's public comments about the US presidential race avoided directly praising President-elect Trump, probably because Kremlin officials thought that any praise from Putin personally would backfire in the United States. Nonetheless, Putin publicly indicated a preference for President-elect Trump's stated policy to work with Russia, and pro-Kremlin figures spoke highly about what they saw as his Russia-friendly positions on Syria and Ukraine. Putin publicly contrasted the President-elect's approach to Russia with Secretary Clinton's "aggressive rhetoric."

- Moscow also saw the election of President-elect Trump as a way to achieve an international counterterrorism coalition against the Islamic State in Iraq and the Levant (ISIL).

- Putin has had many positive experiences working with Western political leaders whose business interests made them more disposed to deal with Russia, such as former Italian Prime Minister Silvio Berlusconi and former German Chancellor Gerhard Schroeder.

- Putin, Russian officials, and other pro-Kremlin pundits stopped publicly criticizing the US election process as unfair almost immediately after the election because Moscow probably assessed it would be counterproductive to building positive relations.

We assess the influence campaign aspired to help President-elect Trump's chances of victory when possible by discrediting Secretary Clinton and publicly contrasting her unfavorably to the President-elect. When it appeared to Moscow that Secretary Clinton was likely to win the presidency the Russian influence campaign focused more on undercutting Secretary Clinton's legitimacy and crippling her presidency from its start, including by impugning the fairness of the election.

- Before the election, Russian diplomats had publicly denounced the US electoral process and were prepared to publicly call into question the validity of the results. Pro-Kremlin bloggers had prepared a Twitter campaign, #DemocracyRIP, on election night in anticipation of Secretary Clinton's victory, judging from their social media activity.

**Russian Campaign Was Multifaceted**

Moscow's use of disclosures during the US election was unprecedented, but its influence campaign otherwise followed a longstanding Russian messaging strategy that blends covert intelligence operations—such as cyber activity—with overt efforts by Russian Government agencies, state-funded media, third-party intermediaries, and paid social media users or "trolls."

- We assess that influence campaigns are approved at the highest levels of the Russian Government—particularly those that would be politically sensitive.

- Moscow's campaign aimed at the US election reflected years of investment in its capabilities, which Moscow has honed in the former Soviet states.

- By their nature, Russian influence campaigns are multifaceted and designed to be deniable because they use a mix of agents of influence, cutouts, front organizations, and false-flag operations. Moscow demonstrated this during the Ukraine crisis in 2014, when Russia deployed forces and advisers to eastern Ukraine and denied it publicly.

The Kremlin's campaign aimed at the US election featured disclosures of data obtained through Russian cyber operations; intrusions into US state and local electoral boards; and overt propaganda. Russian intelligence collection both informed and enabled the influence campaign.

***Cyber Espionage Against US Political Organizations.*** Russia's intelligence services conducted cyber operations against targets associated with the 2016 US presidential election, including targets associated with both major US political parties.

We assess Russian intelligence services collected against the US primary campaigns, think tanks, and lobbying groups they viewed as likely to shape future US policies. In July 2015, Russian intelligence gained access to Democratic National Committee (DNC) networks and maintained that access until at least June 2016.

- The General Staff Main Intelligence Directorate (GRU) probably began cyber operations aimed at the US election by March 2016. We assess that the GRU operations resulted in the compromise of the personal e-mail accounts of Democratic Party officials and political figures. By May, the GRU had exfiltrated large volumes of data from the DNC.

***Public Disclosures of Russian-Collected Data.*** We assess with high confidence that the GRU used the Guccifer 2.0 persona, DCLeaks.com, and WikiLeaks to release US victim data obtained in

2

cyber operations publicly and in exclusives to media outlets.

- Guccifer 2.0, who claimed to be an independent Romanian hacker, made multiple contradictory statements and false claims about his likely Russian identity throughout the election. Press reporting suggests more than one person claiming to be Guccifer 2.0 interacted with journalists.

- Content that we assess was taken from e-mail accounts targeted by the GRU in March 2016 appeared on DCLeaks.com starting in June.

We assess with high confidence that the GRU relayed material it acquired from the DNC and senior Democratic officials to WikiLeaks. Moscow most likely chose WikiLeaks because of its self-proclaimed reputation for authenticity. Disclosures through WikiLeaks did not contain any evident forgeries.

- In early September, Putin said publicly it was important the DNC data was exposed to WikiLeaks, calling the search for the source of the leaks a distraction and denying Russian "state-level" involvement.

- The Kremlin's principal international propaganda outlet RT (formerly Russia Today) has actively collaborated with WikiLeaks. RT's editor-in-chief visited WikiLeaks founder Julian Assange at the Ecuadorian Embassy in London in August 2013, where they discussed renewing his broadcast contract with RT, according to Russian and Western media. Russian media subsequently announced that RT had become "the only Russian media company" to partner with WikiLeaks and had received access to "new leaks of secret information." RT routinely gives Assange sympathetic coverage and provides him a platform to denounce the United States.

These election-related disclosures reflect a pattern of Russian intelligence using hacked information in targeted influence efforts against targets such as Olympic athletes and other foreign governments. Such efforts have included releasing or altering personal data, defacing websites, or releasing e-mails.

- A prominent target since the 2016 Summer Olympics has been the World Anti-Doping Agency (WADA), with leaks that we assess to have originated with the GRU and that have involved data on US athletes.

Russia collected on some Republican-affiliated targets but did not conduct a comparable disclosure campaign.

**Russian Cyber Intrusions Into State and Local Electoral Boards.** Russian intelligence accessed elements of multiple state or local electoral boards. Since early 2014, Russian intelligence has researched US electoral processes and related technology and equipment.

- DHS assesses that the types of systems we observed Russian actors targeting or compromising are not involved in vote tallying.

**Russian Propaganda Efforts.** Russia's state-run propaganda machine—comprised of its domestic media apparatus, outlets targeting global audiences such as RT and Sputnik, and a network of quasi-government trolls—contributed to the influence campaign by serving as a platform for Kremlin messaging to Russian and international audiences. State-owned Russian media made increasingly favorable comments about President-elect Trump as the 2016 US general and primary election campaigns progressed while consistently offering negative coverage of Secretary Clinton.

- Starting in March 2016, Russian Government–linked actors began openly supporting President-elect Trump's candidacy in media aimed at English-speaking audiences. RT and Sputnik—another government-funded outlet producing pro-Kremlin radio and online content in a variety of languages for international audiences—consistently cast President-elect Trump as the target of unfair coverage from traditional US media outlets that they claimed were subservient to a corrupt political establishment.

- Russian media hailed President-elect Trump's victory as a vindication of Putin's advocacy of global populist movements—the theme of Putin's annual conference for Western academics in October 2016—and the latest example of Western liberalism's collapse.

- Putin's chief propagandist Dmitriy Kiselev used his flagship weekly newsmagazine program this fall to cast President-elect Trump as an outsider victimized by a corrupt political establishment and faulty democratic election process that aimed to prevent his election because of his desire to work with Moscow.

- Pro-Kremlin proxy Vladimir Zhirinovskiy, leader of the nationalist Liberal Democratic Party of Russia, proclaimed just before the election that if President-elect Trump won, Russia would "drink champagne" in anticipation of being able to advance its positions on Syria and Ukraine.

RT's coverage of Secretary Clinton throughout the US presidential campaign was consistently negative and focused on her leaked e-mails and accused her of corruption, poor physical and mental health, and ties to Islamic extremism. Some Russian officials echoed Russian lines for the influence campaign that Secretary Clinton's election could lead to a war between the United States and Russia.

- In August, Kremlin-linked political analysts suggested avenging negative Western reports on Putin by airing segments devoted to Secretary Clinton's alleged health problems.

- On 6 August, RT published an English-language video called "Julian Assange Special: Do WikiLeaks Have the E-mail That'll Put Clinton in Prison?" and an exclusive interview with Assange entitled "Clinton and ISIS Funded by the Same Money." RT's most popular video on Secretary Clinton, "How 100% of the Clintons' 'Charity' Went to...Themselves," had more than 9 million views on social media platforms. RT's most popular English language video about the President-elect, called "Trump Will Not Be Permitted To Win," featured Assange and had 2.2 million views.

- For more on Russia's past media efforts—including portraying the 2012 US electoral process as undemocratic—please see Annex A: Russia—Kremlin's TV Seeks To Influence Politics, Fuel Discontent in US.

Russia used trolls as well as RT as part of its influence efforts to denigrate Secretary Clinton. This effort amplified stories on scandals about Secretary Clinton and the role of WikiLeaks in the election campaign.

- The likely financier of the so-called Internet Research Agency of professional trolls located in Saint Petersburg is a close Putin ally with ties to Russian intelligence.

- A journalist who is a leading expert on the Internet Research Agency claimed that some social media accounts that appear to be tied to Russia's professional trolls—because they previously were devoted to supporting Russian actions in Ukraine—started to advocate for President-elect Trump as early as December 2015.

4

## Influence Effort Was Boldest Yet in the US

Russia's effort to influence the 2016 US presidential election represented a significant escalation in directness, level of activity, and scope of effort compared to previous operations aimed at US elections. We assess the 2016 influence campaign reflected the Kremlin's recognition of the worldwide effects that mass disclosures of US Government and other private data—such as those conducted by WikiLeaks and others—have achieved in recent years, and their understanding of the value of orchestrating such disclosures to maximize the impact of compromising information.

- During the Cold War, the Soviet Union used intelligence officers, influence agents, forgeries, and press placements to disparage candidates perceived as hostile to the Kremlin, according to a former KGB archivist.

Since the Cold War, Russian intelligence efforts related to US elections have primarily focused on foreign intelligence collection. For decades, Russian and Soviet intelligence services have sought to collect insider information from US political parties that could help Russian leaders understand a new US administration's plans and priorities.

- The Russian Foreign Intelligence Service (SVR) Directorate S (Illegals) officers arrested in the United States in 2010 reported to Moscow about the 2008 election.

- In the 1970s, the KGB recruited a Democratic Party activist who reported information about then-presidential hopeful Jimmy Carter's campaign and foreign policy plans, according to a former KGB archivist.

## Election Operation Signals "New Normal" in Russian Influence Efforts

We assess Moscow will apply lessons learned from its campaign aimed at the US presidential election to future influence efforts in the United States and worldwide, including against US allies and their election processes. We assess the Russian intelligence services would have seen their election influence campaign as at least a qualified success because of their perceived ability to impact public discussion.

- Putin's public views of the disclosures suggest the Kremlin and the intelligence services will continue to consider using cyber-enabled disclosure operations because of their belief that these can accomplish Russian goals relatively easily without significant damage to Russian interests.

- Russia has sought to influence elections across Europe.

We assess Russian intelligence services will continue to develop capabilities to provide Putin with options to use against the United States, judging from past practice and current efforts. Immediately after Election Day, we assess Russian intelligence began a spearphishing campaign targeting US Government employees and individuals associated with US think tanks and NGOs in national security, defense, and foreign policy fields. This campaign could provide material for future influence efforts as well as foreign intelligence collection on the incoming administration's goals and plans.

# Annex A

**_Russia_ -- Kremlin's TV Seeks To Influence Politics, Fuel Discontent in US***

*RT America TV, a Kremlin-financed channel operated from within the United States, has substantially expanded its repertoire of programming that highlights criticism of alleged US shortcomings in democracy and civil liberties. The rapid expansion of RT's operations and budget and recent candid statements by RT's leadership point to the channel's importance to the Kremlin as a messaging tool and indicate a Kremlin-directed campaign to undermine faith in the US Government and fuel political protest. The Kremlin has committed significant resources to expanding the channel's reach, particularly its social media footprint. A reliable UK report states that RT recently was the most-watched foreign news channel in the UK. RT America has positioned itself as a domestic US channel and has deliberately sought to obscure any legal ties to the Russian Government.*

In the runup to the 2012 US presidential election in November, English-language channel RT America -- created and financed by the Russian Government and part of Russian Government-sponsored RT TV (see textbox 1) -- intensified its usually critical coverage of the United States. The channel portrayed the US electoral process as undemocratic and featured calls by US protesters for the public to rise up and "take this government back."

- RT introduced two new shows -- "Breaking the Set" on 4 September and "Truthseeker" on 2 November -- both overwhelmingly focused on criticism of US and Western governments as well as the promotion of radical discontent.

- From August to November 2012, RT ran numerous reports on alleged US election fraud and voting machine vulnerabilities, contending that US election results cannot be trusted and do not reflect the popular will.

*Messaging on RT prior to the US presidential election (RT, 3 November)*

- In an effort to highlight the alleged "lack of democracy" in the United States, RT broadcast, hosted, and advertised third-party candidate debates and ran reporting supportive of the political agenda of these candidates. The RT hosts asserted that the US two-party system does not represent the views of at least one-third of the population and is a "sham."

---

* This annex was originally published on 11 December 2012 by the Open Source Center, now the Open Source Enterprise.

- RT aired a documentary about the Occupy Wall Street movement on 1, 2, and 4 November. RT framed the movement as a fight against "the ruling class" and described the current US political system as corrupt and dominated by corporations. RT advertising for the documentary featured Occupy movement calls to "take back" the government. The documentary claimed that the US system cannot be changed democratically, but only through "revolution." After the 6 November US presidential election, RT aired a documentary called "Cultures of Protest," about active and often violent political resistance (RT, 1-10 November).

*RT new show "Truthseeker" (RT, 11 November)*

## RT Conducts Strategic Messaging for Russian Government

RT's criticism of the US election was the latest facet of its broader and longer-standing anti-US messaging likely aimed at undermining viewers' trust in US democratic procedures and undercutting US criticism of Russia's political system. RT Editor in Chief Margarita Simonyan recently declared that the United States itself lacks democracy and that it has "no moral right to teach the rest of the world" (*Kommersant*, 6 November).

- Simonyan has characterized RT's coverage of the Occupy Wall Street movement as "information warfare" that is aimed at promoting popular dissatisfaction with the US Government. RT created a *Facebook* app to connect Occupy Wall Street protesters via social media. In addition, RT featured its own hosts in Occupy rallies ("Minaev Live," 10 April; RT, 2, 12 June).

- RT's reports often characterize the United States as a "surveillance state" and allege widespread infringements of civil liberties, police brutality, and drone use (RT, 24, 28 October, 1-10 November).

*Simonyan steps over the White House in the introduction from her short-lived domestic show on REN TV (REN TV, 26 December 2011)*

- RT has also focused on criticism of the US economic system, US currency policy, alleged Wall Street greed, and the US national debt. Some of RT's hosts have compared the United States to Imperial Rome and have predicted that government corruption and "corporate greed" will lead to US financial collapse (RT, 31 October, 4 November).

RT broadcasts support for other Russian interests in areas such as foreign and energy policy.

- RT runs anti-fracking programming, highlighting environmental issues and the impacts on public health. This is likely reflective of the Russian Government's concern about the impact of fracking and US natural gas production on the global energy market and the potential challenges to Gazprom's profitability (5 October).

- RT is a leading media voice opposing Western intervention in the Syrian conflict and blaming the West for waging "information wars" against the Syrian Government (RT, 10 October-9 November).

*RT anti-fracking reporting (RT, 5 October)*

- In an earlier example of RT's messaging in support of the Russian Government, during the Georgia-Russia military conflict the channel accused Georgians of killing civilians and organizing a genocide of the Ossetian people. According to Simonyan, when "the Ministry of Defense was at war with Georgia," RT was "waging an information war against the entire Western world" (*Kommersant*, 11 July).

In recent interviews, RT's leadership has candidly acknowledged its mission to expand its US audience and to expose it to Kremlin messaging. However, the leadership rejected claims that RT interferes in US domestic affairs.

- Simonyan claimed in popular arts magazine *Afisha* on 3 October: "It is important to have a channel that people get used to, and then, when needed, you show them what you need to show. In some sense, not having our own foreign broadcasting is the same as not having a ministry of defense. When there is no war, it looks like we don't need it. However, when there is a war, it is critical."

- According to Simonyan, "the word 'propaganda' has a very negative connotation, but indeed, there is not a single international foreign TV channel that is doing something other than promotion of the values of the country that it is broadcasting from." She added that "when Russia is at war, we are, of course, on Russia's side" (*Afisha*, 3 October; *Kommersant*, 4 July).

- TV-Novosti director Nikolov said on 4 October to the Association of Cable Television that RT builds on worldwide demand for "an alternative view of the entire world." Simonyan asserted on 3 October in *Afisha* that RT's goal is "to make an alternative channel that shares information unavailable elsewhere" in order to "conquer the audience" and expose it to Russian state messaging (*Afisha*, 3 October; *Kommersant*, 4 July).

- On 26 May, Simonyan tweeted with irony: "Ambassador McFaul hints that our channel is interference with US domestic affairs. And we, sinful souls, were thinking that it is freedom of speech."

8

## RT Leadership Closely Tied to, Controlled by Kremlin

RT Editor in Chief Margarita Simonyan has close ties to top Russian Government officials, especially Presidential Administration Deputy Chief of Staff Aleksey Gromov, who reportedly manages political TV coverage in Russia and is one of the founders of RT.

- Simonyan has claimed that Gromov shielded her from other officials and their requests to air certain reports. Russian media consider Simonyan to be Gromov's protege (*Kommersant*, 4 July; Dozhd TV, 11 July).

- Simonyan replaced Gromov on state-owned Channel One's Board of Directors. Government officials, including Gromov and Putin's Press Secretary Peskov were involved in creating RT and appointing Simonyan (*Afisha*, 3 October).

- According to Simonyan, Gromov oversees political coverage on TV, and he has periodic meetings with media managers where he shares classified information and discusses their coverage plans. Some opposition journalists, including Andrey Loshak, claim that he also ordered media attacks on opposition figures (*Kommersant*, 11 July).

*Simonyan shows RT facilities to then Prime Minister Putin. Simonyan was on Putin's 2012 presidential election campaign staff in Moscow (Rospress, 22 September 2010, Ria Novosti, 25 October 2012).*

The Kremlin staffs RT and closely supervises RT's coverage, recruiting people who can convey Russian strategic messaging because of their ideological beliefs.

- The head of RT's Arabic-language service, Aydar Aganin, was rotated from the diplomatic service to manage RT's Arabic-language expansion, suggesting a close relationship between RT and Russia's foreign policy apparatus. RT's London Bureau is managed by Darya Pushkova, the daughter of Aleksey Pushkov, the current chair of the Duma Russian Foreign Affairs Committee and a former Gorbachev speechwriter (*DXB*, 26 March 2009; *MK.ru*, 13 March 2006).

- According to Simonyan, the Russian Government sets rating and viewership requirements for RT and, "since RT receives budget from the state, it must complete tasks given by the state." According to Nikolov, RT news stories are written and edited "to become news" exclusively in RT's Moscow office (Dozhd TV, 11 July; *AKT*, 4 October).

- In her interview with pro-Kremlin journalist Sergey Minaev, Simonyan complimented RT staff in the United States for passionately defending Russian positions on the air and in social media. Simonyan said: "I wish you could see...how these guys, not just on air, but on their own social networks, *Twitter*, and when giving interviews, how they defend the positions that we stand on!" ("Minaev Live," 10 April).

## RT Focuses on Social Media, Building Audience

RT aggressively advertises its social media accounts and has a significant and fast-growing social media footprint. In line with its efforts to present itself as anti-mainstream and to provide viewers alternative news content, RT is making its social media operations a top priority, both to avoid broadcast TV regulations and to expand its overall audience.

- According to RT management, RT's website receives at least 500,000 unique viewers every day. Since its inception in 2005, RT videos received more than 800 million views on *YouTube* (1 million views per day), which is the highest among news outlets (see graphics for comparison with other news channels) (*AKT*, 4 October).

- According to Simonyan, the TV audience worldwide is losing trust in traditional TV broadcasts and stations, while the popularity of "alternative channels" like RT or Al Jazeera grows. RT markets itself as an "alternative channel" that is available via the Internet everywhere in the world, and it encourages interaction and social networking (*Kommersant*, 29 September).

- According to Simonyan, RT uses social media to expand the reach of its political reporting and uses well-trained people to monitor public opinion in social media commentaries (*Kommersant*, 29 September).

- According to Nikolov, RT requires its hosts to have social media accounts, in part because social media allows the distribution of content that would not be allowed on television (*Newreporter.org*, 11 October).

- Simonyan claimed in her 3 October interview to independent TV channel Dozhd that Occupy Wall Street coverage gave RT a significant audience boost.

The Kremlin spends $190 million a year on the distribution and dissemination of RT programming, focusing on hotels and satellite, terrestrial, and cable broadcasting. The Kremlin is rapidly expanding RT's availability around the world and giving it a reach comparable to channels such as Al Jazeera English. According to Simonyan, the United Kingdom and the United States are RT's most successful markets. RT does not, however, publish audience information.

- According to market research company Nielsen, RT had the most rapid growth (40 percent) among all international news channels in the United States over the past year (2012). Its audience in New York tripled and in Washington DC grew by 60% (*Kommersant*, 4 July).

- RT claims that it is surpassing Al Jazeera in viewership in New York and Washington DC (*BARB*, 20 November; RT, 21 November).

- RT states on its website that it can reach more than 550 million people worldwide and 85 million people in the United States; however, it does not publicize its actual US audience numbers (RT, 10 December).

## TV News Broadcasters: Comparative Social Media Footprint

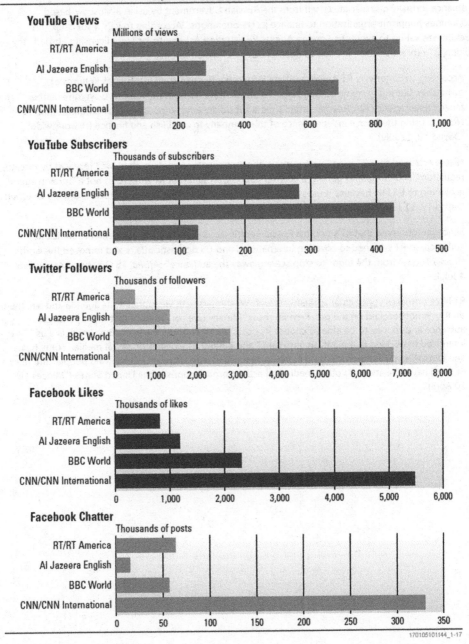

### YouTube Views
Millions of views

- RT/RT America
- Al Jazeera English
- BBC World
- CNN/CNN International

0 — 200 — 400 — 600 — 800 — 1,000

### YouTube Subscribers
Thousands of subscribers

- RT/RT America
- Al Jazeera English
- BBC World
- CNN/CNN International

0 — 100 — 200 — 300 — 400 — 500

### Twitter Followers
Thousands of followers

- RT/RT America
- Al Jazeera English
- BBC World
- CNN/CNN International

0 — 1,000 — 2,000 — 3,000 — 4,000 — 5,000 — 6,000 — 7,000 — 8,000

### Facebook Likes
Thousands of likes

- RT/RT America
- Al Jazeera English
- BBC World
- CNN/CNN International

0 — 1,000 — 2,000 — 3,000 — 4,000 — 5,000 — 6,000

### Facebook Chatter
Thousands of posts

- RT/RT America
- Al Jazeera English
- BBC World
- CNN/CNN International

0 — 50 — 100 — 150 — 200 — 250 — 300 — 350

170105101144_1-17

11

## Formal Disassociation From Kremlin Facilitates RT US Messaging

RT America formally disassociates itself from the Russian Government by using a Moscow-based autonomous nonprofit organization to finance its US operations. According to RT's leadership, this structure was set up to avoid the Foreign Agents Registration Act and to facilitate licensing abroad. In addition, RT rebranded itself in 2008 to deemphasize its Russian origin.

- According to Simonyan, RT America differs from other Russian state institutions in terms of ownership, but not in terms of financing. To disassociate RT from the Russian Government, the federal news agency RIA Novosti established a subsidiary autonomous nonprofit organization, TV-Novosti, using the formal independence of this company to establish and finance RT worldwide (Dozhd TV, 11 July).

- Nikolov claimed that RT is an "autonomous noncommercial entity," which is "well received by foreign regulators" and "simplifies getting a license." Simonyan said that RT America is not a "foreign agent" according to US law because it uses a US commercial organization for its broadcasts (*AKT*, 4 October; Dozhd TV, 11 July).

- Simonyan observed that RT's original Russia-centric news reporting did not generate sufficient audience, so RT switched to covering international and US domestic affairs and removed the words "Russia Today" from the logo "to stop scaring away the audience" (*Afisha*, 18 October; *Kommersant*, 4 July).

- RT hires or makes contractual agreements with Westerners with views that fit its agenda and airs them on RT. Simonyan said on the pro-Kremlin show "Minaev Live" on 10 April that RT has enough audience and money to be able to choose its hosts, and it chooses the hosts that "think like us," "are interested in working in the anti-mainstream," and defend RT's beliefs on social media. Some hosts and journalists do not present themselves as associated with RT when interviewing people, and many of them have affiliations to other media and activist organizations in the United States ("Minaev Live," 10 April).

# Annex B

## ESTIMATIVE LANGUAGE

Estimative language consists of two elements: judgments about the likelihood of developments or events occurring and levels of confidence in the sources and analytic reasoning supporting the judgments. Judgments are not intended to imply that we have proof that shows something to be a fact. Assessments are based on collected information, which is often incomplete or fragmentary, as well as logic, argumentation, and precedents.

**Judgments of Likelihood.** The chart below approximates how judgments of likelihood correlate with percentages. Unless otherwise stated, the Intelligence Community's judgments are not derived via statistical analysis. Phrases such as "we judge" and "we assess"—and terms such as "probable" and "likely"—convey analytical assessments.

*Percent*

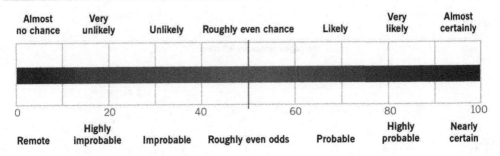

| Almost no chance | Very unlikely | | Unlikely | Roughly even chance | | Likely | | Very likely | Almost certainly |
|---|---|---|---|---|---|---|---|---|---|
| 0 | 20 | | 40 | | 60 | | 80 | | 100 |
| Remote | Highly improbable | | Improbable | Roughly even odds | | Probable | | Highly probable | Nearly certain |

**Confidence in the Sources Supporting Judgments.** Confidence levels provide assessments of the quality and quantity of the source information that supports judgments. Consequently, we ascribe high, moderate, or low levels of confidence to assessments:

- **High confidence** generally indicates that judgments are based on high-quality information from multiple sources. High confidence in a judgment does not imply that the assessment is a fact or a certainty; such judgments might be wrong.

- **Moderate confidence** generally means that the information is credibly sourced and plausible but not of sufficient quality or corroborated sufficiently to warrant a higher level of confidence.

- **Low confidence** generally means that the information's credibility and/or plausibility is uncertain, that the information is too fragmented or poorly corroborated to make solid analytic inferences, or that reliability of the sources is questionable.

This page intentionally left blank.

# APPENDIX B

## Steele Dossier

COMPANY INTELLIGENCE REPORT 2016/080

**US PRESIDENTIAL ELECTION: REPUBLICAN CANDIDATE DONALD TRUMP'S ACTIVITIES IN RUSSIA AND COMPROMISING RELATIONSHIP WITH THE KREMLIN**

### Summary

- Russian regime has been cultivating, supporting and assisting TRUMP for at least 5 years. Aim, endorsed by PUTIN, has been to encourage splits and divisions in western alliance

- So far TRUMP has declined various sweetener real estate business deals offered him in Russia in order to further the Kremlin's cultivation of him. However he and his inner circle have accepted a regular flow of intelligence from the Kremlin, including on his Democratic and other political rivals

- Former top Russian intelligence officer claims FSB has compromised TRUMP through his activities in Moscow sufficiently to be able to blackmail him. According to several knowledgeable sources, his conduct in Moscow has included perverted sexual acts which have been arranged/monitored by the FSB

- A dossier of compromising material on Hillary CLINTON has been collated by the Russian Intelligence Services over many years and mainly comprises bugged conversations she had on various visits to Russia and intercepted phone calls rather than any embarrassing conduct. The dossier is controlled by Kremlin spokesman, PESKOV, directly on PUTIN's orders. However it has not as yet been distributed abroad, including to TRUMP. Russian intentions for its deployment still unclear

### Detail

1. Speaking to a trusted compatriot in June 2016 sources A and B, a senior Russian Foreign Ministry figure and a former top level Russian intelligence officer still active inside the Kremlin respectively, the Russian authorities had been cultivating and supporting US Republican presidential candidate, Donald TRUMP for at least 5 years. Source B asserted that the TRUMP operation was both supported and directed by Russian President Vladimir PUTIN. Its aim was to sow discord and

disunity both within the US itself, but more especially within the Transatlantic alliance which was viewed as inimical to Russia's interests. Source C, a senior Russian financial official said the TRUMP operation should be seen in terms of PUTIN's desire to return to Nineteenth Century 'Great Power' politics anchored upon countries' interests rather than the ideals-based international order established after World War Two. S/he had overheard PUTIN talking in this way to close associates on several occasions.

2. In terms of specifics, Source A confided that the Kremlin had been feeding TRUMP and his team valuable intelligence on his opponents, including Democratic presidential candidate Hillary CLINTON, for several years (see more below). This was confirmed by Source D, a close associate of TRUMP who had organized and managed his recent trips to Moscow, and who reported, also in June 2016, that this Russian intelligence had been "very helpful". The Kremlin's cultivation operation on TRUMP also had comprised offering him various lucrative real estate development business deals in Russia, especially in relation to the ongoing 2018 World Cup soccer tournament. However, so far, for reasons unknown, TRUMP had not taken up any of these.

3. However, there were other aspects to TRUMP's engagement with the Russian authorities. One which had borne fruit for them was to exploit TRUMP's personal obsessions and sexual perversion in order to obtain suitable 'kompromat' (compromising material) on him. According to Source D, where s/he had been present, TRUMP's (perverted) conduct in Moscow included hiring the presidential suite of the Ritz Carlton Hotel, where he knew President and Mrs OBAMA (whom he hated) had stayed on one of their official trips to Russia, and defiling the bed where they had slept by employing a number of prostitutes to perform a 'golden showers' (urination) show in front of him. The hotel was known to be under FSB control with microphones and concealed cameras in all the main rooms to record anything they wanted to.

4. The Moscow Ritz Carlton episode involving TRUMP reported above was confirmed by Source E, ▓▓▓▓▓▓▓▓▓▓▓▓▓▓▓▓▓▓▓▓▓▓▓▓▓▓▓, who said that s/he and several of the staff were aware of it at the time and subsequently. S/he believed it had happened in 2013. Source E provided an introduction for a company ethnic Russian operative to Source F, a female staffer at the hotel when TRUMP had stayed there, who also confirmed the story. Speaking separately in June 2016, Source B (the former top level Russian intelligence officer) asserted that TRUMP's unorthodox behavior in Russia over the years had provided the authorities there with enough embarrassing material on the now Republican presidential candidate to be able to blackmail him if they so wished.

5. Asked about the Kremlin's reported intelligence feed to TRUMP over recent years and rumours about a Russian dossier of 'kompromat' on

Hillary CLINTON (being circulated), Source B confirmed the file's existence. S/he confided in a trusted compatriot that it had been collated by Department K of the FSB for many years, dating back to her husband Bill's presidency, and comprised mainly eavesdropped conversations of various sorts rather than details/evidence of unorthodox or embarrassing behavior. Some of the conversations were from bugged comments CLINTON had made on her various trips to Russia and focused on things she had said which contradicted her current position on various issues. Others were most probably from phone intercepts.

6. Continuing on this theme, Source G, a senior Kremlin official, confided that the CLINTON dossier was controlled exclusively by chief Kremlin spokesman, Dmitriy PESKOV, who was responsible for compiling/handling it on the explicit instructions of PUTIN himself. The dossier however had not as yet been made available abroad, including to TRUMP or his campaign team. At present it was unclear what PUTIN's intentions were in this regard.

20 June 2016

COMPANY INTELLIGENCE REPORT 2016/086

## RUSSIA/CYBER CRIME: A SYNOPSIS OF RUSSIAN STATE SPONSORED AND OTHER CYBER OFFENSIVE (CRIMINAL) OPERATIONS

### Summary

- Russia has extensive programme of state-sponsored offensive cyber operations. External targets include foreign governments and big corporations, especially banks. FSB leads on cyber within Russian apparatus. Limited success in attacking top foreign targets like G7 governments, security services and IFIs but much more on second tier ones through IT back doors, using corporate and other visitors to Russia

- FSB often uses coercion and blackmail to recruit most capable cyber operatives in Russia into its state-sponsored programmes. Heavy use also, both wittingly and unwittingly, of CIS emigres working in western corporations and ethnic Russians employed by neighbouring governments e.g. Latvia

- Example cited of successful Russian cyber operation targeting senior Western business visitor. Provided back door into important Western institutions.

- Example given of US citizen of Russian origin approached by FSB and offered incentive of "investment" in his business when visiting Moscow.

- Problems however for Russian authorities themselves in countering local hackers and cyber criminals, operating outside state control. Central Bank claims there were over 20 serious attacks on correspondent accounts held by CBR in 2015, comprising Roubles several billion in fraud

- Some details given of leading non-state Russian cyber criminal groups

### Details

1. Speaking in June 2016, a number of Russian figures with a detailed knowledge of national cyber crime, both state-sponsored and otherwise, outlined the current situation in this area. A former senior intelligence officer divided Russian state-sponsored offensive cyber operations into four categories (in order of priority):- targeting foreign, especially

western governments; penetrating leading foreign business corporations, especially banks; domestic monitoring of the elite; and attacking political opponents both at home and abroad. The former intelligence officer reported that the Federal Security Service (FSB) was the lead organization within the Russian state apparatus for cyber operations.

2. In terms of the success of Russian offensive cyber operations to date, a senior government figure reported that there had been only limited success in penetrating the "first tier" foreign targets. These comprised western (especially G7 and NATO) governments, security and intelligence services and central banks, and the IFIs. To compensate for this shortfall, massive effort had been invested, with much greater success, in attacking the "secondary targets", particularly western private banks and the governments of smaller states allied to the West. S/he mentioned Latvia in this regard. Hundreds of agents, either consciously cooperating with the FSB or whose personal and professional IT systems had been unwittingly compromised, were recruited. Many were people who had ethnic and family ties to Russia and/or had been incentivized financially to cooperate. Such people often would receive monetary inducements or contractual favours from the Russian state or its agents in return. This had created difficulties for parts of the Russian state apparatus in obliging/indulging them e.g. the Central Bank of Russia knowingly having to cover up for such agents' money laundering operations through the Russian financial system.

3. In terms of the FSB's recruitment of capable cyber operatives to carry out its, ideally deniable, offensive cyber operations, a Russian IT specialist with direct knowledge reported in June 2016 that this was often done using coercion and blackmail. In terms of 'foreign' agents, the FSB was approaching US citizens of Russian (Jewish) origin on business trips to Russia. In one case a US citizen of Russian ethnicity had been visiting Moscow to attract investors in his new information technology program. The FSB clearly knew this and had offered to provide seed capital to this person in return for them being able to access and modify his IP, with a view to targeting priority foreign targets by planting a Trojan virus in the software. The US visitor was told this was common practice. The FSB also had implied significant operational success as a result of installing cheap Russian IT games containing their own malware unwittingly by targets on their PCs and other platforms.

4. In a more advanced and successful FSB operation, an IT operator inside a leading Russian SOE, who previously had been employed on conventional (defensive) IT work there, had been under instruction for the last year to conduct an offensive cyber operation against a foreign director of the company. Although the latter was apparently an infrequent visitor to Russia, the FSB now successfully had penetrated his personal IT and through this had managed to access various important institutions in the West through the back door.

5. In terms of other technical IT platforms, an FSB cyber operative flagged up the 'Telegram' enciphered commercial system as having been of especial concern and therefore heavily targeted by the FSB, not least because it was used frequently by Russian internal political activists and oppositionists. His/her understanding was that the FSB now successfully had cracked this communications software and therefore it was no longer secure to use.

6. The senior Russian government figure cited above also reported that non-state sponsored cyber crime was becoming an increasing problem inside Russia for the government and authorities there. The Central Bank of Russia claimed that in 2015 alone there had been more than 20 attempts at serious cyber embezzlement of money from corresponding accounts held there, comprising several billions Roubles. More generally, s/he understood there were circa 15 major organised crime groups in the country involved in cyber crime, all of which continued to operate largely outside state and FSB control. These included the so-called 'Anunak', 'Buktrap' and 'Metel' organisations.

26 July 2015

COMPANY INTELLIGENCE REPORT 2016/095

RUSSIA/US PRESIDENTIAL ELECTION: FURTHER INDICATIONS OF
EXTENSIVE CONSPIRACY BETWEEN TRUMP'S CAMPAIGN TEAM AND THE
KREMLIN

Summary

- Further evidence of extensive conspiracy between TRUMP's campaign
  team and Kremlin, sanctioned at highest levels and involving Russian
  diplomatic staff based in the US

- TRUMP associate admits Kremlin behind recent appearance of DNC e-
  mails on WikiLeaks, as means of maintaining plausible deniability

- Agreed exchange of information established in both directions. TRUMP's
  team using moles within DNC and hackers in the US as well as outside in
  Russia. PUTIN motivated by fear and hatred of Hillary CLINTON. Russians
  receiving intel from TRUMP's team on Russian oligarchs and their families
  in US

- Mechanism for transmitting this intelligence involves "pension"
  disbursements to Russian emigres living in US as cover, using consular
  officials in New York, DC and Miami

- Suggestion from source close to TRUMP and MANAFORT that Republican
  campaign team happy to have Russia as media bogeyman to mask more
  extensive corrupt business ties to China and other emerging countries

Detail

1. Speaking in confidence to a compatriot in late July 2016, Source E, an
   ethnic Russian close associate of Republican US presidential candidate
   Donald TRUMP, admitted that there was a well-developed conspiracy of
   co-operation between them and the Russian leadership. This was
   managed on the TRUMP side by the Republican candidate's campaign
   manager, Paul MANAFORT, who was using foreign policy advisor, Carter
   PAGE, and others as intermediaries. The two sides had a mutual interest
   in defeating Democratic presidential candidate Hillary CLINTON, whom
   President PUTIN apparently both hated and feared.

2. Inter alia, Source E, acknowledged that the Russian regime had been
   behind the recent leak of embarrassing e-mail messages, emanating from
   the Democratic National Committee (DNC), to the WikiLeaks platform.

CONFIDENTIAL/SENSITIVE SOURCE

The reason for using WikiLeaks was "plausible deniability" and the operation had been conducted with the full knowledge and support of TRUMP and senior members of his campaign team. In return the TRUMP team had agreed to sideline Russian intervention in Ukraine as a campaign issue and to raise US/NATO defence commitments in the Baltics and Eastern Europe to deflect attention away from Ukraine, a priority for PUTIN who needed to cauterise the subject.

3. In the wider context of TRUMP campaign/Kremlin co-operation, Source E claimed that the intelligence network being used against CLINTON comprised three elements. Firstly there were agents/facilitators within the Democratic Party structure itself; secondly Russian émigré and associated offensive cyber operators based in the US; and thirdly, state-sponsored cyber operatives working in Russia. All three elements had played an important role to date. On the mechanism for rewarding relevant assets based in the US, and effecting a two-way flow of intelligence and other useful information, Source E claimed that Russian diplomatic staff in key cities such as New York, Washington DC and Miami were using the émigré 'pension' distribution system as cover. The operation therefore depended on key people in the US Russian émigré community for its success. Tens of thousands of dollars were involved.

4. In terms of the intelligence flow from the TRUMP team to Russia, Source E reported that much of this concerned the activities of business oligarchs and their families' activities and assets in the US, with which PUTIN and the Kremlin seemed preoccupied.

5. Commenting on the negative media publicity surrounding alleged Russian interference in the US election campaign in support of TRUMP, Source E said he understood that the Republican candidate and his team were relatively relaxed about this because it deflected media and the Democrats' attention away from TRUMP's business dealings in China and other emerging markets. Unlike in Russia, these were substantial and involved the payment of large bribes and kickbacks which, were they to become public, would be potentially very damaging to their campaign.

6. Finally, regarding TRUMP's claimed minimal investment profile in Russia, a separate source with direct knowledge said this had not been for want of trying. TRUMP's previous efforts had included exploring the real estate sector in St Petersburg as well as Moscow but in the end TRUMP had had to settle for the use of extensive sexual services there from local prostitutes rather than business success.

**COMPANY INTELLIGENCE REPORT 2016/94**

**RUSSIA: SECRET KREMLIN MEETINGS ATTENDED BY TRUMP ADVISOR, CARTER PAGE IN MOSCOW (JULY 2016)**

**Summary**

- TRUMP advisor Carter PAGE holds secret meetings in Moscow with SECHIN and senior Kremlin Internal Affairs official, DIVYEKIN

- SECHIN raises issues of future bilateral US-Russia energy co-operation and associated lifting of western sanctions against Russia over Ukraine. PAGE non-committal in response

- DIVEYKIN discusses release of Russian dossier of 'kompromat' on TRUMP's opponent, Hillary CLINTON, but also hints at Kremlin possession of such material on TRUMP

**Detail**

1. Speaking in July 2016, a Russian source close to Rosneft President, PUTIN close associate and US-sanctioned individual, Igor SECHIN, confided the details of a recent secret meeting between him and visiting Foreign Affairs Advisor to Republican presidential candidate Donald TRUMP, Carter PAGE.

2. According to SECHIN's associate, the Rosneft President (CEO) had raised with PAGE the issues of future bilateral energy cooperation and prospects for an associated move to lift Ukraine-related western sanctions against Russia. PAGE had reacted positively to this demarche by SECHIN but had been generally non-committal in response.

3. Speaking separately, also in July 2016, an official close to Presidential Administration Head, S. IVANOV, confided in a compatriot that a senior colleague in the Internal Political Department of the PA, DIVYEKIN (nfd) also had met secretly with PAGE on his recent visit. Their agenda had included DIVEYKIN raising a dossier of 'kompromat' the Kremlin possessed on TRUMP's Democratic presidential rival, Hillary CLINTON, and its possible release to the Republican's campaign team.

4. However, the Kremlin official close to S. IVANOV added that s/he believed DIVEYKIN also had hinted (or indicated more strongly) that the Russian leadership also had 'kompromat' on TRUMP which the latter should bear in mind in his dealings with them.

**19 July 2016**

10

COMPANY INTELLIGENCE REPORT 2016/097

**RUSSIA-US PRESIDENTIAL ELECTION: KREMLIN CONCERN THAT POLITICAL FALLOUT FROM DNC E-MAIL HACKING AFFAIR SPIRALLING OUT OF CONTROL**

**Summary**

- Kremlin concerned that political fallout from DNC e-mail hacking operation is spiralling out of control. Extreme nervousness among TRUMP's associates as result of negative media attention/accusations

- Russians meanwhile keen to cool situation and maintain 'plausible deniability' of existing /ongoing pro-TRUMP and anti-CLINTON operations. Therefore unlikely to be any ratcheting up offensive plays in immediate future

- Source close to TRUMP campaign however confirms regular exchange with Kremlin has existed for at least 8 years, including intelligence fed back to Russia on oligarchs' activities in US

- Russians apparently have promised not to use 'kompromat' they hold on TRUMP as leverage, given high levels of voluntary co-operation forthcoming from his team

**Detail**

1. Speaking in confidence to a trusted associate in late July 2016, a Russian émigré figure close to the Republican US presidential candidate Donald TRUMP's campaign team commented on the fallout from publicity surrounding the Democratic National Committee (DNC) e-mail hacking scandal. The émigré said there was a high level of anxiety within the TRUMP team as a result of various accusations levelled against them and indications from the Kremlin that President PUTIN and others in the leadership thought things had gone too far now and risked spiralling out of control.

2. Continuing on this theme, the émigré associate of TRUMP opined that the Kremlin wanted the situation to calm but for 'plausible deniability' to be maintained concerning its (extensive) pro-TRUMP and anti-CLINTON operations. S/he therefore judged that it was unlikely these would be ratcheted up, at least for the time being.

3. However, in terms of established operational liaison between the TRUMP team and the Kremlin, the émigré confirmed that an intelligence exchange had been running between them for at least 8 years. Within this context PUTIN's priority requirement had been for intelligence on the activities, business and otherwise, in the US of leading Russian oligarchs and their families. TRUMP and his associates duly had obtained and supplied the Kremlin with this information.

4. Finally, the émigré said s/he understood the Kremlin had more intelligence on CLINTON and her campaign but he did not know the details or when or if it would be released. As far as 'kompromat' (compromising information) on TRUMP were concerned, although there was plenty of this, he understood the Kremlin had given its word that it would not be deployed against the Republican presidential candidate given how helpful and co-operative his team had been over several years, and particularly of late.

**30 July 2016**

12

COMPANY INTELLIGENCE REPORT 2016/100

RUSSIA/USA: GROWING BACKLASH IN KREMLIN TO DNC HACKING AND
TRUMP SUPPORT OPERATIONS

Summary

- Head of PA IVANOV laments Russian intervention in US presidential
  election and black PR against CLINTON and the DNC. Vows not to supply
  intelligence to Kremlin PR operatives again. Advocates now sitting tight
  and denying everything

- Presidential spokesman PESKOV the main protagonist in Kremlin
  campaign to aid TRUMP and damage CLINTON. He is now scared and
  fears being made scapegoat by leadership for backlash in US. Problem
  compounded by his botched intervention in recent Turkish crisis

- Premier MEDVEDEV's office furious over DNC hacking and associated
  anti-Russian publicity. Want good relations with US and ability to travel
  there. Refusing to support or help cover up after PESKOV

- Talk now in Kremlin of TRUMP withdrawing from presidential race
  altogether, but this still largely wishful thinking by more liberal elements
  in Moscow

Detail

1. Speaking in early August 2016, two well-placed and established Kremlin
   sources outlined the divisions and backlash in Moscow arising from the
   leaking of Democratic National Committee (DNC) e-mails and the wider
   pro-TRUMP operation being conducted in the US. Head of Presidential
   Administration, Sergei IVANOV, was angry at the recent turn of events.
   He believed the Kremlin "team" involved, led by presidential spokesman
   Dmitriy PESKOV, had gone too far in interfering in foreign affairs with
   their "elephant in a china shop black PR". IVANOV claimed always to have
   opposed the handling and exploitation of intelligence by this PR "team".
   Following the backlash against such foreign interference in US politics,
   IVANOV was advocating that the only sensible course of action now for
   the Russian leadership was to "sit tight and deny everything".

2. Continuing on this theme the source close to IVANOV reported that
   PESKOV now was "scared shitless" that he would be scapegoated by
   PUTIN and the Kremlin and held responsible for the backlash against
   Russian political interference in the US election. IVANOV was determined

to stop PESKOV playing an independent role in relation to the US going forward and the source fully expected the presidential spokesman now to lay low. PESKOV's position was not helped by a botched attempt by him also to interfere in the recent failed coup in Turkey from a government relations (GR) perspective (no further details).

3. The extent of disquiet and division within Moscow caused by the backlash against Russian interference in the US election was underlined by a second source, close to premier Dmitriy MEDVEDEV (DAM). S/he said the Russian prime minister and his colleagues wanted to have good relations with the US, regardless of who was in power there, and not least so as to be able to travel there in future, either officially or privately. They were openly refusing to cover up for PESKOV and others involved in the DNC/TRUMP operations or to support his counter-attack of allegations against the USG for its alleged hacking of the Russian government and state agencies.

4. According to the first source, close to IVANOV, there had been talk in the Kremlin of TRUMP being forced to withdraw from the presidential race altogether as a result of recent events, ostensibly on grounds of his psychological state and unsuitability for high office. This might not be so bad for Russia in the circumstances but in the view of the source, it remained largely wishful thinking on the part of those in the regime opposed to PESKOV and his "botched" operations, at least for the time being.

**5 August 2016**

COMPANY INTELLIGENCE REPORT 2016/101

RUSSIA/US PRESIDENTIAL ELECTION: SENIOR KREMLIN FIGURE OUTLINES EVOLVING RUSSIAN TACTICS IN PRO-TRUMP, ANTI-CLINTON OPERATION

Summary

- Head of PA, IVANOV assesses Kremlin intervention in US presidential election and outlines leadership thinking on operational way forward

- No new leaks envisaged, as too politically risky, but rather further exploitation of (WikiLeaks) material already disseminated to exacerbate divisions

- Educated US youth to be targeted as protest (against CLINTON) and swing vote in attempt to turn them over to TRUMP

- Russian leadership, including PUTIN, celebrating perceived success to date in splitting US hawks and elite

- Kremlin engaging with several high profile US players, including STEIN, PAGE and (former DIA Director Michael Flynn), and funding their recent visits to Moscow

Details

1. Speaking in confidence to a close colleague in early August 2016, Head of the Russian Presidential Administration (PA), Sergei IVANOV, assessed the impact and results of Kremlin intervention in the US presidential election to date. Although most commentators believed that the Kremlin was behind the leaked DNC/CLINTON e-mails, this remained technically deniable. Therefore the Russians would not risk their position for the time being with new leaked material, even to a third party like WikiLeaks. Rather the tactics would be to spread rumours and misinformation about the content of what already had been leaked and make up new content.

2. Continuing on this theme, IVANOV said that the audience to be targeted by such operations was the educated youth in America as the PA assessed that there was still a chance they could be persuaded to vote for Republican candidate Donald TRUMP as a protest against the Washington establishment (in the form of Democratic candidate Hillary CLINTON). The hope was that even if she won, as a result of this CLINTON in power would be bogged down in working for internal reconciliation in the US, rather than being able to focus on foreign policy which would damage Russia's interests. This also should give President PUTIN more room for manoeuvre in the run-up to Russia's own presidential election in 2018.

3. IVANOV reported that although the Kremlin had underestimated the strength of US media and liberal reaction to the DNC hack and TRUMP's links to Russia, PUTIN was generally satisfied with the progress of the anti-CLINTON operation to date. He recently had had a drink with PUTIN to mark this. In IVANOV's view, the US had tried to divide the Russian elite with sanctions but failed, whilst they, by contrast, had succeeded in splitting the US hawks inimical to Russia and the Washington elite more generally, half of whom had refused to endorse any presidential candidate as a result of Russian intervention.

4. Speaking separately, also in early August 2016, a Kremlin official involved in US relations commented on aspects of the Russian operation to date. Its goals had been threefold- asking sympathetic US actors how Moscow could help them; gathering relevant intelligence; and creating and disseminating compromising information ('kompromat'). This had involved the Kremlin supporting various US political figures, including funding indirectly their recent visits to Moscow. S/he named a delegation from Lyndon LAROUCHE; presidential candidate Jill STEIN of the Green Party; TRUMP foreign policy adviser

Carter PAGE; and former DIA Director Michael Flynn, in this regard and as successful in terms of perceived outcomes.

**10 August 2016**

16

COMPANY INTELLIGENCE REPORT 2016/102

RUSSIA/US PRESIDENTIAL ELECTION: REACTION IN TRUMP CAMP TO RECENT NEGATIVE PUBLICITY ABOUT
RUSSIAN INTERFERENCE AND LIKELY RESULTING TACTICS GOING FORWARD

Summary

- TRUMP campaign insider reports recent DNC e-mail leaks were aimed at switching SANDERS (protest)
  voters away from CLINTON and over to TRUMP

- Admits Republican campaign underestimated resulting negative reaction from US liberals, elite and
  media and forced to change course as result

- Need now to turn tables on CLINTON's use of PUTIN as bogeyman in election, although some
  resentment at Russian president's perceived attempt to undermine USG and system over and above
  swinging presidential election

Detail

1. Speaking in confidence on 9 August 2016, an ethnic Russian associate of Republican US presidential
   candidate Donald TRUMP discussed the reaction inside his camp, and revised tactics therein resulting
   from recent negative publicity concerning Moscow's clandestine involvement in the campaign.
   TRUMP's associate reported that the aim of leaking the DNC e-mails to WikiLeaks during the Democratic
   Convention had been to swing supporters of Bernie SANDERS away from Hillary CLINTON and across to
   TRUMP. These voters were perceived as activist and anti-status quo and anti-establishment and in that
   regard sharing many features with the TRUMP campaign, including a visceral dislike of Hillary CLINTON.
   This objective had been conceived and promoted, inter alia, by TRUMP's foreign policy adviser Carter
   PAGE who had discussed it directly with the ethnic Russian associate.

2. Continuing on this theme, the ethnic Russian associate of TRUMP assessed that the problem was that
   the TRUMP campaign had underestimated the strength of the negative reaction from liberals and
   especially the conservative elite to Russian interference. This was forcing a rethink and a likely change
   of tactics. The main objective in the short term was to check Democratic candidate Hillary CLINTON's
   successful exploitation of the PUTIN as bogeyman/Russian interference story to tarnish TRUMP and
   bolster her own (patriotic) credentials. The TRUMP campaign was focusing on tapping into support in
   the American television media to achieve this, as they reckoned this resource had been underused by
   them to date.

3. However, TRUMP's associate also admitted that there was a fair amount of anger and resentment
   within the Republican candidate's team at what was perceived by PUTIN as going beyond the objective
   of weakening CLINTON and bolstering TRUMP, by attempting to exploit the situation to undermine the
   US government and democratic system more generally. It was unclear at present how this aspect of
   the situation would play out in the weeks to come.

10 August 2016

COMPANY INTELLIGENCE REPORT 2016/136

## RUSSIA/US PRESIDENTIAL ELECTION: FURTHER DETAILS OF TRUMP LAWYER COHEN'S SECRET LIAISON WITH THE KREMLIN

### Summary

- Kremlin insider reports TRUMP lawyer COHEN's secret meeting/s with Kremlin officials in August 2016 was/were held in Prague

- Russian parastatal organisation Rossotrudnichestvo used as cover for this liaison and premises in Czech capital may have been used for the meeting/s

- Pro-PUTIN leading Duma figure, KOSACHEV, reportedly involved as "plausibly deniable" facilitator and may have participated in the August meeting/s with COHEN

### Detail

1. Speaking to a compatriot and friend on 19 October 2016, a Kremlin insider provided further details of reported clandestine meeting/s between Republican presidential candidate, Donald TRUMP's lawyer Michael COHEN and Kremlin representatives in August 2016. Although the communication between them had to be cryptic for security reasons, the Kremlin insider clearly indicated to his/her friend that the reported contact/s took place in Prague, Czech Republic.

2. Continuing on this theme, the Kremlin insider highlighted the importance of the Russian parastatal organisation, Rossotrudnichestvo, in this contact between TRUMP campaign representative/s and Kremlin officials. Rossotrudnichestvo was being used as cover for this relationship and its office in Prague may well have been used to host the COHEN/Russian Presidential Administration (PA) meeting/s. It was considered a "plausibly deniable" vehicle for this, whilst remaining entirely under Kremlin control.

3. The Kremlin insider went on to identify leading pro-PUTIN Duma figure, Konstantin KOSACHEV (Head of the Foreign Relations Committee) as an important figure in the TRUMP campaign-Kremlin liaison operation. KOSACHEV, also "plausibly deniable" being part of the Russian legislature rather than executive, had facilitated the contact in Prague and by implication, may have attended the meeting/s with COHEN there in August.

### Company Comment

We reported previously, in our Company Intelligence Report 2016/135 of 19 October 2016 from the same source, that COHEN met officials from the PA Legal Department clandestinely in an EU country in August 2016. This was in order to clean up the mess left behind by western media revelations of TRUMP ex-campaign manager MANAFORT's corrupt relationship with the former pro-Russian YANUKOVYCH regime in Ukraine and TRUMP foreign policy advisor, Carter PAGE's secret meetings in Moscow with senior regime figures in July 2016. According to the Kremlin advisor, these meeting/s were originally scheduled for COHEN in Moscow but shifted to what was considered an operationally "soft" EU country when it was judged too compromising for him to travel to the Russian capital.

20 October 2016

COMPANY INTELLIGENCE REPORT 2016/105

## RUSSIA/UKRAINE: THE DEMISE OF TRUMP'S CAMPAIGN MANAGER PAUL MANAFORT

### Summary

- Ex-Ukrainian President YANUKOVYCH confides directly to PUTIN that he authorised kick-back payments to MANAFORT, as alleged in western media. Assures Russian President however there is no documentary evidence/trail

- PUTIN and Russian leadership remain worried however and sceptical that YANUKOVYCH has fully covered the traces of these payments to TRUMP's former campaign manager

- Close associate of TRUMP explains reasoning behind MANAFORT's recent resignation. Ukraine revelations played part but others wanted MANAFORT out for various reasons, especially LEWANDOWSKI who remains influential

### Detail

1. Speaking in late August 2016, in the immediate aftermath of Paul MANAFORT's resignation as campaign manager for US Republican presidential candidate Donald TRUMP, a well-placed Russian figure reported on a recent meeting between President PUTIN and ex-President YANUKOVYCH of Ukraine. This had been held in secret on 15 August near Volgograd, Russia and the western media revelations about MANAFORT and Ukraine had featured prominently on the agenda. YANUKOVYCH had confided in PUTIN that he did authorise and order substantial kick-back payments to MANAFORT as alleged but sought to reassure him that there was no documentary trail left behind which could provide clear evidence of this.

2. Given YANUKOVYCH's (unimpressive) record in covering up his own corrupt tracks in the past, PUTIN and others in the Russian leadership were sceptical about the ex-Ukrainian president's reassurances on this as relating to MANAFORT. They therefore still feared the scandal had legs, especially as MANAFORT had been commercially active in Ukraine right up to the time (in March 2016) when he joined TRUMP's campaign team. For them it therefore remained a point of potential political vulnerability and embarrassment.

3. Speaking separately, also in late August 2016, an American political figure associated with Donald TRUMP and his campaign outlined the reasons behind MANAFORT's recent demise. S/he said it was true that the Ukraine corruption revelations had played a part in this but also, several senior players close to TRUMP had wanted MANAFORT out, primarily to loosen his control on strategy and policy formulation. Of particular importance in this regard was MANAFORT's predecessor as campaign manager, Corey LEWANDOWSKI, who hated MANAFORT personally and remained close to TRUMP with whom he discussed the presidential campaign on a regular basis.

**22 August 2016**

Z-1

COMPANY INTELLIGENCE REPORT 2016/111

RUSSIA/US: KREMLIN FALLOUT FROM MEDIA EXPOSURE OF MOSCOW'S
INTERFERENCE IN THE US PRESIDENTIAL CAMPAIGN

## Summary

- Kremlin orders senior staff to remain silent in media and private on allegations of Russian interference in US presidential campaign

- Senior figure however confirms gist of allegations and reports IVANOV sacked as Head of Administration on account of giving PUTIN poor advice on issue. VAINO selected as his replacement partly because he was not involved in pro-TRUMP, anti-CLINTON operation/s

- Russians do have further 'kompromat' on CLINTON (e-mails) and considering disseminating it after Duma (legislative elections) in late September. Presidential spokesman PESKOV continues to lead on this

- However, equally important is Kremlin objective to shift policy consensus favourably to Russia in US post-OBAMA whoever wins. Both presidential candidates' opposition to TPP and TTIP viewed as a result in this respect

- Senior Russian diplomat withdrawn from Washington embassy on account of potential exposure in US presidential election operation/s

## Detail

1. Speaking in confidence to a trusted compatriot in mid-September 2016, a senior member of the Russian Presidential Administration (PA) commented on the political fallout from recent western media revelations about Moscow's intervention, in favour of Donald TRUMP and against Hillary CLINTON, in the US presidential election. The PA official reported that the issue had become incredibly sensitive and that President PUTIN had issued direct orders that Kremlin and government insiders should not discuss it in public or even in private.

2. Despite this, the PA official confirmed, from direct knowledge, that the gist of the allegations was true. PUTIN had been receiving conflicting advice on interfering from three separate and expert groups. On one side had been the Russian ambassador to the US, Sergei KISLYAK, and the Ministry of Foreign Affairs, together with an independent and informal network run by presidential foreign policy advisor, Yuri USHAKOV

22

(KISLYAK's predecessor in Washington) who had urged caution and the potential negative impact on Russia from the operation/s. On the other side was former PA Head, Sergei IVANOV, backed by Russian Foreign Intelligence (SVR), who had advised PUTIN that the pro-TRUMP, anti-CLINTON operation/s would be both effective and plausibly deniable with little blowback. The first group/s had been proven right and this had been the catalyst in PUTIN's decision to sack IVANOV (unexpectedly) as PA Head in August. His successor, Anton VAINO, had been selected for the job partly because he had not been involved in the US presidential election operation/s.

3. Continuing on this theme, the senior PA official said the situation now was that the Kremlin had further 'kompromat' on candidate CLINTON and had been considering releasing this via "plausibly deniable" channels after the Duma (legislative) elections were out of the way in mid-September. There was however a growing train of thought and associated lobby, arguing that the Russians could still make candidate CLINTON look "weak and stupid" by provoking her into railing against PUTIN and Russia without the need to release more of her e-mails. Presidential Spokesman, Dmitriy PESKOV remained a key figure in the operation, although any final decision on dissemination of further material would be taken by PUTIN himself.

4. The senior PA official also reported that a growing element in Moscow's intervention in the US presidential election campaign was the objective of shifting the US political consensus in Russia's perceived interests regardless of who won. It basically comprised of pushing candidate CLINTON away from President OBAMA's policies. The best example of this was that both candidates now openly opposed the draft trade agreements, TPP and TTIP, which were assessed by Moscow as detrimental to Russian interests. Other issues where the Kremlin was looking to shift the US policy consensus were Ukraine and Syria. Overall however, the presidential election was considered still to be too close to call.

5. Finally, speaking separately to the same compatriot, a senior Russian MFA official reported that as a prophylactic measure, a leading Russian diplomat, Mikhail KULAGIN, had been withdrawn from Washington at short notice because Moscow feared his heavy involvement in the US presidential election operation, including the so-called veterans' pensions ruse (reported previously), would be exposed in the media there. His replacement, Andrei BONDAREV however was clean in this regard.

23

**Company Comment**

The substance of what was reported by the senior Russian PA official in paras 1 and 2 above, including the reasons for Sergei IVANOV's dismissal, was corroborated independently by a former top level Russian intelligence officer and Kremlin insider, also in mid-September.

**14 September 2016**

24

COMPANY INTELLIGENCE REPORT 2016/112

**RUSSIA/US PRESIDENTIAL ELECTION: KREMLIN-ALPHA GROUP CO-OPERATION**

**Summary**

- Top level Russian official confirms current closeness of Alpha Group-PUTIN relationship. Significant favours continue to be done in both directions and FRIDMAN and AVEN still giving informal advice to PUTIN, especially on the US

- Key intermediary in PUTIN-Alpha relationship identified as Oleg GOVORUN, currently Head of a Presidential Administration department but throughout the 1990s, the Alpha executive who delivered illicit cash directly to PUTIN

- PUTIN personally unbothered about Alpha's current lack of investment in Russia but under pressure from colleagues over this and able to exploit it as lever over Alpha interlocutors

**Detail**

1. Speaking to a trusted compatriot in mid-September 2016, a top level Russian government official commented on the history and current state of relations between President PUTIN and the Alpha Group of businesses led by oligarchs Mikhail FRIDMAN, Petr AVEN and German KHAN. The Russian government figure reported that although they had had their ups and downs, the leading figures in Alpha currently were on very good terms with PUTIN. Significant favours continued to be done in both directions, primarily political ones for PUTIN and business/legal ones for Alpha. Also, FRIDMAN and AVEN continued to give informal advice to PUTIN on foreign policy, and especially about the US where he distrusted advice being given to him by officials.

2. Although FRIDMAN recently had met directly with PUTIN in Russia, much of the dialogue and business between them was mediated through a senior Presidential Administration official, Oleg GOVORUN, who currently headed the department therein responsible for Social Co-operation With the CIS. GOVORUN was trusted by PUTIN and recently had accompanied him to Uzbekistan to pay respects at the tomb of former president KARIMOV. However according to the top level Russian government official, during the 1990s GOVORUN had been Head of Government Relations at Alpha Group and in reality, the "driver" and "bag carrier"

25

used by FRIDMAN and AVEN to deliver large amounts of illicit cash to the Russian president, at that time deputy Mayor of St Petersburg. Given that and the continuing sensitivity of the PUTIN-Alpha relationship, and need for plausible deniability, much of the contact between them was now indirect and entrusted to the relatively low profile GOVORUN.

3. The top level Russian government official described the PUTIN-Alpha relationship as both carrot and stick. Alpha held 'kompromat' on PUTIN and his corrupt business activities from the 1990s whilst although not personally overly bothered by Alpha's failure to reinvest the proceeds of its TNK oil company sale into the Russian economy since, the Russian president was able to use pressure on this count from senior Kremlin colleagues as a lever on FRIDMAN and AVEN to make them do his political bidding.

**14 September 2016**

26

COMPANY INTELLIGENCE REPORT 2016/113

## RUSSIA/US PRESIDENTIAL ELECTION- REPUBLICAN CANDIDATE TRUMP'S PRIOR ACTIVITIES IN ST PETERSBURG

### Summary

- Two knowledgeable St Petersburg sources claim Republican candidate TRUMP has paid bribes and engaged in sexual activities there but key witnesses silenced and evidence hard to obtain

- Both believe Azeri business associate of TRUMP, Araz AGALAROV will know the details

### Detail

1. Speaking to a trusted compatriot in September 2016, two well-placed sources based in St Petersburg, one in the political/business elite and the other involved in the local services and tourist industry, commented on Republican US presidential candidate Donald TRUMP's prior activities in the city.

2. Both knew TRUMP had visited St Petersburg on several occasions in the past and had been interested in doing business deals there involving real estate. The local business/political elite figure reported that TRUMP had paid bribes there to further his interests but very discreetly and only through affiliated companies, making it very hard to prove. The local services industry source reported that TRUMP had participated in sex parties in the city too, but that all direct witnesses to this recently had been "silenced" i.e. bribed or coerced to disappear.

3. The two St Petersburg figures cited believed an Azeri business figure, Araz AGALAROV (with offices in Baku and London) had been closely involved with TRUMP in Russia and would know most of the details of what the Republican presidential candidate had got up to there.

**14 September 2016**

27

COMPANY INTELLIGENCE REPORT 2016/130

## RUSSIA: KREMLIN ASSESSMENT OF TRUMP AND RUSSIAN INTERFERENCE IN US PRESIDENTIAL ELECTION

Summary

- Buyer's remorse sets in with Kremlin over TRUMP support operation in US presidential election. Russian leadership disappointed that leaked e-mails on CLINTON have not had greater impact in campaign

- Russians have injected further anti-CLINTON material into the 'plausibly deniable' leaks pipeline which will continue to surface, but best material already in public domain

- PUTIN angry with senior officials who "overpromised" on TRUMP and further heads likely to roll as result. Foreign Minister LAVROV may be next

- TRUMP supported by Kremlin because seen as divisive, anti-establishment candidate who would shake up current international status quo in Russia's favor. Lead on TRUMP operation moved from Foreign Ministry to FSB and then to presidential administration where it now sits

Detail

1. Speaking separately in confidence to a trusted compatriot in early October 2016, a senior Russian leadership figure and a Foreign Ministry official reported on recent developments concerning the Kremlin's operation to support Republican candidate Donald TRUMP in the US presidential election. The senior leadership figure said that a degree of buyer's remorse was setting in among Russian leaders concerning TRUMP. PUTIN and his colleagues were surprised and disappointed that leaks of Democratic candidate, Hillary CLINTON's hacked e-mails had not had greater impact on the campaign.
2. Continuing on this theme, the senior leadership figure commented that a stream of further hacked CLINTON material already had been injected by the Kremlin into compliant western media outlets like Wikileaks, which remained at least "plausibly deniable", so the stream of these would continue through October and up to the election. However s/he understood that the best material the Russians had already was out and there were no real game-changers to come.
3. The Russian Foreign Ministry official, who had direct access to the TRUMP support operation, reported that PUTIN was angry at his subordinate's "over-promising" on the Republican presidential candidate, both in terms of his chances and reliability and being able to cover and/or contain the US backlash over Kremlin interference. More heads therefore were likely to roll, with the MFA the easiest target. Ironically, despite his consistent urging of caution on the issue, Foreign Minister LAVROV could be the next one to go.
4. Asked to explain why PUTIN and the Kremlin had launched such an aggressive TRUMP support operation in the first place, the MFA official said that Russia needed to upset the liberal international status quo, including on Ukraine-related sanctions, which was seriously

disadvantaging the country. TRUMP was viewed as divisive in disrupting the whole US political system; anti-Establishment; and a pragmatist with whom they could do business. As the TRUMP support operation had gained momentum, control of it had passed from the MFA to the FSB and then into the presidential administration where it remained, a reflection of its growing significance over time. There was still a view in the Kremlin that TRUMP would continue as a (divisive) political force even if he lost the presidency and may run for and be elected to another public office.

12 October 2016

COMPANY INTELLIGENCE REPORT 2016/134

RUSSIA/US PRESIDENTIAL ELECTION: FURTHER DETAILS OF KREMLIN LIAISON WITH TRUMP CAMPAIGN

Summary

- Close associate of SECHIN confirms his secret meeting in Moscow with Carter PAGE in July

- Substance included offer of large stake in Rosneft in return for lifting sanctions on Russia. PAGE confirms this is TRUMP's intention

- SECHIN continued to think TRUMP could win presidency up to 17 October. Now looking to reorientate his engagement with the US

- Kremlin insider highlights importance of TRUMP's lawyer, Michael COHEN in covert relationship with Russia. COHEN's wife is of Russian descent and her father a leading property developer in Moscow

Detail

1. Speaking to a trusted compatriot in mid October 2016, a close associate of Rosneft President and PUTIN ally Igor' SECHIN elaborated on the reported secret meeting between the latter and Carter PAGE, of US Republican presidential candidate's foreign policy team, in Moscow in July 2016. The secret meeting had been confirmed to him/her by a senior member of SECHIN's staff, in addition to by the Rosneft President himself. It took place on either 7 or 8 July, the same day or the one after Carter PAGE made a public speech to the Higher Economic School in Moscow.

2. In terms of the substance of their discussion, SECHIN's associate said that the Rosneft President was so keen to lift personal and corporate western sanctions imposed on the company, that he offered PAGE/TRUMP's associates the brokerage of up to a 19 per cent (privatised) stake in Rosneft in return. PAGE had expressed interest and confirmed that were TRUMP elected US president, then sanctions on Russia would be lifted.

3. According to SECHIN's close associate, the Rosneft President had continued to believe that TRUMP could win the US presidency right up to 17 October, when he assessed this was no longer possible. SECHIN was keen to re-adapt accordingly and put feelers out to other business and political contacts in the US instead.

4. Speaking separately to the same compatriot in mid-October 2016, a Kremlin insider with direct access to the leadership confirmed that a key role in the secret TRUMP campaign/Kremlin relationship was being played by the Republican candidate's personal lawyer Michael COHEN. ████████████████████████████████████████

30

**Source Comment**

5.  SECHIN's associate opined that although PAGE had not stated it explicitly to SECHIN, he had clearly implied that in terms of his comment on TRUMP's intention to lift Russian sanctions if elected president, he was speaking with the Republican candidate's authority.

**Company Comment**

6.

18 October 2016

COMPANY INTELLIGENCE REPORT 2016/135

**RUSSIA/US PRESIDENTIAL ELECTION: THE IMPORTANT ROLE OF TRUMP
LAWYER, COHEN IN CAMPAIGN'S SECRET LIAISON WITH THE KREMLIN**

**Summary**

- Kremlin insider outlines important role played by TRUMP's lawyer
  COHEN in secret liaison with Russian leadership

- COHEN engaged with Russians in trying to cover up scandal of
  MANAFORT and exposure of PAGE and meets Kremlin officials secretly in
  the EU in August in pursuit of this goal

- These secret contacts continue but are now farmed out to trusted agents
  in Kremlin-linked institutes so as to remain "plausibly deniable" for
  Russian regime

- Further confirmation that sacking of IVANOV and appointments of VAINO
  and KIRIYENKO linked to need to cover up Kremlin's TRUMP support
  operation

**Detail**

1. Speaking in confidence to a longstanding compatriot friend in mid-
   October 2016, a Kremlin insider highlighted the importance of
   Republican presidential candidate Donald TRUMP's lawyer, Michael
   COHEN, in the ongoing secret liaison relationship between the New York
   tycoon's campaign and the Russian leadership. COHEN's role had grown
   following the departure of Paul MANNAFORT as TRUMP's campaign
   manager in August 2016. Prior to that MANNAFORT had led for the
   TRUMP side.

2. According to the Kremlin insider, COHEN now was heavily engaged in a
   cover up and damage limitation operation in the attempt to prevent the
   full details of TRUMP's relationship with Russia being exposed. In
   pursuit of this aim, COHEN had met secretly with several Russian
   Presidential Administration (PA) Legal Department officials in an EU
   country in August 2016. The immediate issues had been to contain
   further scandals involving MANNAFORT's commercial and political role
   in Russia/Ukraine and to limit the damage arising from exposure of
   former TRUMP foreign policy advisor, Carter PAGE's secret meetings
   with Russian leadership figures in Moscow the previous month. The

32

overall objective had been to "to sweep it all under the carpet and make sure no connections could be fully established or proven"

3. Things had become even "hotter" since August on the TRUMP-Russia track. According to the Kremlin insider, this had meant that direct contact between the TRUMP team and Russia had been farmed out by the Kremlin to trusted agents of influence working in pro-government policy institutes like that of Law and Comparative Jurisprudence. COHEN however continued to lead for the TRUMP team.

4. Referring back to the (surprise) sacking of Sergei IVANOV as Head of PA in August 2016, his replacement by Anton VAINO and the appointment of former Russian premier Sergei KIRIYENKO to another senior position in the PA, the Kremlin insider repeated that this had been directly connected to the TRUMP support operation and the need to cover up now that it was being exposed by the USG and in the western media.

**Company Comment**

The Kremlin insider was unsure of the identities of the PA officials with whom COHEN met secretly in August, or the exact date/s and locations of the meeting/s. There were significant internal security barriers being erected in the PA as the TRUMP issue became more controversial and damaging. However s/he continued to try to obtain these.

**19 October 2016**

# COMPANY INTELLIGENCE REPORT 2016/166

## US/RUSSIA: FURTHER DETAILS OF SECRET DIALOGUE BETWEEN TRUMP CAMPAIGN TEAM, KREMLIN AND ASSOCIATED HACKERS IN PRAGUE

### Summary

- TRUMP's representative COHEN accompanied to Prague in August/September 2016 by 3 colleagues for secret discussions with Kremlin representatives and associated operators/hackers

- Agenda included how to process deniable cash payments to operatives; contingency plans for covering up operations; and action in event of a CLINTON election victory

- Some further details of Russian representatives/operatives involved; Romanian hackers employed; and use of Bulgaria as bolt hole to "lie low"

- Anti-CLINTON hackers and other operatives paid by both TRUMP team and Kremlin, but with ultimate loyalty to Head of PA, IVANOV and his successor/s

### Detail

1. We reported previously (2016/135 and /136) on secret meeting/s held in Prague, Czech Republic in August 2016 between then Republican presidential candidate Donald TRUMP's representative, Michael COHEN and his interlocutors from the Kremlin working under cover of Russian 'NGO' Rossotrudnichestvo.

2. ███████████████████████████████████████ provided further details of these meeting/s and associated anti-CLINTON/Democratic Party operations. COHEN had been accompanied to Prague by 3 colleagues and the timing of the visit was either in the last week of August or the first week of September. One of their main Russian interlocutors was Oleg SOLODUKHIN operating under Rossotrudnichestvo cover. According to ███████████████████, the agenda comprised questions on how deniable cash payments were to be made to hackers who had worked in Europe under Kremlin direction against the CLINTON campaign and various contingencies for covering up these operations and Moscow's secret liaison with the TRUMP team more generally.

3. ████████████ reported that over the period March-September 2016 a company called ████████ and its affiliates had been using botnets and porn traffic to transmit viruses, plant bugs, steal data and conduct "altering operations" against the Democratic Party leadership. Entities linked to one ████████████ were involved and he and another hacking expert, both recruited under duress by the FSB, ████ ████████ were significant players in this operation. In Prague, COHEN agreed contingency plans for various scenarios to protect the operation, but in particular what was to be done in the event that Hillary CLINTON won the presidency. It was important in this event that all cash payments owed were made quickly and discreetly and that cyber and other operators were stood down/able to go effectively to ground to cover their traces. (We reported earlier that the involvement of political operatives Paul MANAFORT and Carter PAGE in the secret TRUMP-Kremlin liaison had been exposed in the media in the run-up to Prague and that damage limitation of these also was discussed by COHEN with the Kremlin representatives).

4. In terms of practical measures to be taken, it was agreed by the two sides in Prague to stand down various "Romanian hackers" (presumably based in their homeland or neighbouring eastern Europe) and that other operatives should head for a bolt-hole in Plovdiv, Bulgaria where they should "lay low". On payments, IVANOV's associate said that the operatives involved had been paid by both TRUMP's team and the Kremlin, though their orders and ultimate loyalty lay with IVANOV, as Head of the PA and thus ultimately responsible for the operation, and his designated successor/s after he was dismissed by president PUTIN in connection with the anti-CLINTON operation in mid August.

13 December 2016

# APPENDIX C

## Memo from Grassley to Comey regarding FBI Investigation into Steele

CHARLES E. GRASSLEY, IOWA, CHAIRMAN

ORRIN G. HATCH, UTAH
LINDSEY O. GRAHAM, SOUTH CAROLINA
JOHN CORNYN, TEXAS
MICHAEL S. LEE, UTAH
TED CRUZ, TEXAS
BEN SASSE, NEBRASKA
JEFF FLAKE, ARIZONA
MIKE CRAPO, IDAHO
THOM TILLIS, NORTH CAROLINA
JOHN KENNEDY, LOUISIANA

DIANNE FEINSTEIN, CALIFORNIA
PATRICK J. LEAHY, VERMONT
RICHARD J. DURBIN, ILLINOIS
SHELDON WHITEHOUSE, RHODE ISLAND
AMY KLOBUCHAR, MINNESOTA
AL FRANKEN, MINNESOTA
CHRISTOPHER A. COONS, DELAWARE
RICHARD BLUMENTHAL, CONNECTICUT
MAZIE K. HIRONO, HAWAII

**United States Senate**

COMMITTEE ON THE JUDICIARY

WASHINGTON, DC 20510–6275

Kolan L. Davis, Chief Counsel and Staff Director
Jennifer Duck, Democratic Staff Director

March 6, 2017

<u>**VIA ELECTRONIC TRANSMISSION**</u>

The Honorable James B. Comey, Jr.
Director
Federal Bureau of Investigation
935 Pennsylvania Avenue, N.W.
Washington, DC 20535

Dear Director Comey:

On February 28, 2017, the *Washington Post* reported that the FBI reached an agreement a few weeks before the Presidential election to pay the author of the unsubstantiated dossier alleging a conspiracy between President Trump and the Russians, Christopher Steele, to continue investigating Mr. Trump.[1] The article claimed that the FBI was aware Mr. Steele was creating these memos as part of work for an opposition research firm connected to Hillary Clinton. The idea that the FBI and associates of the Clinton campaign would pay Mr. Steele to investigate the Republican nominee for President in the run-up to the election raises further questions about the FBI's independence from politics, as well as the Obama administration's use of law enforcement and intelligence agencies for political ends. It is additionally troubling that the FBI reportedly agreed to such an arrangement given that, in January of 2017, then-Director Clapper issued a statement stating that "the IC has not made any judgment that the information in this document is reliable, and we did not rely upon it in any way for our conclusions." According to the *Washington Post*, the FBI's arrangement with Mr. Steele fell through when the media published his dossier and revealed his identity.

The Committee requires additional information to evaluate this situation. Please provide the following information and respond to these questions by March 20, 2017. Please also schedule a briefing by that date by FBI personnel with knowledge of these issues.

1. All FBI records relating to the agreement with Mr. Steele regarding his investigation of President Trump and his associates, including the agreement itself, all drafts, all internal FBI

---

[1] Tom Hamburger and Rosalind Helderman, *FBI Once Planned to Pay Former British Spy Who Authored Controversial Trump Dossier*, THE WASHINGTON POST (Feb. 28, 2017).

communications about the agreement, all FBI communications with Mr. Steele about the agreement, all FBI requests for authorization for the agreement, and all records documenting the approval of the agreement.

2. All records, including 302s, of any FBI meetings or interviews with Mr. Steele.

3. All FBI policies, procedures, and guidelines applicable when the FBI seeks to fund an investigator associated with a political opposition research firm connected to a political candidate, or with any outside entity.

4. All FBI records relating to agreements and payments made to Mr. Steele in connection with any other investigations, including the reported agreements relating to his investigation of FIFA.

5. Were any other government officials outside of the FBI involved in discussing or authorizing the agreement with Mr. Steele, including anyone from the Department of Justice or the Obama White House? If so, please explain who was involved and provide all related records.

6. How did the FBI first obtain Mr. Steele's Trump investigation memos? Has the FBI obtained additional memos from this same source that were not published by *Buzzfeed*? If so, please provide copies.

7. Has the FBI created, or contributed to the creation of, any documents based on or otherwise referencing these memos or the information in the memos? If so, please provide copies of all such documents and, where necessary, clarify which portions are based on or related to the memos.

8. Has the FBI verified or corroborated any of the allegations made in the memos? Were any allegations or other information from the memo included in any documents created by the FBI, or which the FBI helped to create, without having been independently verified or corroborated by the FBI beforehand? If so, why?

9. Has the FBI relied on or otherwise referenced the memos or any information in the memos in seeking a FISA warrant, other search warrant, or any other judicial process? Did the FBI rely on or otherwise reference the memos in relation to any National Security Letters? If so, please include copies of all relevant applications and other documents.

10. Who decided to include the memos in the briefings received by Presidents Obama and Trump? What was the basis for that decision?

11. Did the agreement with Mr. Steele ever enter into force? If so, for how long? If it did not, why not?

12. You have previously stated that you will not comment on pending investigations, including confirming or denying whether they exist. You have also acknowledged that statements about closed investigations are a separate matter, sometimes warranting disclosures or public

comment. Given the inflammatory nature of the allegations in Mr. Steele's dossier, if the FBI is undertaking or has undertaken any investigation of the claims, will you please inform the Committee at the conclusion of any such investigations as to what information the investigations discovered and what conclusions the FBI reached? Simply put, when allegations like these are put into the public domain prior to any FBI assessment of their reliability, then if subsequent FBI investigation of the allegations finds them false, unsupported, or unreliable, the FBI should make those rebuttals public.

I anticipate that your responses to these questions may contain both classified and unclassified information. Please send all unclassified material directly to the Committee. In keeping with the requirements of Executive Order 13526, if any of the responsive documents do contain classified information, please segregate all unclassified material within the classified documents, provide all unclassified information directly to the Committee, and provide a classified addendum to the Office of Senate Security. Although the Committee complies with all laws and regulations governing the handling of classified information, it is not bound, absent its prior agreement, by any handling restrictions or instructions on unclassified information unilaterally asserted by the Executive Branch.

Thank you for your prompt attention to this important matter. If you have any questions, please contact Patrick Davis of my Committee staff at (202) 224-5225.

Sincerely,

Charles E. Grassley
Chairman
Committee on the Judiciary

cc:     The Honorable Diane Feinstein
        Ranking Member
        Senate Committee on the Judiciary

# APPENDIX D

## Letters from Trump, Sessions, and Rosenstein on firing Comey

THE WHITE HOUSE

WASHINGTON

May 9, 2017

Dear Director Comey:

I have received the attached letters from the Attorney General and Deputy Attorney General of the United States recommending your dismissal as the Director of the Federal Bureau of Investigation. I have accepted their recommendation and you are hereby terminated and removed from office, effective immediately.

While I greatly appreciate you informing me, on three separate occasions, that I am not under investigation, I nevertheless concur with the judgment of the Department of Justice that you are not able to effectively lead the Bureau.

It is essential that we find new leadership for the FBI that restores public trust and confidence in its vital law enforcement mission.

I wish you the best of luck in your future endeavors.

Donald J. Trump

May 9, 2017

President Donald J. Trump
The White House
Washington, DC  20500

Dear Mr. President:

    As Attorney General, I am committed to a high level of discipline, integrity, and the rule of law to the Department of Justice—an institution that I deeply respect. Based on my evaluation, and for the reasons expressed by the Deputy Attorney General in the attached memorandum, I have concluded that a fresh start is needed at the leadership of the FBI. It is essential that this Department of Justice clearly reaffirm its commitment to longstanding principles that ensure the integrity and fairness of federal investigations and prosecutions. The Director of the FBI must be someone who follows faithfully the rules and principles of the Department of Justice and who sets the right example for our law enforcement officials and others in the Department. Therefore, I must recommend that you remove Director James B. Comey, Jr. and identify an experienced and qualified individual to lead the great men and women of the FBI.

Sincerely

Jeff Sessions
Attorney General

JS:ph
Attachment

The Deputy Attorney General                                    *Washington, D.C. 20530*

May 9, 2017

MEMORANDUM FOR THE ATTORNEY GENERAL

FROM:             ROD J. ROSENSTEIN
                  DEPUTY ATTORNEY GENERAL

SUBJECT:          RESTORING PUBLIC CONFIDENCE IN THE FBI

The Federal Bureau of Investigation has long been regarded as our nation's premier federal investigative agency. Over the past year, however, the FBI's reputation and credibility have suffered substantial damage, and it has affected the entire Department of Justice. That is deeply troubling to many Department employees and veterans, legislators and citizens.

The current FBI Director is an articulate and persuasive speaker about leadership and the immutable principles of the Department of Justice. He deserves our appreciation for his public service. As you and I have discussed, however, I cannot defend the Director's handling of the conclusion of the investigation of Secretary Clinton's emails, and I do not understand his refusal to accept the nearly universal judgment that he was mistaken. Almost everyone agrees that the Director made serious mistakes; it is one of the few issues that unites people of diverse perspectives.

The Director was wrong to usurp the Attorney General's authority on July 5, 2016, and announce his conclusion that the case should be closed without prosecution. It is not the function of the Director to make such an announcement. At most, the Director should have said the FBI had completed its investigation and presented its findings to federal prosecutors. The Director now defends his decision by asserting that he believed Attorney General Loretta Lynch had a conflict. But the FBI Director is never empowered to supplant federal prosecutors and assume command of the Justice Department. There is a well-established process for other officials to step in when a conflict requires the recusal of the Attorney General. On July 5, however, the Director announced his own conclusions about the nation's most sensitive criminal investigation, without the authorization of duly appointed Justice Department leaders.

Compounding the error, the Director ignored another longstanding principle: we do not hold press conferences to release derogatory information about the subject of a declined criminal investigation. Derogatory information sometimes is disclosed in the course of criminal investigations and prosecutions, but we never release it gratuitously. The Director laid out his version of the facts for the news media as if it were a closing argument, but without a trial. It is a textbook example of what federal prosecutors and agents are taught not to do.

In response to skeptical questions at a congressional hearing, the Director defended his remarks by saying that his "goal was to say what is true. What did we do, what did we find, what do we think about it." But the goal of a federal criminal investigation is not to announce our thoughts at a press conference. The goal is to determine whether there is sufficient evidence to justify a federal criminal prosecution, then allow a federal prosecutor who exercises authority delegated by the Attorney General to make a prosecutorial decision, and then – if prosecution is warranted – let the judge and jury determine the facts. We sometimes release information about closed investigations in appropriate ways, but the FBI does not do it sua sponte.

Concerning his letter to the Congress on October 28, 2016, the Director cast his decision as a choice between whether he would "speak" about the FBI's decision to investigate the newly-discovered email messages or "conceal" it. "Conceal" is a loaded term that misstates the issue. When federal agents and prosecutors quietly open a criminal investigation, we are not concealing anything; we are simply following the longstanding policy that we refrain from publicizing non-public information. In that context, silence is not concealment.

My perspective on these issues is shared by former Attorneys General and Deputy Attorneys General from different eras and both political parties. Judge Laurence Silberman, who served as Deputy Attorney General under President Ford, wrote that "it is not the bureau's responsibility to opine on whether a matter should be prosecuted." Silberman believes that the Director's "performance was so inappropriate for an FBI director that [he] doubt[s] the bureau will ever completely recover." Jamie Gorelick, Deputy Attorney General under President Clinton, joined with Larry Thompson, Deputy Attorney General under President George W. Bush, to opine that the Director had "chosen personally to restrike the balance between transparency and fairness, departing from the department's traditions." They concluded that the Director violated his obligation to "preserve, protect and defend" the traditions of the Department and the FBI.

Former Attorney General Michael Mukasey, who served under President George W. Bush, observed that the Director "stepped way outside his job in disclosing the recommendation in that fashion" because the FBI director "doesn't make that decision." Alberto Gonzales, who also served as Attorney General under President George W. Bush, called the decision "an error in judgment." Eric Holder, who served as Deputy Attorney General under President Clinton and Attorney General under President Obama, said that the Director's decision "was incorrect. It violated long-standing Justice Department policies and traditions. And it ran counter to guidance that I put in place four years ago laying out the proper way to conduct investigations during an election season." Holder concluded that the Director "broke with these fundamental principles" and "negatively affected public trust in both the Justice Department and the FBI."

Former Deputy Attorneys General Gorelick and Thompson described the unusual events as "real-time, raw-take transparency taken to its illogical limit, a kind of reality TV of federal criminal investigation," that is "antithetical to the interests of justice."

Donald Ayer, who served as Deputy Attorney General under President George H.W. Bush, along with other former Justice Department officials, was "astonished and perplexed" by the decision to "break[] with longstanding practices followed by officials of both parties during past elections." Ayer's letter noted, "Perhaps most troubling ... is the precedent set by this departure from the Department's widely-respected, non-partisan traditions."

We should reject the departure and return to the traditions.

Although the President has the power to remove an FBI director, the decision should not be taken lightly. I agree with the nearly unanimous opinions of former Department officials. The way the Director handled the conclusion of the email investigation was wrong. As a result, the FBI is unlikely to regain public and congressional trust until it has a Director who understands the gravity of the mistakes and pledges never to repeat them. Having refused to admit his errors, the Director cannot be expected to implement the necessary corrective actions.

THE WHITE HOUSE
Office of the Press Secretary

FOR IMMEDIATE RELEASE
May 9, 2017

### Statement from the Press Secretary

Today, President Donald J. Trump informed FBI Director James Comey that he has been terminated and removed from office. President Trump acted based on the clear recommendations of both Deputy Attorney General Rod Rosenstein and Attorney General Jeff Sessions.

"The FBI is one of our Nation's most cherished and respected institutions and today will mark a new beginning for our crown jewel of law enforcement," said President Trump.

A search for a new permanent FBI Director will begin immediately.

### ###

# APPENDIX E

## Appointment of Special Counsel from the Office of the Deputy Attorney General

**Office of the Deputy Attorney General**
Washington, D.C. 20530

ORDER NO. 3915-2017

APPOINTMENT OF SPECIAL COUNSEL
TO INVESTIGATE RUSSIAN INTERFERENCE WITH THE
2016 PRESIDENTIAL ELECTION AND RELATED MATTERS

By virtue of the authority vested in me as Acting Attorney General, including 28 U.S.C. §§ 509, 510, and 515, in order to discharge my responsibility to provide supervision and management of the Department of Justice, and to ensure a full and thorough investigation of the Russian government's efforts to interfere in the 2016 presidential election, I hereby order as follows:

(a)     Robert S. Mueller III is appointed to serve as Special Counsel for the United States Department of Justice.

(b)     The Special Counsel is authorized to conduct the investigation confirmed by then-FBI Director James B. Comey in testimony before the House Permanent Select Committee on Intelligence on March 20, 2017, including:

    (i)     any links and/or coordination between the Russian government and individuals associated with the campaign of President Donald Trump; and

    (ii)    any matters that arose or may arise directly from the investigation; and

    (iii)   any other matters within the scope of 28 C.F.R. § 600.4(a).

(c)     If the Special Counsel believes it is necessary and appropriate, the Special Counsel is authorized to prosecute federal crimes arising from the investigation of these matters.

(d)     Sections 600.4 through 600.10 of Title 28 of the Code of Federal Regulations are applicable to the Special Counsel.

_5/17/17_
Date

Rod J. Rosenstein
Acting Attorney General

# APPENDIX F

## Memo from Grassley and Graham to Rosenstein and Wray, regarding Steele communication with US media

CHARLES E. GRASSLEY, IOWA, CHAIRMAN

ORRIN G. HATCH, UTAH
LINDSEY O. GRAHAM, SOUTH CAROLINA
JOHN CORNYN, TEXAS
MICHAEL S. LEE, UTAH
TED CRUZ, TEXAS
BEN SASSE, NEBRASKA
JEFF FLAKE, ARIZONA
MIKE CRAPO, IDAHO
THOM TILLIS, NORTH CAROLINA
JOHN KENNEDY, LOUISIANA

DIANNE FEINSTEIN, CALIFORNIA
PATRICK J. LEAHY, VERMONT
RICHARD J. DURBIN, ILLINOIS
SHELDON WHITEHOUSE, RHODE ISLAND
AMY KLOBUCHAR, MINNESOTA
AL FRANKEN, MINNESOTA
CHRISTOPHER A. COONS, DELAWARE
RICHARD BLUMENTHAL, CONNECTICUT
MAZIE K. HIRONO, HAWAII

Kolan L. Davis, Chief Counsel and Staff Director
Jennifer Duck, Democratic Staff Director

**United States Senate**

COMMITTEE ON THE JUDICIARY
WASHINGTON, DC 20510-6275

January 4, 2018

**VIA ELECTRONIC TRANSMISSION**

The Honorable Rod J. Rosenstein
Deputy Attorney General
U.S. Department of Justice
950 Pennsylvania Avenue, NW
Washington, DC 20530

The Honorable Christopher A. Wray
Director
Federal Bureau of Investigation
935 Pennsylvania Avenue, NW
Washington, DC 20535

Dear Deputy Attorney General Rosenstein and Director Wray:

Attached please find a classified memorandum related to certain communications between Christopher Steele and multiple U.S. news outlets regarding the so-called "Trump dossier" that Mr. Steele compiled on behalf of Fusion GPS for the Clinton Campaign and the Democratic National Committee and also provided to the FBI.

Based on the information contained therein, we are respectfully referring Mr. Steele to you for investigation of potential violations of 18 U.S.C. § 1001, for statements the Committee has reason to believe Mr. Steele made regarding his distribution of information contained in the dossier.

Thank you for your prompt attention to this important matter. If you have any questions, please contact Patrick Davis or DeLisa Lay of Chairman Grassley's staff at (202) 224-5225.

Sincerely,

Charles E. Grassley
Chairman
Committee on the Judiciary

Lindsey O. Graham
Chairman
Subcommittee on Crime and Terrorism
Committee on the Judiciary

Enclosure: As stated.

cc:     The Honorable Dianne Feinstein
        Ranking Member
        Committee on the Judiciary

        The Honorable Richard Burr
        Chairman
        Senate Select Committee on Intelligence

        The Honorable Mark Warner
        Vice Chairman
        Senate Select Committee on Intelligence

        The Honorable Devin Nunes
        Chairman
        House Permanent Select Committee on Intelligence

        The Honorable Adam Schiff
        Ranking Member
        House Permanent Select Committee on Intelligence

MEMORANDUM

(U)   FROM:        Charles E. Grassley, Chairman, U.S. Senate Committee on the Judiciary
                   Lindsey O. Graham, Chairman, Subcommittee on Crime and Terrorism,
                   U.S. Senate Committee on the Judiciary

      TO:          The Honorable Rod J. Rosenstein, Deputy Attorney General, U.S.
                   Department of Justice

                   The Honorable Christopher A. Wray, Director, Federal Bureau of
                   Investigation

      RE:          Referral of Christopher Steele for Potential Violation of 18 U.S.C. § 1001

(U) As you know, former British Intelligence Officer Christopher Steele was hired by the private firm Fusion GPS in June 2016 to gather information about "links between Russia and [then-presidential candidate] Donald Trump."[1] Pursuant to that business arrangement, Mr. Steele prepared a series of documents styled as intelligence reports, some of which were later compiled into a "dossier" and published by *BuzzFeed* in January 2017.[2] On the face of the dossier, it appears that Mr. Steele gathered much of his information from Russian government sources inside Russia.[3] According to the law firm Perkins Coie, Mr. Steele's dossier-related efforts were funded through Fusion GPS by that law firm on behalf of the Democratic National Committee and the Clinton Campaign.[4]

(U) In response to reporting by the *Washington Post* about Mr. Steele's relationship with the FBI relating to this partisan dossier project, the Judiciary Committee began raising a series of questions to the FBI and the Justice Department about these matters as part of the Committee's constitutional oversight responsibilities.[5]

(U) The FBI has since provided the Committee access to classified documents relevant to the FBI's relationship with Mr. Steele and whether the FBI relied on his dossier work. As explained in greater detail below, when information in those classified documents is evaluated in light of sworn statements by Mr. Steele in British litigation, it appears that either Mr. Steele lied to the FBI or the British court, or that the classified documents reviewed by the Committee contain materially false statements.

---

[1] (U) Defence, *Gubarev et. Al v. Orbis Business Intelligence Limited and Christobpher Steele*, Claim No. HQ17D00413, Queen's Bench (Apr. 4, 2017), para. 9 [Hereinafter "Steele Statement 1"] [Attachment A].
[2] (U) *Id.* at para. 10; Ken Bensinger, Miriam Elder, and Mark Schoofs, *These Reports Allege Trump Has Deep Ties to Russia*, BUZZFEED (Jan. 10, 2017).
[3] (U) *Id.*
[4] (U) Adam Entous, Devlin Barrett and Rosalind S. Helderman, *Clinton Campaign, DNC Paid for Research that Led to Russia Dossier*, THE WASHINGTON POST (Oct. 24, 2017).
[5] (U) Tom Hamburger and Rosalind S. Helderman, *FBI Once Planned to Pay Former British Spy who Authored Controversial Trump Dossier*, THE WASHINGTON POST (Feb. 28, 2017).

(U) In response to the Committee's inquiries, the Chairman and Ranking Member received a briefing on March 15, 2017, from then-Director James B. Comey, Jr.

██████ That briefing addressed the Russia investigation, the FBI's relationship with Mr. Steele, and the FBI's reliance on Mr. Steele's dossier in two applications it filed for surveillance under the Foreign Intelligence Surveillance Act (FISA). Then, on March 17, 2017, the Chairman and Ranking Member were provided copies of the two relevant FISA applications, which requested authority to conduct surveillance of Carter Page. Both relied heavily on Mr. Steele's dossier claims, and both applications were granted by the Foreign Intelligence Surveillance Court (FISC). In December of 2017, the Chairman, Ranking Member, and Subcommittee Chairman Graham were allowed to review a total of four FISA applications relying on the dossier to seek surveillance of Mr. Carter Page, as well as numerous other FBI documents relating to Mr. Steele.

██████ In the March 2017 briefing with then-Director Comey, he stated that ███████

██████████████████████████████████████████████
██████████████████████████████████████████████
██████████████████████████████████████████████

(U) Similarly, in June 2017, former FBI Director Comey testified publicly before the Senate Select Committee on Intelligence that he had briefed President-Elect Trump on the dossier allegations in January 2017, which Mr. Comey described as "salacious" and "unverified."[6]

██████ When asked at the March 2017 briefing why the FBI relied on the dossier in the FISA applications absent meaningful corroboration—and in light of the highly political motives surrounding its creation—then-Director Comey stated that the FBI included the dossier allegations about Carter Page in the FISA applications because Mr. Steele himself was considered reliable due to his past work with the Bureau.

██████ Indeed, the documents we have reviewed show that the FBI took important investigative steps largely based on Mr. Steele's information—and relying heavily on his credibility. Specifically, on October 21, 2016, the FBI filed its first warrant application under FISA for Carter Page. ████████████████████████████████████
███████████████████████████████████ The bulk of the application consists of allegations against Page that were disclosed to the FBI by Mr. Steele and are also outlined in the Steele dossier. The application appears to contain no additional information corroborating the dossier allegations against Mr. Page, although it does cite to a news article that appears to be sourced to Mr. Steele's dossier as well.

---

[6] (U) Statement of James B. Comey, Jr., Hearing of the U.S. Sen. Select Comm. on Intelligence (June 8, 2017).

████████ The FBI discussed the reliability of this unverified information provided by Mr. Steele in footnotes 8 and 18 of the FISA warrant application. First, the FBI noted to a vaguely limited extent the political origins of the dossier. In footnote 8 the FBI stated that the dossier information was compiled pursuant to the direction of a law firm who had hired an "identified U.S. person"—now known as Glenn Simpson of Fusion GPS—████████████████████ ████████████████████████████████████████████████████ The application failed to disclose that the identities of Mr. Simpson's ultimate clients were the Clinton campaign and the DNC.

████████ The FBI stated to the FISC that "based on [Steele's] previous reporting history with the FBI, whereby [Steele] provided reliable information to the FBI, the FBI believes [Steele's] reporting to be credible." In short, it appears the FBI relied on admittedly uncorroborated information, funded by and obtained for Secretary Clinton's presidential campaign, in order to conduct surveillance of an associate of the opposing presidential candidate. It did so based on Mr. Steele's personal credibility and presumably having faith in his process of obtaining the information.

(U) But there is substantial evidence suggesting that Mr. Steele materially misled the FBI about a key aspect of his dossier efforts, one which bears on his credibility.

████████████████████████████████████████████████████████████████
████████████████████████████████████████████████████████████████
████████████████████████████████████████████████████████████████
████████████████████████████████████████████████████████████████
████████████████████

████████ Yet the FISA applications note the existence of a news article dated September 23, 2016, which in particular contained some of the same dossier information about Mr. Page compiled by Mr. Steele and on which the FBI relied in its application. While not explicitly stated, this is presumably the article by Michael Isikoff of *Yahoo News*, titled "U.S. Intel Officials Probe Ties Between Trump Adviser and Kremlin." ████████████████████████ ████████████, the application attempts to explain away the inconsistency between Mr. Steele's assertion to the FBI and the existence of the article, apparently to shield Mr. Steele's credibility on which it still relied for the renewal request. The application to the FISC said: "Given that the information contained in the September 23rd news article generally matches the information about Page that [Steele] discovered doing his/her research, ████ ██████ ████████████████████████ ████████████████████████████████████████████████████████████

---

[7] ████████ The FBI has failed to provide the Committee the 1023s documenting all of Mr. Steele's statements to the FBI, so the Committee is relying on the accuracy of the FBI's representation to the FISC regarding those statements.

████████████████████████

█████████████████  ███████████████████

█████████████████████ *The FBI does not believe* that [Steele] directly provided this information to the press" (emphasis added).

████████ In footnote 9 of its January 2017 application to renew the FISA warrant for Mr. Page, the FBI again addressed Mr. Steele's credibility. At that time, the FBI noted that it had suspended its relationship with Mr. Steele in October 2016 because of Steele's "unauthorized disclosure of information to the press." The FBI relayed that Steele had been bothered by the FBI's notification to Congress in October 2016 about the reopening of the Clinton investigation, and as a result "[Steele] independently and against the prior admonishment from the FBI to speak only with the FBI on this matter, released the reporting discussed herein [dossier allegations against Page] to an identified news organization." However, the FBI continued to cite to Mr. Steele's past work as evidence of his reliability, and stated that "the incident that led to the FBI suspending its relationship with [Mr. Steele] occurred after [Mr. Steele] provided" the FBI with the dossier information described in the application. The FBI further asserted in footnote 19 that it did not believe that Steele directly gave information to *Yahoo News* that "published the September 23 News Article."

████████ So, as documented in the FISA renewals, the FBI still seemed to believed Mr. Steele's earlier claim that he had only provided the dossier information to the FBI and Fusion—and not to the media—prior to his October media contact that resulted in the FBI suspending the relationship. Accordingly, the FBI still deemed the information he provided prior to the October disclosure to be reliable. After all, the FBI already believed Mr. Steele was reliable, he had previously told the FBI he had not shared the information with the press – and lying to the FBI is a crime. In defending Mr. Steele's credibility to the FISC, the FBI had posited an innocuous explanation for the September 23 article, based on the assumption that Mr. Steele had told the FBI the truth about his press contacts. The FBI then vouched for him twice more, using the same rationale, in subsequent renewal applications filed with the Foreign Intelligence Surveillance Court in April and June 2017.

(U) However, public reports, court filings, and information obtained by the Committee during witness interviews in the course of its ongoing investigation indicate that Mr. Steele not only provided dossier information to the FBI, but also to numerous media organizations **prior to** the end of his relationship with the FBI in October 2016.[8]

(U) In Steele's sworn court filings in litigation in London, he admitted that he "gave off the record briefings to a small number of journalists about the pre-election memoranda [*i.e.*, the dossier] in late summer/autumn 2016."[9] In another sworn filing in that case, Mr. Steele further

---

[8] (U) *See* Steele Statement 1; Defendants' Response to Claimants' Request for Further Information Pursuant to CPR Part 18, *Gubarev et. Al v. Orbis Business Intelligence Limited and Christopher Steele*, Claim No. HQ17D00413, Queen's Bench (May 18, 2017), [Hereinafter "Steele Statement 2"] [Attachment B]; Tom Hamburger and Rosalind S. Helderman, *FBI Once Planned to Pay Former British Spy who Authored Controversial Trump Dossier*, THE WASHINGTON POST (Feb. 28, 2017); Simpson Transcript, on File with Sen. Comm. on the Judiciary.
[9] (U) Steele Statement 1 at para. 32.

stated that journalists from "the New York Times, the Washington Post, **Yahoo News**, the New Yorker, and CNN" were "briefed **at the end of September 2016** *by [Steele]* and Fusion at Fusion's instruction."[10] The filing further states that Mr. Steele "subsequently participated in further meetings at Fusion's instruction with Fusion and the New York Times, the Washington Post, and Yahoo News, which took place mid-October 2016."[11] According to these court filings, "[t]he briefings involved the disclosure of limited intelligence regarding indications of Russian interference in the US election process and the possible co-ordination of members of Trump's campaign team and Russian government officials."[12] In his interview with the Committee, Glenn Simpson of Fusion GPS confirmed this account by Mr. Steele and his company as filed in the British court.[13]

▮▮▮▮▮ The first of these filings was publicly reported in the U.S. media in April of 2017, yet the FBI did not subsequently disclose to the FISC this evidence suggesting that Mr. Steele had lied to the FBI. Instead the application still relied primarily on his credibility prior to the October media incident.

▮▮▮▮▮ The FBI received similar information from a Justice Department official, Bruce Ohr, who maintained contacts with Mr. Simpson and Mr. Steele about their dossier work, and whose wife also worked for Fusion GPS on the Russia project. ▮▮▮▮▮

▮▮▮▮▮▮▮▮▮▮▮▮▮▮▮▮▮▮▮▮▮▮▮▮▮▮▮▮▮▮▮▮▮▮▮▮▮▮▮▮▮▮▮▮▮▮▮▮▮▮▮▮▮▮▮▮▮▮▮▮

▮▮▮▮▮▮▮▮▮▮▮▮▮▮▮▮▮▮▮▮▮▮▮▮▮▮▮▮▮▮▮▮▮▮▮▮▮▮▮▮▮▮▮▮▮▮▮▮▮▮▮▮▮▮▮▮▮▮▮▮

▮▮▮▮▮▮▮▮▮▮▮▮▮▮▮▮▮▮▮▮▮▮▮▮▮▮▮▮▮▮▮▮▮▮▮▮▮▮▮▮▮▮▮▮▮▮▮▮▮▮▮▮▮▮▮▮▮▮▮▮

▮▮▮▮▮▮▮▮▮▮▮▮▮▮▮▮▮▮▮▮▮▮▮▮▮▮▮▮▮▮▮▮▮▮▮▮▮▮▮▮▮ He also noted in the same interview that Mr. Steele was "desperate" to see that Mr. Trump was not elected president.[16] None of the information provided by Mr. Ohr in his interviews with the FBI was included in the FISA renewal applications, despite its relevance to whether Mr. Steele had lied to the FBI about his contacts with the media as well as its broader relevance to his credibility and his stated political motive.

---

[10] (U) Steele Statement 2 at para. 18. (emphasis added).
[11] ▮▮▮▮ *Id.* The filing also apparently described the media contact that resulted in the FBI's suspension of its relationship with Mr. Steele, stating: "In addition, and again at Fusion's instruction, in late October 2016 the Second Defendant briefed a journalist from Mother Jones by Skype."
[12] (U) *Id.*
[13] (U) Simpson Transcript, On File with the Sen. Comm. on the Judiciary at 205-07.
[14] ▮▮▮▮▮▮ Ohr FD-302 (Nov. 22, 2016).
[15] ▮▮▮▮▮▮ Ohr FD-302 (Dec. 12, 2016).
[16] ▮▮▮▮▮ Ohr FD-302 (Nov. 22, 2016).

███████ Whether Mr. Steele lied to the FBI about his media contacts is relevant for at least two reasons. First, it is relevant to his credibility as a source, particularly given the lack of corroboration for his claims, at least at the time they were included in the FISA applicdations. Second, it is relevant to the reliability of his information-gathering efforts.

(U) Mr. Steele conducted his work for Fusion GPS compiling the "pre-election memoranda" "[b]etween June and early November 2016."[17] In the British litigation, Mr. Steele acknowledged briefing journalists about the dossier memoranda "in late summer/autumn 2016."[18] Unsurprisingly, during the summer of 2016, reports of at least some of the dossier allegations began circulating among reporters and people involved in Russian issues.[19] Mr. Steele also admitted in the British litigation to briefing journalists from the *Washington Post*, *Yahoo News*, the *New Yorker*, and *CNN* in September of 2016.[20] Simply put, the more people who contemporaneously knew that Mr. Steele was compiling his dossier, the more likely it was vulnerable to manipulation. In fact, in the British litigation, which involves a post-election dossier memorandum, Mr. Steele admitted that he received and included in it ***unsolicited***—and unverified—allegations.[21] That filing implies that he similarly received unsolicited intelligence on these matters prior to the election as well, stating that Mr. Steele "***continued to receive unsolicited intelligence*** on the matters covered by the pre-election memoranda after the US Presidential election."[22]

███████████████████████████████████████████
███████████████████████████████████████████
███████████████████████████████████████████

(U) One memorandum by Mr. Steele that was not published by *Buzzfeed* is dated October 19, 2016. The report alleges ██████████████████, as well as ████████ ████. Mr. Steele's memorandum states that his company "received this report from ██ ████ US State Department," that the report was the second in a series, and that the report was information that came from a foreign sub-source who "is in touch with ██████████, a contact of ██████████, a friend of the Clintons, who passed it to ██████." It is troubling enough that the Clinton Campaign funded Mr. Steele's work, but that these Clinton associates were contemporaneously feeding Mr. Steele allegations raises additional concerns about his credibility.

---

[17] (U) Steele Statement 1 at para. 9.
[18] (U) Steele Statement 1 at para. 32
[19] (U) Ahkmetshin Transcript, On File with the Sen. Comm. on the Judiciary (Mr. Ahkmetshin informed the Committee that he began hearing from journalists about the dossier before it was published, and thought it was the summer of 2016).
[20] (U) Steele Statement 2 at para. 18 (emphasis added).
[21] (U) Steele Statement 1 at para. 18 and 20c.
[22] (U) *Id.*; *see* Steele Statement 2 at 4 ("Such intelligence was not actively sought, it was merely received.")

█████ Simply put, Mr. Steele told the FBI he had not shared the Carter Page dossier information beyond his client and the FBI. The Department repeated that claim to the FISC. Yet Mr. Steele acknowledged in sworn filings that he did brief *Yahoo News* and other media organizations about the dossier around the time of the publication of the *Yahoo News* article that seems to be based on the dossier.

(U) On September 23, 2016, *Yahoo News* published its article entitled "U.S. Intel Officials Probe Ties Between Trump Adviser and Kremlin."[23] That article described claims about meetings between Carter Page and Russians, including Igor Sechin. Mr. Sechin is described in the article as "a longtime Putin associate and former Russian deputy prime minister" under sanction by the Treasury Department in response to Russia's actions in the Ukraine.[24] The article attributes the information to "a well-placed Western intelligence source," who reportedly said that "[a]t their alleged meeting, Sechin raised the issue of the lifting of sanctions with Page."[25] This information also appears in multiple "memoranda" that make up the dossier.[26]

(U) In sum, around the same time *Yahoo News* published its article containing dossier information about Carter Page, *Mr. Steele and* Fusion GPS had briefed *Yahoo News* and other news outlets about information contained in the dossier.

█████ These facts appear to directly contradict the FBI's assertions in its initial application for the Page FISA warrant, as well as subsequent renewal applications. The FBI repeatedly represented to the court that Mr. Steele told the FBI he did *not* have unauthorized contacts with the press about the dossier prior to October 2016. The FISA applications make these claims specifically in the context of the September 2016 *Yahoo News* article. But Mr. Steele has admitted—publicly before a court of law—that he *did* have such contacts with the press at this time, and his former business partner Mr. Simpson has confirmed it to the Committee. Thus, the FISA applications are either materially false in claiming that Mr. Steele said he did not provide dossier information to the press prior to October 2016, or Mr. Steele made materially false statements to the FBI when he claimed he only provided the dossier information to his business partner and the FBI.

█████ In this case, Mr. Steele's apparent deception seems to have posed significant, material consequences on the FBI's investigative decisions and representations to the court. Mr. Steele's information formed a significant portion of the FBI's warrant application, and the FISA application relied more heavily on Steele's credibility than on any independent verification or corroboration for his claims. Thus the basis for the warrant authorizing surveillance on a U.S. citizen rests largely on Mr. Steele's credibility. The Department of Justice has a responsibility to

---

[23] (U) Michael Isikoff, *U.S. Intel Officials Probe Ties Between Trump Adviser and Kremlin*, YAHOO NEWS (Sept. 23, 2016).
[24] (U) *Id.*
[25] (U) *Id.*
[26] (U) Bensinger *et. al*, BUZZFEED.

determine whether Mr. Steele provided false information to the FBI and whether the FBI's representations to the court were in error.

(U) Accordingly, we are referring Christopher Steele to the Department of Justice for investigation of potential violation(s) of 18 U.S.C. § 1001.

# APPENDIX G

## Nunes memo

**THE WHITE HOUSE**

WASHINGTON

February 2, 2018

The Honorable Devin Nunes
Chairman, House Permanent Select Committee on Intelligence
United States Capitol
Washington, DC 20515

Dear Mr. Chairman:

On January 29, 2018, the House Permanent Select Committee on Intelligence (hereinafter "the Committee") voted to disclose publicly a memorandum containing classified information provided to the Committee in connection with its oversight activities (the "Memorandum," which is attached to this letter). As provided by clause 11(g) of Rule X of the House of Representatives, the Committee has forwarded this Memorandum to the President based on its determination that the release of the Memorandum would serve the public interest.

The Constitution vests the President with the authority to protect national security secrets from disclosure. As the Supreme Court has recognized, it is the President's responsibility to classify, declassify, and control access to information bearing on our intelligence sources and methods and national defense. *See, e.g., Dep't of Navy v. Egan*, 484 U.S. 518, 527 (1988). In order to facilitate appropriate congressional oversight, the Executive Branch may entrust classified information to the appropriate committees of Congress, as it has done in connection with the Committee's oversight activities here. The Executive Branch does so on the assumption that the Committee will responsibly protect such classified information, consistent with the laws of the United States.

The Committee has now determined that the release of the Memorandum would be appropriate. The Executive Branch, across Administrations of both parties, has worked to accommodate congressional requests to declassify specific materials in the public interest.[1] However, public release of classified information by unilateral action of the Legislative Branch is extremely rare and raises significant separation of powers concerns. Accordingly, the Committee's request to release the Memorandum is interpreted as a request for declassification pursuant to the President's authority.

The President understands that the protection of our national security represents his highest obligation. Accordingly, he has directed lawyers and national security staff to assess the

---

[1] *See, e.g.*, S. Rept. 114-8 at 12 (Administration of Barack Obama) ("On April 3, 2014 . . . the Committee agreed to send the revised Findings and Conclusions, and the updated Executive Summary of the Committee Study, to the President for declassification and public release."); H. Rept. 107-792 (Administration of George W. Bush) (similar); E.O. 12812 (Administration of George H.W. Bush) (noting Senate resolution requesting that President provide for declassification of certain information via Executive Order).

declassification request, consistent with established standards governing the handling of classified information, including those under Section 3.1(d) of Executive Order 13526. Those standards permit declassification when the public interest in disclosure outweighs any need to protect the information. The White House review process also included input from the Office of the Director of National Intelligence and the Department of Justice. Consistent with this review and these standards, the President has determined that declassification of the Memorandum is appropriate.

Based on this assessment and in light of the significant public interest in the memorandum, the President has authorized the declassification of the Memorandum. To be clear, the Memorandum reflects the judgments of its congressional authors. The President understands that oversight concerning matters related to the Memorandum may be continuing. Though the circumstances leading to the declassification through this process are extraordinary, the Executive Branch stands ready to work with Congress to accommodate oversight requests consistent with applicable standards and processes, including the need to protect intelligence sources and methods.

Sincerely,

Donald F. McGahn II
Counsel to the President

cc: The Honorable Paul Ryan
Speaker of the House of Representatives

The Honorable Adam Schiff
Ranking Member, House Permanent Select Committee on Intelligence

January 18, 2018

Declassified by order of the President
February 2, 2018

To:       HPSCI Majority Members

From:     HPSCI Majority Staff

Subject:  Foreign Intelligence Surveillance Act Abuses at the Department of Justice and the
          Federal Bureau of Investigation

## Purpose

This memorandum provides Members an update on significant facts relating to the
Committee's ongoing investigation into the Department of Justice (DOJ) and Federal Bureau of
Investigation (FBI) and their use of the Foreign Intelligence Surveillance Act (FISA) during the
2016 presidential election cycle. Our findings, which are detailed below, 1) raise concerns with
the legitimacy and legality of certain DOJ and FBI interactions with the Foreign Intelligence
Surveillance Court (FISC), and 2) represent a troubling breakdown of legal processes established
to protect the American people from abuses related to the FISA process.

## Investigation Update

On October 21, 2016, DOJ and FBI sought and received a FISA probable cause order
(not under Title VII) authorizing electronic surveillance on Carter Page from the FISC. Page is a
U.S. citizen who served as a volunteer advisor to the Trump presidential campaign. Consistent
with requirements under FISA, the application had to be first certified by the Director or Deputy
Director of the FBI. It then required the approval of the Attorney General, Deputy Attorney
General (DAG), or the Senate-confirmed Assistant Attorney General for the National Security
Division.

The FBI and DOJ obtained one initial FISA warrant targeting Carter Page and three FISA
renewals from the FISC. As required by statute (50 U.S.C. §1805(d)(1)), a FISA order on an
American citizen must be renewed by the FISC every 90 days and each renewal requires a
separate finding of probable cause. Then-Director James Comey signed three FISA applications
in question on behalf of the FBI, and Deputy Director Andrew McCabe signed one. Then-DAG
Sally Yates, then-Acting DAG Dana Boente, and DAG Rod Rosenstein each signed one or more
FISA applications on behalf of DOJ.

Due to the sensitive nature of foreign intelligence activity, FISA submissions (including
renewals) before the FISC are classified. As such, the public's confidence in the integrity of the
FISA process depends on the court's ability to hold the government to the highest standard—
particularly as it relates to surveillance of American citizens. However, the FISC's rigor in
protecting the rights of Americans, which is reinforced by 90-day renewals of surveillance
orders, is necessarily dependent on the government's production to the court of all material and
relevant facts. This should include information potentially favorable to the target of the FISA

application that is known by the government. In the case of Carter Page, the government had at least four independent opportunities before the FISC to accurately provide an accounting of the relevant facts. However, our findings indicate that, as described below, material and relevant information was omitted.

1) The "dossier" compiled by Christopher Steele (Steele dossier) on behalf of the Democratic National Committee (DNC) and the Hillary Clinton campaign formed an essential part of the Carter Page FISA application. Steele was a longtime FBI source who was paid over $160,000 by the DNC and Clinton campaign, via the law firm Perkins Coie and research firm Fusion GPS, to obtain derogatory information on Donald Trump's ties to Russia.

   a) Neither the initial application in October 2016, nor any of the renewals, disclose or reference the role of the DNC, Clinton campaign, or any party/campaign in funding Steele's efforts, even though the political origins of the Steele dossier were then known to senior DOJ and FBI officials.

   b) The initial FISA application notes Steele was working for a named U.S. person, but does not name Fusion GPS and principal Glenn Simpson, who was paid by a U.S. law firm (Perkins Coie) representing the DNC (even though it was known by DOJ at the time that political actors were involved with the Steele dossier). The application does not mention Steele was ultimately working on behalf of—and paid by—the DNC and Clinton campaign, or that the FBI had separately authorized payment to Steele for the same information.

2) The Carter Page FISA application also cited extensively a September 23, 2016, *Yahoo News* article by Michael Isikoff, which focuses on Page's July 2016 trip to Moscow. This article does not corroborate the Steele dossier because it is derived from information leaked by Steele himself to *Yahoo News*. The Page FISA application incorrectly assesses that Steele did not directly provide information to *Yahoo News*. Steele has admitted in British court filings that he met with *Yahoo News*—and several other outlets—in September 2016 at the direction of Fusion GPS. Perkins Coie was aware of Steele's initial media contacts because they hosted at least one meeting in Washington D.C. in 2016 with Steele and Fusion GPS where this matter was discussed.

   a) Steele was suspended and then terminated as an FBI source for what the FBI defines as the most serious of violations—an unauthorized disclosure to the media of his relationship with the FBI in an October 30, 2016, *Mother Jones* article by David Corn. Steele should have been terminated for his previous undisclosed contacts with Yahoo and other outlets in September—before the Page application was submitted to

# UNCLASSIFIED

the FISC in October—but Steele improperly concealed from and lied to the FBI about those contacts.

b) Steele's numerous encounters with the media violated the cardinal rule of source handling—maintaining confidentiality—and demonstrated that Steele had become a less than reliable source for the FBI.

3) Before and after Steele was terminated as a source, he maintained contact with DOJ via then-Associate Deputy Attorney General Bruce Ohr, a senior DOJ official who worked closely with Deputy Attorneys General Yates and later Rosenstein. Shortly after the election, the FBI began interviewing Ohr, documenting his communications with Steele. For example, in September 2016, Steele admitted to Ohr his feelings against then-candidate Trump when Steele said he **"was desperate that Donald Trump not get elected and was passionate about him not being president."** This clear evidence of Steele's bias was recorded by Ohr at the time and subsequently in official FBI files—but not reflected in any of the Page FISA applications.

a) During this same time period, Ohr's wife was employed by Fusion GPS to assist in the cultivation of opposition research on Trump. Ohr later provided the FBI with all of his wife's opposition research, paid for by the DNC and Clinton campaign via Fusion GPS. The Ohrs' relationship with Steele and Fusion GPS was inexplicably concealed from the FISC.

4) According to the head of the FBI's counterintelligence division, Assistant Director Bill Priestap, corroboration of the Steele dossier was in its "infancy" at the time of the initial Page FISA application. After Steele was terminated, a source validation report conducted by an independent unit within FBI assessed Steele's reporting as only minimally corroborated. Yet, in early January 2017, Director Comey briefed President-elect Trump on a summary of the Steele dossier, even though it was—according to his June 2017 testimony—"salacious and unverified." While the FISA application relied on Steele's past record of credible reporting on other unrelated matters, it ignored or concealed his anti-Trump financial and ideological motivations. Furthermore, Deputy Director McCabe testified before the Committee in December 2017 that no surveillance warrant would have been sought from the FISC without the Steele dossier information.

# UNCLASSIFIED

5) The Page FISA application also mentions information regarding fellow Trump campaign advisor George Papadopoulos, but there is no evidence of any cooperation or conspiracy between Page and Papadopoulos. The Papadopoulos information triggered the opening of an FBI counterintelligence investigation in late July 2016 by FBI agent Pete Strzok. Strzok was reassigned by the Special Counsel's Office to FBI Human Resources for improper text messages with his mistress, FBI Attorney Lisa Page (no known relation to Carter Page), where they both demonstrated a clear bias against Trump and in favor of Clinton, whom Strzok had also investigated. The Strzok/Lisa Page texts also reflect extensive discussions about the investigation, orchestrating leaks to the media, and include a meeting with Deputy Director McCabe to discuss an "insurance" policy against President Trump's election.

# UNCLASSIFIED

# APPENDIX H

## Schiff memo

UNCLASSIFIED

~~TOP SECRET//NOFORN~~

TO: All Members of the House of Representatives
FROM: HPSCI Minority
DATE: January 29, 2018
RE: Correcting the Record – The Russia Investigations

The HPSCI Majority's move to release to the House of Representatives its allegations against the Federal Bureau of Investigation (FBI) and the Department of Justice (DOJ) is a transparent effort to undermine those agencies, the Special Counsel, and Congress' investigations. It also risks public exposure of sensitive sources and methods for no legitimate purpose.

FBI and DOJ officials did not "abuse" the Foreign Intelligence Surveillance Act (FISA) process, omit material information, or subvert this vital tool to spy on the Trump campaign.

In fact, DOJ and the FBI would have been remiss in their duty to protect the country had they not sought a FISA warrant and repeated renewals to conduct temporary surveillance of Carter Page, someone the FBI assessed to be an agent of the Russian government. DOJ met the rigor, transparency, and evidentiary basis needed to meet FISA's probable cause requirement, by demonstrating:

- o contemporaneous evidence of Russia's election interference;
- o concerning Russian links and outreach to Trump campaign officials;
- o Page's history with Russian intelligence; and
- o ▮▮▮▮▮▮▮▮▮▮▮ Page's suspicious activities in 2016, including in Moscow.

The Committee's Minority has therefore prepared this memorandum to correct the record:

- **Christopher Steele's raw intelligence reporting did not inform the FBI's decision to initiate its counterintelligence investigation in late July 2016.** In fact, the FBI's closely-held investigative team only received Steele's reporting in mid-September – more than seven weeks later. The FBI – and, subsequently, the Special Counsel's – investigation into links between the Russian government and Trump campaign associates has been based on troubling law enforcement and intelligence information unrelated to the "dossier."

- **DOJ's October 21, 2016 FISA application and three subsequent renewals carefully outlined for the Court a multi-pronged rationale for surveilling Page,** who, at the time of the first application, was no longer with the Trump campaign. DOJ detailed Page's past relationships with Russian spies and interaction with Russian officials during the 2016 campaign, ▮▮▮▮▮▮▮▮▮▮. DOJ cited multiple sources to support the case for surveilling Page — but made only narrow use of information from Steele's sources about Page's specific activities in 2016, chiefly his suspected July 2016 meetings in Moscow with Russian officials, ▮▮▮▮▮▮▮▮▮▮▮▮▮▮▮▮▮▮▮. In fact, the FBI interviewed Page in March 2016 about his contact with Russian intelligence, the very month candidate Donald Trump named him a foreign policy advisor.

As DOJ informed the Court in subsequent renewals, ▮▮▮▮▮▮▮▮▮▮▮▮▮▮ **Steele's reporting about Page's Moscow meetings** ▮▮▮▮▮▮▮▮▮. DOJ's applications did not otherwise rely on Steele's reporting, including any "salacious" allegations

1

~~TOP SECRET//NOFORN~~

UNCLASSIFIED

about Trump, and the FBI never paid Steele for this reporting. While explaining why the FBI viewed Steele's reporting and sources as reliable and credible, DOJ also disclosed:
  o   Steele's prior relationship with the FBI;
  o   the fact of and reason for his termination as a source; and
  o   the assessed political motivation of those who hired him.

- **The Committee Majority's memorandum, which draws selectively on highly sensitive classified information, includes other distortions and misrepresentations** that are contradicted by the underlying classified documents, which the vast majority of Members of the Committee and the House have not had the opportunity to review – and which Chairman Nunes chose not to read himself.[1]

## Background

On January 18, 2018, the Committee Majority, during an unrelated business meeting, forced a surprise vote to release to the full House a profoundly misleading memorandum alleging serious abuses by the FBI and DOJ. Majority staff drafted the document in secret on behalf of Chairman Devin Nunes (and reportedly with guidance and input from Rep. Trey Gowdy), and then rushed a party-line vote without prior notice.

This was by design. The overwhelming majority of Committee Members never received DOJ authorization to access the underlying classified information, and therefore could not judge the veracity of Chairman Nunes' claims. Due to sensitive sources and methods, DOJ provided access only to the Committee's Chair and Ranking Member (or respective designees), and limited staff, to facilitate the Committee's investigation into Russia's covert campaign to influence the 2016 U.S. elections.[2] As DOJ has confirmed publicly, it did not authorize the broader release of this information within Congress or to the public, and Chairman Nunes refused to allow DOJ and the FBI to review his document until he permitted the FBI Director to see it for the first time in HPSCI's secure spaces late on Sunday, January 28 – 10 days after disclosure to the House.[3]

## FBI's Counterintelligence Investigation

In its October 2016 FISA application and subsequent renewals, DOJ accurately informed the Court that the FBI initiated its counterintelligence investigation on July 31, 2016, after receiving information ████████████. George Papadopoulos revealed ████████ that individuals linked to Russia, who took interest in Papadopoulos as a Trump campaign foreign policy adviser, informed him in late April 2016 that Russia ████████ ████████████████████████████████████████████████████.[4] Papadopoulos's disclosure, moreover, occurred against **the backdrop of Russia's aggressive covert campaign to influence our elections, which the FBI was already monitoring.** We would later learn in Papadopoulos's plea that that the information the Russians could assist by anonymously releasing were thousands of Hillary Clinton's emails.[5]

DOJ told the Court the truth. Its representation was consistent with the FBI's underlying investigative record, which current and former senior officials later corroborated in extensive

Committee testimony. Christopher Steele's reporting, which he began to share with an FBI agent ███████ ████████████████ through the end of October 2016, **played no role** in launching the FBI's counterintelligence investigation into Russian interference and links to the Trump campaign. In fact, Steele's reporting did not reach the counterintelligence team investigating Russia at FBI headquarters until mid-September 2016, more than seven weeks after the FBI opened its investigation, because the probe's existence was so closely held within the FBI.[6] By then, the FBI had already opened sub-inquiries into ███ individuals linked to the Trump campaign: ████████████ █████████████████████████████████████████████████████████ and former campaign foreign policy advisor **Carter Page**.

As Committee testimony bears out, the FBI would have continued its investigation, including against ██████ individuals, even if it had never received information from Steele, never applied for a FISA warrant against Page, or if the FISC had rejected the application.[7]

### DOJ's FISA Application and Renewals

The initial warrant application and subsequent renewals received independent scrutiny and approval by four different federal judges, ~~three~~ of whom were appointed by President George W. *one by George-* Bush and one by President Ronald Reagan. DOJ first applied to the FISC on October 21, 2016 *H.W Bush* for a warrant to permit the FBI to initiate electronic surveillance and physical search of Page for 90 days, consistent with FISA requirements. The Court approved three renewals – in early January 2017, early April 2017, and late June 2017 – which authorized the FBI to maintain surveillance on Page until late September 2017. Senior DOJ and FBI officials appointed by the Obama and Trump Administrations, including acting Attorney General Dana Boente and Deputy Attorney General Rod Rosenstein, certified the applications with the Court.

**FISA was _not_ used to spy on Trump or his campaign.** As the Trump campaign and Page have acknowledged, Page ended his formal affiliation with the campaign months **before** DOJ applied for a warrant. DOJ, moreover, submitted the initial application **less than three weeks** before the election, even though the FBI's investigation had been ongoing since the end of July 2016.

DOJ's warrant request was based on compelling evidence and probable cause to believe Page was knowingly assisting clandestine Russian intelligence activities in the U.S.:

- **Page's Connections to Russian Government and Intelligence Officials:** The FBI had an independent basis for investigating Page's motivations and actions during the campaign, transition, and following the inauguration. As DOJ described in detail to the Court, Page had an extensive record as ███████████████████████████████████████████████████ ████████████████[8] prior to joining the Trump campaign. He resided in Moscow from 2004-2007 and pursued business deals with Russia's state-owned energy company Gazprom—█████████████████████████████████████████████████████████████████
As early as ████, a Russian intelligence officer ███████████████████ targeted Page for recruitment. Page showed ████████████████████████

**Page remained on the radar of Russian intelligence and the FBI.** In 2013, prosecutors indicted three other Russian spies, two of whom targeted Page for recruitment. The FBI also interviewed Page multiple times about his Russian intelligence contacts, including in March 2016.[10] The FBI's concern about and knowledge of Page's activities therefore long predate the FBI's receipt of Steele's information.

- **Page's Suspicious Activity During the 2016 Campaign:** The FISA applications also detail Page's suspicious activity after joining the Trump campaign in March 2016. ████████████ ████████████████████████████████████ Page traveled to Moscow in July 2016, during which he gave a university commencement address – an honor usually reserved for well-known luminaries.

  o **It is in this specific sub-section of the applications that DOJ refers to Steele's reporting on Page and his alleged coordination with Russian officials.** Steele's information about Page was consistent with the FBI's assessment of Russian intelligence efforts to recruit him and his connections to Russian persons of interest.

  o In particular, Steele's sources reported that Page met separately while in Russia with Igor Sechin, a close associate of Vladimir Putin and executive chairman of Rosneft, Russia's state-owned oil company, and Igor Divyekin, a senior Kremlin official. Sechin allegedly discussed the prospect of future U.S.-Russia energy cooperation and "an associated move to lift Ukraine-related western sanctions against Russia." Divyekin allegedly disclosed to Page that the Kremlin possessed compromising information on Clinton ("kompromat") and noted "the possibility of its being released to Candidate #1's campaign."[11] [*Note*: "Candidate #1" refers to candidate Trump.] This closely tracks what other Russian contacts were informing another Trump foreign policy advisor, George Papadopoulos.

- In subsequent FISA renewals, **DOJ provided additional information obtained through multiple independent sources that corroborated Steele's reporting.**

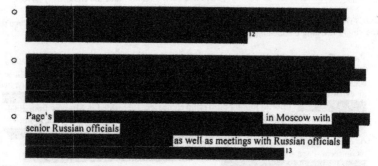

  o ████████████████████████████████████████████████ [12]

  o ████████████████████████████████████████████████

  o Page's ████████████████ in Moscow with ████ senior Russian officials ████████████████████ ████████████████ as well as meetings with Russian officials ████ [13]

This information contradicts Page's November 2, 2017 testimony to the Committee, in which he initially denied any such meetings and then was forced to admit speaking with

Dvorkovich and meeting with Rosneft's Sechin-tied investor relations chief, Andrey
Baranov.

- **The Court-approved surveillance of Page allowed FBI to collect valuable intelligence.**
  The FISA renewals demonstrate that the FBI collected important investigative information
  and leads by conducting Court-approved surveillance. For instance, ███████████████

  ██████████████████████████████████████████████

  DOJ also documented evidence that Page ██████████████ , anticipated
  ████████████ and repeatedly contacted ██████████
  ████████ in an effort to present himself as ████████████████
  ████████████████████████████ [15]
  ████████████████████████████████████ [16]
  Page's efforts to ████████████████████████████ also contradict his
  sworn testimony to our Committee.

### DOJ's Transparency about Christopher Steele

Far from "omitting" material facts about Steele, as the Majority claims,[17] DOJ repeatedly
informed the Court about Steele's background, credibility, and potential bias. DOJ
explained in detail Steele's prior relationship with and compensation from the FBI; his
credibility, reporting history, and source network; the fact of and reason for his termination as a
source in late October 2016; and the likely political motivations of those who hired Steele.

- **DOJ was transparent with Court about Steele's sourcing:** The Committee Majority,
  which had earlier accused Obama Administration officials of improper "unmasking," faults
  DOJ for not revealing the names of specific U.S. persons and entities in the FISA application
  and subsequent renewals. In fact, DOJ appropriately upheld its longstanding practice of
  protecting U.S. citizen information by purposefully not "unmasking" U.S. person and entity
  names, unless they were themselves the subject of a counterintelligence investigation. DOJ
  instead used generic identifiers that provided the Court with more than sufficient information
  to understand the political context of Steele's research. In an extensive explanation to the
  Court, DOJ discloses that Steele

  *"was approached by an identified U.S. Person,[18] who indicated to Source #1 [Steele][19] that a
  U.S.-based law firm[20] had hired the identified U.S. Person to conduct research regarding
  Candidate #1's[21] ties to Russia. (The identified U.S. Person and Source #1 have a longstanding business relationship.) The identified U.S. person hired Source #1 to conduct this
  research. The identified U.S. Person never advised Source #1 as to the motivation behind the
  research into Candidate #1's ties to Russia. The FBI speculates that the identified U.S. Person
  was likely looking for information that could be used to discredit Candidate #1's campaign."[22]*

  Contrary to the Majority's assertion that DOJ fails to mention that Steele's research was
  commissioned by "political actors" to "obtain derogatory information on Donald Trump's
  ties to Russia,"[23] **DOJ in fact informed the Court accurately that Steele was hired by**

5

politically-motivated U.S. persons and entities and that his research appeared intended for use "to discredit" Trump's campaign.

- **DOJ explained the FBI's reasonable basis for finding Steele credible:** The applications correctly described Steele as ███████████████ ███████████████████████. The applications also reviewed Steele's multi-year history of credible reporting on Russia and other matters, including information DOJ used in criminal proceedings.[24] Senior FBI and DOJ officials have repeatedly affirmed to the Committee the reliability and credibility of Steele's reporting, an assessment also reflected in the FBI's underlying source documents.[25] The FBI has undertaken a rigorous process to vet allegations from Steele's reporting, including with regard to Page.[26]

- **The FBI properly notified the FISC after it terminated Steele as a source for making unauthorized disclosures to the media.** The Majority cites no evidence that the FBI, prior to filing its initial October 21, 2016 application, actually knew or should have known of any allegedly inappropriate media contacts by Steele. Nor do they cite evidence that Steele disclosed to *Yahoo!* details included in the FISA warrant, since the British Court filings to which they refer do not address what Steele may have said to *Yahoo!*.

  DOJ informed the Court in its renewals that the FBI acted promptly to terminate Steele after learning from him (<u>after</u> DOJ filed the first warrant application) that he had discussed his work with a media outlet in late October. The January 2018 renewal further explained to the Court that Steele told the FBI that he made his unauthorized media disclosure because of his frustration at Director Comey's public announcement shortly before the election that the FBI reopened its investigation into candidate Clinton's email use.

- **DOJ never paid Steele for the "dossier":** The Majority asserts that the FBI had "separately authorized payment" to Steele for his research on Trump but neglects to mention that payment was cancelled and never made. As the FBI's records and Committee testimony confirms, although the FBI initially considered compensation ███████████████ ██████████████████, **Steele ultimately never received payment from the FBI for any "dossier"-related information.**[27] DOJ accurately informed the Court that Steele had been an FBI confidential human source since ███, for which he was "compensated ██████████████████ by the FBI" -- payment for previously-shared information of value unrelated to the FBI's Russia investigation.[28]

### Additional Omissions, Errors, and Distortions in the Majority's Memorandum

- **DOJ appropriately provided the Court with a comprehensive explanation of Russia's election interference, including evidence that Russia courted another Trump campaign advisor, Papadopoulos, and that Russian agents previewed their hack and dissemination of stolen emails.** In claiming that there is "no evidence of any cooperation or conspiracy between Page and Papadopoulos,"[29] the Majority misstates the reason why DOJ specifically explained Russia's courting of Papadopoulos. Papadopoulos's interaction with Russian agents, coupled with real-time evidence of Russian election interference, provided the Court with a broader context in which to evaluate Russia's clandestine activities and Page's history and alleged contact with Russian officials. Moreover, since only Page ███████

███████████████, no evidence of a separate conspiracy between him and Papadopoulos was required. **DOJ would have been negligent in omitting vital information about Papadopoulos and Russia's concerted efforts.**

- **In its Court filings, DOJ made proper use of news coverage.** The Majority falsely claims that the FISA materials "relied heavily" on a September 23, 2016 *Yahoo!* News article by Michael Isikoff and that this article "does not corroborate the Steele Dossier because it is derived from information leaked by Steele himself."[30] In fact, DOJ referenced Isikoff's article, alongside another article the Majority fails to mention, not to provide separate corroboration for Steele's reporting, but instead to inform the Court of Page's public denial of his suspected meetings in Moscow, which Page also echoed in a September 25, 2016 letter to FBI Director Comey. ████████████████████████████████████████[31]

- **The Majority's reference to Bruce Ohr is misleading.** The Majority mischaracterizes Bruce Ohr's role, overstates the significance of his interactions with Steele, and misleads about the timeframe of Ohr's communication with the FBI. In late November 2016, Ohr informed the FBI of his prior professional relationship with Steele and information that Steele shared with him (including Steele's concern about Trump being compromised by Russia). He also described his wife's contract work with Fusion GPS, the firm that hired Steele separately. This occurred weeks <u>after</u> the election and more than a month <u>after</u> the Court approved the initial FISA application. The Majority describes Bruce Ohr as a senior DOJ official who "worked closely with the Deputy Attorney General, Yates and later Rosenstein," in order to imply that Ohr was somehow involved in the FISA process, but there is no indication this is the case.

  Bruce Ohr is a well-respected career professional whose portfolio is drugs and organized crime, not counterintelligence. There is no evidence that he would have known about the Page FISA applications and their contents. The Majority's assertions, moreover, are irrelevant in determining the veracity of Steele's reporting. By the time Ohr debriefs with the FBI, it had already terminated Steele as a source and was independently corroborating Steele's reporting about Page's activities. Bruce Ohr took the initiative to inform the FBI of what he knew, and the Majority does him a grave disservice by suggesting he is part of some malign conspiracy.

- **Finally, Peter Strzok and Lisa Page's text messages are irrelevant to the FISA application.** The Majority gratuitously includes reference to Strzok and Page at the end of their memorandum, in an effort to imply that political bias infected the FBI's investigation and DOJ's FISA applications. In fact, neither Strzok nor Page served as affiants on the applications, which were the product of extensive and senior DOJ and FBI review.[32] In demonizing both career professionals, the Majority accuses them of "orchestrating leaks to the media" – a serious charge; omits inconvenient text messages, in which they critiqued a wide range of other officials and candidates from both parties; does not disclose that FBI Deputy Director McCabe testified to the Committee that he had no idea what Page and Strzok were referring to in their "insurance policy" texts;[33] and ignores Strzok's acknowledged role in preparing a public declaration, by then Director Comey, about former Secretary Clinton's "extreme carelessness" in handling classified information—which greatly damaged Clinton's public reputation in the days just prior to the presidential election.

---

[1] Letter to HPSCI Chairman Devin Nunes, Assistant Attorney General Stephen Boyd, Department of Justice, January 24, 2018.

[2] Letter to HPSCI Chairman Devin Nunes, Assistant Attorney General Stephen Boyd, Department of Justice, January 24, 2018. DOJ also confirmed in writing to Minority Staff DOJ and FBI's terms of review:

> the Department has accommodated HPSCI's oversight request by allowing repeated in camera reviews of the material in an appropriate secure facility under the general stipulations that (1) **the Chair (or his delegate) and the Ranking Member (or his delegate) and two staff each, with appropriate security clearances, be allowed to review on behalf of the Committee, (2)** that the review take place in a reading room set up at the Department, and (3) that the documents not leave the physical control of the Department, and (5) that the review opportunities be bipartisan in nature. Though we originally requested that no notes be taken, in acknowledgment of a request by the Committee and recognizing that the volume of documents had increased with time, the Department eventually allowed notes to be taken to facilitate HPSCI's review. Also, initial reviews of the material include [sic] short briefings by Department officials to put the material in context and to provide some additional information.

Email from Stephen Boyd to HPSCI Minority Staff, January 18, 2018 (emphasis supplied).

[3] Letter to HPSCI Chairman Devin Nunes, Assistant Attorney General Stephen Boyd, Department of Justice, January 24, 2018.

[4]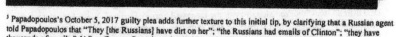

[5] Papadopoulos's October 5, 2017 guilty plea adds further texture to this initial tip, by clarifying that a Russian agent told Papadopoulos that "They [the Russians] have dirt on her"; "the Russians had emails of Clinton"; "they have thousands of emails." *U.S. v. George Papadopoulos* (1:17-cr-182, District of Columbia), p. 7.

[6]

[7] Under the Special Counsel's direction, Flynn and Papadopoulos have both pleaded guilty to lying to federal investigators and are cooperating with the Special Counsel's investigation, while Manafort and his long-time aide, former Trump deputy campaign manager Rick Gates, have been indicted on multiple counts and are awaiting trial. See *U.S. v. Michael T. Flynn* (1:17-cr-232, District of Columbia); *U.S. v. Paul J. Manafort, Jr., and Richard W. Gates III* (1:17-cr-201, District of Columbia); *U.S. v. George Papadopoulos* (1:17-cr-182, District of Columbia).

[10] See also, *U.S. v. Evgeny Buryakov, a/k/a "Zhenya," Igor Sporyshev, and Victor Podobnyy*, U.S. Southern District of New York, January 23, 2015.

[11] Department of Justice, Foreign Intelligence Surveillance Court Application, October 21, 2016, p.18. Repeated in subsequent renewal applications

[12] Department of Justice, Foreign Intelligence Surveillance Court Application, June 29, 2017, pp. 20-21.

[13] ██████████████████████████████████████████

[14] ████████████████████████████████ the FBI and broader Intelligence Community's high confidence assessment that the Russian government was engaged in a covert interference campaign to influence the 2016 election, including that Russian intelligence actors "compromised the DNC" and WikiLeaks subsequently leaked in July 2016 "a trove" of DNC emails. Department of Justice, Foreign Intelligence Surveillance Court Application, October 21, 2016, pp. 6-7. Repeated and updated with new information in subsequent renewal applications. Department of Justice, Foreign Intelligence Surveillance Court Application, June 29, 2017, pp. 20-21.

[15] Department of Justice, Foreign Intelligence Surveillance Court Application, June 29, 2017, pp. 36, 46, 48.

[16] Department of Justice, Foreign Intelligence Surveillance Court Application, June 29, 2017, p. 56.

[17] HPSCI Majority Memorandum, *Foreign Intelligence Surveillance Act Abuses at the Department of Justice and the Federal Bureau of Investigation,* January 18, 2018, pp. 2-3 (enumerating "omissions" of fact, regarding Steele and his activities, from the Page FISA applications).

[18] Glenn Simpson.

[19] Christopher Steele.

[20] Perkins Coie LLP.

[21] Donald Trump.

[22] Department of Justice, Foreign Intelligence Surveillance Court Application, October 21, 2016, pp. 15-16, n. 8. Repeated in subsequent renewal applications.

[23] HPSCI Majority Memorandum, *Foreign Intelligence Surveillance Act Abuses at the Department of Justice and the Federal Bureau of Investigation,* January 18, 2018, p. 2.

[24] Department of Justice, Foreign Intelligence Surveillance Court Application, October 21, 2016, p. 15, footnote 8. Repeated in subsequent renewal applications.

[25] Interview of Andrew McCabe (FBI Deputy Director), House Permanent Select Committee on Intelligence, December 19, 2017, p. 46, 100; Interview of Sally Yates (former Deputy Attorney General), House Permanent Select Committee on Intelligence, November 3, 2017, p. 16; Interview with John Carlin (former Assistant Attorney General for National Security), House Permanent Select Committee on Intelligence, July, 2017, p. 35.

[26] Interview of Andrew McCabe (FBI Deputy Director), House Permanent Select Committee on Intelligence, December 19, 2017, p. 100-101, 115.

[27] Interview of FBI Agent, House Permanent Select Committee on Intelligence, December 20, 2017, p. 112.

[28] Department of Justice, Foreign Intelligence Surveillance Court Application, October 21, 2016, pp. 15-16, n. 8. Repeated in subsequent renewal applications.

[29] HPSCI Majority Memorandum, *Foreign Intelligence Surveillance Act Abuses at the Department of Justice and the Federal Bureau of Investigation,* January 18, 2018, p. 4 ("The Page FISA application also mentions information regarding fellow Trump campaign advisor George Papadopoulos, but there is no evidence of any cooperation or conspiracy between Page and Papadopoulos.")

[30] HPSCI Majority Memorandum, *Foreign Intelligence Surveillance Act Abuses at the Department of Justice and the Federal Bureau of Investigation,* January 18, 2018, p. 2. Neither Isikoff nor *Yahoo!* are specifically identified in the FISA Materials, in keeping with the FBI's general practice of not identifying U.S. persons.

[31] Department of Justice, Foreign Intelligence Surveillance Court Application, October 21, 2016, p. 25; Department of Justice, Foreign Intelligence Surveillance Court Application, January 12. 2017, p. 31; Carter Page, Letter to FBI Director James Comey, September 25, 2016.

~~TOP SECRET//NOFORN~~

[33] Interview of Andrew McCabe (FBI Deputy Director), House Permanent Select Committee on Intelligence, December 19, 2017, p. 157.

~~TOP SECRET//NOFORN~~

# APPENDIX I

## Statement of the Offense, filed against Flynn by the Special Counsel's office

UNITED STATES DISTRICT COURT
FOR THE DISTRICT OF COLUMBIA

| | |
|---|---|
| UNITED STATES OF AMERICA | Criminal No.: |
| v. | Violation: 18 U.S.C. § 1001 (False Statements) |
| MICHAEL T. FLYNN, | |
| Defendant. | |

### STATEMENT OF THE OFFENSE

Pursuant to Federal Rule of Criminal Procedure 11, the United States of America and the defendant, MICHAEL T. FLYNN, stipulate and agree that the following facts are true and accurate. These facts do not constitute all of the facts known to the parties concerning the charged offense; they are being submitted to demonstrate that sufficient facts exist that the defendant committed the offense to which he is pleading guilty.

1.    The defendant, MICHAEL T. FLYNN, who served as a surrogate and national security advisor for the presidential campaign of Donald J. Trump ("Campaign"), as a senior member of President-Elect Trump's Transition Team ("Presidential Transition Team"), and as the National Security Advisor to President Trump, made materially false statements and omissions during an interview with the Federal Bureau of Investigation ("FBI") on January 24, 2017, in Washington, D.C. At the time of the interview, the FBI had an open investigation into the Government of Russia's ("Russia") efforts to interfere in the 2016 presidential election, including the nature of any links between individuals associated with the Campaign and Russia, and whether there was any coordination between the Campaign and Russia's efforts.

2.    FLYNN's false statements and omissions impeded and otherwise had a material impact on the FBI's ongoing investigation into the existence of any links or coordination

between individuals associated with the Campaign and Russia's efforts to interfere with the 2016 presidential election.

*False Statements Regarding FLYNN's Request to the Russian Ambassador that Russia Refrain from Escalating the Situation in Response to U.S. Sanctions against Russia*

3.     On or about January 24, 2017, FLYNN agreed to be interviewed by agents from the FBI ("January 24 voluntary interview"). During the interview, FLYNN falsely stated that he did not ask Russia's Ambassador to the United States ("Russian Ambassador") to refrain from escalating the situation in response to sanctions that the United States had imposed against Russia. FLYNN also falsely stated that he did not remember a follow-up conversation in which the Russian Ambassador stated that Russia had chosen to moderate its response to those sanctions as a result of FLYNN's request. In truth and in fact, however, FLYNN then and there knew that the following had occurred:

a.     On or about December 28, 2016, then-President Barack Obama signed Executive Order 13757, which was to take effect the following day. The executive order announced sanctions against Russia in response to that government's actions intended to interfere with the 2016 presidential election ("U.S. Sanctions").

b.     On or about December 28, 2016, the Russian Ambassador contacted FLYNN.

c.     On or about December 29, 2016, FLYNN called a senior official of the Presidential Transition Team ("PTT official"), who was with other senior ·members of the Presidential Transition Team at the Mar-a-Lago resort in Palm Beach, Florida, to discuss what, if anything, to communicate to the Russian Ambassador about the U.S. Sanctions. On that call, FLYNN and

2

the PTT official discussed the U.S. Sanctions, including the potential impact of those sanctions on the incoming administration's foreign policy goals. The PTT official and FLYNN also discussed that the members of the Presidential Transition Team at Mar-a-Lago did not want Russia to escalate the situation.

d.     Immediately after his phone call with the PTT official, FLYNN called the Russian Ambassador and requested that Russia not escalate the situation and only respond to the U.S. Sanctions in a reciprocal manner.

e.     Shortly after his phone call with the Russian Ambassador, FLYNN spoke with the PTT official to report on the substance of his call with the Russian Ambassador, including their discussion of the U.S. Sanctions.

f.     On or about December 30, 2016, Russian President Vladimir Putin released a statement indicating that Russia would not take retaliatory measures in response to the U.S. Sanctions at that time.

g.     On or about December 31, 2016, the Russian Ambassador called FLYNN and informed him that Russia had chosen not to retaliate in response to FLYNN's request.

h.     After his phone call with the Russian Ambassador, FLYNN spoke with senior members of the Presidential Transition Team about FLYNN's conversations with the Russian Ambassador regarding the U.S. Sanctions and Russia's decision not to escalate the situation.

3

*False Statements Regarding FLYNN's Request that Foreign Officials Vote Against or*
*Delay a United Nations Security Council Resolution*

4.      During the January 24 voluntary interview, FLYNN made additional false

statements about calls he made to Russia and several other countries regarding a resolution

submitted by Egypt to the United Nations Security Council on December 21, 2016. Specifically

FLYNN falsely stated that he only asked the countries' positions on the vote, and that he did not

request that any of the countries take any particular action on the resolution. FLYNN also

falsely stated that the Russian Ambassador never described to him Russia's response to

FLYNN's request regarding the resolution. In truth and in fact, however, FLYNN then and there

knew that the following had occurred:

a.      On or about December 21, 2016, Egypt submitted a resolution to the

United Nations Security Council on the issue of Israeli settlements

("resolution"). The United Nations Security Council was scheduled to

vote on the resolution the following day.

b.      On or about December 22, 2016, a very senior member of the Presidential

Transition Team directed FLYNN to contact officials from foreign

governments, including Russia, to learn where each government stood on

the resolution and to influence those governments to delay the vote or

defeat the resolution.

c.      On or about December 22, 2016, FLYNN contacted the Russian

Ambassador about the pending vote. FLYNN informed the Russian

Ambassador about the incoming administration's opposition to the

resolution, and requested that Russia vote against or delay the resolution.

4

d.      On or about December 23, 2016, FLYNN again spoke with the Russian Ambassador, who informed FLYNN that if it came to a vote Russia would not vote against the resolution.

*Other False Statements Regarding FLYNN's Contacts with Foreign Governments*

5.      On March 7, 2017, FLYNN filed multiple documents with the Department of Justice pursuant to the Foreign Agents Registration Act ("FARA") pertaining to a project performed by him and his company, the Flynn Intel Group, Inc. ("FIG"), for the principal benefit of the Republic of Turkey ("Turkey project"). In the FARA filings, FLYNN made materially false statements and omissions, including by falsely stating that (a) FIG did not know whether or the extent to which the Republic of Turkey was involved in the Turkey project, (b) the Turkey project was focused on improving U.S. business organizations' confidence regarding doing business in Turkey, and (c) an op-ed by FLYNN published in *The Hill* on November 8, 2016, was written at his own initiative; and by omitting that officials from the Republic of Turkey provided supervision and direction over the Turkey project.

ROBERT S. MUELLER, III
Special Counsel

By: _____
Brandon L. Van Grack
Zainab N. Ahmad
Senior Assistant Special Counsels
The Special Counsel's Office

## DEFENDANT'S ACCEPTANCE

The preceding statement is a summary, made for the purpose of providing the Court with a factual basis for my guilty plea to the charge against me. It does not include all of the facts known to me regarding this offense. I make this statement knowingly and voluntarily and because I am, in fact, guilty of the crime charged. No threats have been made to me nor am I under the influence of anything that could impede my ability to understand this Statement of the Offense fully.

I have read every word of this Statement of the Offense, or have had it read to me. Pursuant to Federal Rule of Criminal Procedure 11, after consulting with my attorneys, I agree and stipulate to this Statement of the Offense, and declare under penalty of perjury that it is true and correct.

Date: 11/30/17

Michael T. Flynn
Defendant

## ATTORNEYS' ACKNOWLEDGMENT

I have read this Statement of the Offense, and have reviewed it with my client fully. I concur in my client's desire to adopt and stipulate to this Statement of the Offense as true and accurate.

Date: 11/30/17

Robert K. Kelner
Attorney for Defendant

Stephen P. Anthony
Attorney for Defendant

# APPENDIX J

**HOUSE PERMANENT SELECT
COMMITTEE ON INTELLIGENCE
RUSSIA INVESTIGATION**

## Overview

Following a more than yearlong, bipartisan investigation into Russia active measures targeting the 2016 U.S. election, the House Intelligence Committee has completed a draft report of 150+ pages, with 600+ citations. The draft report addresses, in detail, <u>each of the questions within the agreed parameters of the investigation, as announced in March 2017</u>. It analyzes:

- Russian active measures directed against the 2016 U.S. election and against our European allies;
- The U.S. government response to that attack;
- Links between Russians and the Trump and Clinton campaigns; and
- Purported leaks of classified information.

## Initial Findings

The draft report contains 40+ initial findings that describe:

- A pattern of Russian attacks on America's European allies;
- Russian cyberattacks on U.S. political institutions in 2015-2016 and their use of social media to sow discord;
- A lackluster pre-election response to Russian active measures;
- Concurrence with the Intelligence Community Assessment's judgments, except with respect to Putin's supposed preference for candidate Trump;
- We have found no evidence of collusion, coordination, or conspiracy between the Trump campaign and the Russians;
- How anti-Trump research made its way from Russian sources to the Clinton campaign; and
- Problematic contacts between senior Intelligence Community officials and the media.

## Proposed Recommendations

The draft report includes 25+ proposed recommendations for Congress and the executive branch to improve:

- Election security, including protecting vote tallies;
- Support to European allies;
- The U.S. government response to cyber-attacks;
- Campaign finance transparency; and
- Counterintelligence practices related to political campaigns and unauthorized disclosures.

## Conclusion

The draft report will be provided to the Committee minority on March 13 for review and comment. After adoption it will be submitted for a declassification review, and a declassified version will be made public. The report's completion will signify the closure of one chapter in the Committee's robust oversight of the threat posed by Moscow—which <u>began well before the investigation</u> and will continue thereafter.

Additional follow-on efforts arising from the investigation include oversight of the unmasking of Americans' names in intelligence reports, FISA abuse, and other matters.

# ABOUT THE AUTHOR

Photo credit: Reuters

TED ROOSEVELT MALLOCH, SCHOLAR-DIPLOMAT-STRATEGIST, IS ALSO Chairman and Chief Executive Officer of the Roosevelt Group, a leading strategic management and thought leadership company.

He has served as Research Professor at Yale University, Senior Fellow at Said Business School, Oxford University, and Professor of Leadership and Governance at Henley Business School.

His most recent books concern the nature of virtuous enterprise, the practices of practical wisdom in business, the pursuit of happiness, and the virtues of generosity, prudence, and thrift. His most recent book is entitled *Common Sense Business*.

He has served on the executive board of the World Economic Forum (Davos); held an ambassadorial level position at the United Nations in Geneva, Switzerland; worked in the US State Department and Senate Committee on Foreign Relations; worked in capital markets at Salomon Brothers on Wall Street; and sat on a number of corporate, mutual fund, and not-for-profit boards.

Ted earned his PhD in international political economy from the University of Toronto, took his BA from Gordon College, and an MLitt from the University of Aberdeen on a St. Andrews Fellowship.